THE LOST LINES OF BRITAIN

AA

THE LOST LINES OF BRITAIN

A NOSTALGIC TRIP ALONG BRITAIN'S LOST RAILWAYS
FEATURING RAILWAY WALKS AND CYCLE PATHS

JULIAN HOLLAND

Published by AA Publishing, a trading name of AA Media Ltd, whose registered office is Fanum House, Basing View, Basingstoke, Hampshire RG21 4EA. Registered Number 06112600

Editor: David Popey
Layout and design: Keith Miller
Picture researcher: Julian Holland
Image manipulation and internal repro: Sarah Montgomery
Verifiers: Matthew Thompson and Alexander Medcalf
Proofreader: Alison Moore
Indexer: Julian Holland
Production: Stephanie Allen

Commissioning Editor: Paul Mitchell

Cartography provided by the Mapping Services Department of AA Publishing

Visit AA Publishing at theAA.com/shop

A CIP catalogue record for this book is available from the British Library.

A04239

ISBN 978 0 7495 6630 2 and ISBN 978 0 7495 6631 9 (SS)

Printed in China by C & C Offset Printing Co., Ltd

Page 1
The Stephenson Locomotive Society's Whitby Moors Railtour crosses Larpool Viaduct at Whitby on the last day of service, 6 March 1965. On the right is the connecting spur from West Cliff station down to the Esk Valley line, which can be seen disappearing behind the gasworks. Pages 190–195 further explore the history of this line.

Pages 2–3
Returning to Leeds City, the Railway Correspondence & Travel Society's 'Solway Ranger' makes a fine sight as it heads out of Keswick behind Ivatt Class 2 2-6-0s Nos 46426 and 46458 on 13 June 1964. This section of trackbed now forms part of the Keswick Railway Footpath (see pages 166–169).

CONTENTS

INTRODUCTION

For such a small country, Britain once possessed one of the most extensive rail systems in the world, which, by the outbreak of the First World War, had reached a peak of 23,440 route miles. Following the war, Britain's 120 or more railway companies were amalgamated to form just four large, mainly regional, companies: the London, Midland & Scottish (LMS); the London & North Eastern Railway (LNER); the Great Western Railway (GWR); and the Southern Railway (SR). Duplication of lines previously built between the same places by the original competing companies soon became redundant and many were closed. Closures also came about due to increasing competition from road transport, and by the outbreak of the Second World War, a total of 1,264 route miles of railway had disappeared in this way.

The Second World War saw a reprieve for Britain's four railway companies, but by the end of hostilities in 1945, they were in a poor and run-down state. Nationalisation followed in 1948 and the newly formed British Transport Commission (BTC) wasted no time in seeking to reduce mounting losses on lightly used rural lines. Years before Dr Beeching came on the scene, the BTC's Branch Line Committee drew up a list of these lines and, over the next 14 years, a further 3,300 route miles were closed.

Despite the Modernisation Plan of 1955, Britain's railways continued to be a drain on the taxpayer. Unable to compete with the roads and saddled with out-of-date working practices, the railways were losing money hand over fist and, by the early 1960s, something needed to be done. Enter

◄ Class 'N' 2-6-0 No. 31862 stands at Horam station on the Cuckoo Line (see pages 56–59) with a northbound train for Eridge, c.1960. An important source of railborne traffic once came from the local Express Dairies depot in the village. Listed for closure in the Beeching Report, it saw its last service in 1965.

▶ North of Pant Glas, the asphalted section of the Lôn Eifion cycleway near Graianog Crossing was once used by lorries serving a nearby quarry. Today, it is easy going for the many cyclists that use this level, traffic-free trail (see pages 144–149).

the new Conservative Minister of Transport, Ernest Marples, and the newly appointed Chairman of British Railways, Dr Richard Beeching. The story of Dr Beeching's 1963 report on the state of the country's railway network, *The Reshaping of Britain's Railways*, is well known. As a direct result of the report, a further 4,065 route miles were closed along with thousands of stations.

By 1975, Britain's countryside was criss-crossed by thousands of miles of disused railways, their tracks ripped up for scrap, stations sold off to discerning buyers for conversion into private residences and land sold off piecemeal to farmers. However, by this time, the railway preservation movement was moving into top gear and, over the following 25 years, succeeded in reopening hundreds of miles of previously closed lines. Despite this there

still remained thousands of miles of disused trackbed, much of which traversed some of Britain's most beautiful countryside. The stage was now set for their renaissance.

The idea of using closed railway lines for recreational purposes can be traced back to 1937 when the LMS gave the 8-mile trackbed of the then recently closed Leek & Manifold Valley Light Railway to the Staffordshire County Council for use as a footpath — today the Manifold Way has become a popular traffic-free footpath and cycleway enjoyed by thousands of visitors each year. Forty years later, a group of Bristol environmentalists, later to become the charity Sustrans, also saw the potential of these closed railway lines as green traffic-free routes for cyclists. From its early beginnings in 1984, with the opening of the Bristol to Bath Railway Path,

Sustrans has, in partnership with local authorities and landowners, built a 10,000-mile network of these routes covering the whole country. Now collectively known as the National Cycle Network, many of these routes incorporate resurfaced former railway lines – their fairly level, traffic-free, linear paths passing through some of Britain's most beautiful scenery have made them a magnet for thousands of walkers and cyclists around the country. In addition to Sustrans' efforts, many local authorities have also seen the wisdom in reopening many of these old railway lines to walkers and cyclists, with local businesses also reaping the financial benefits. Some of the routes are so popular today that they carry far more 'passengers' than they once did during the age of the railway!

Despite all of this rebirth, there are still a few hidden railway treasures still waiting to be discovered out there by the more hardy adventurer, suitably equipped with sturdy walking boots, map and compass. Whether you are a weekend walker, keen cyclist, railway enthusiast or a combination of any of these, *The Lost Lines of Britain* is a ticket to the hidden world of Britain's railway heritage.

Julian Holland

FOLLOWING THE LOST LINES OF BRITAIN

THE LINES TODAY

Thousands of miles of railway lines were closed down throughout the 20th century, not least following the implementation of the Beeching Report in the 1960s. Since then many have been converted to footpaths and cycleways, the latter mainly by the charity Sustrans. Apart from these well-worn routes there are, fortunately, both for the railway enthusiast and walker, many other hidden byways – often in the most beautiful parts of the countryside – that follow the routes of long-closed railways and that can be enjoyed in peace and tranquillity.

Every line is accompanied by a map to show the route of the original railway and the sections that can be walked today (see map legend, right). A panel at the end of each section describes key features on the route and provides a useful guide to the closest local heritage railways and other nearby attractions. Practical information lists the nearest open railway station and tourist information office and recommends an Ordnance Survey map. Addresses and contact details of the nearest cycle-hire establishments are provided where they exist close to the route of the lost line.

MAP LEGEND

——	Existing railway
———	Closed railway
———	Lost line
———	Walkable section of lost line
———	Heritage line
● *Alloa*	Station

SAFETY

No walk or cycle ride can be considered to be completely free from risk and both will always require a degree of common sense and judgement to ensure they are as safe as possible.

- It is essential that those who explore Britain's lost railways should make sure that they are on public rights of way and respect landowners' privacy.

- Be careful around remnants of old railways, especially if you have children with you. It is important to keep away from potentially dangerous structures, such as bridges, viaducts and tunnels, that are not on the official path.

- Some sections of route are by, or cross, busy roads. Take care and remember traffic can be dangerous even on minor country lanes.

- Be particularly careful on cliff paths and in upland terrain.

- Be aware of the consequences of changes in the weather and check the forecast before you set out. Carry spare clothing and a torch if you are walking in the winter months. Remember that the weather can change very quickly at any time of the year, and in moorland and heathland areas, mist and fog can make route finding much harder. Don't set out in these conditions unless you are confident of your navigation skills in poor visibility. In summer, remember to take account of the heat and sun; wear a hat and sunscreen, and carry spare water.

- On walks away from centres of population, carry a whistle and survival bag. If you do have an accident requiring the emergency services, make a note of your position as accurately as possible and dial 999.

▶A 4-mile stretch of the Cockermouth, Keswick and Penrith Railway trackbed between Keswick and Threlkeld is now a popular traffic-free footpath and cycleway known as the Keswick Railway Footpath. Car parking is available at either end of the path, which threads its way up the wooded Greta Valley, passing through short tunnels and crossing and recrossing the river on bridges no fewer than eight times. For further information, see pages 166–169.

THE WEST COUNTRY

◀ Introduced in 1899, the ex-LSWR 'T9' 4-4-0s were affectionately known as 'Greyhounds' due to their excellent steaming qualities and were a common sight on the North Cornwall lines until the early 1960s. Here, No. 30711, allocated to 72A Exmouth Junction shed, waits to depart from Wadebridge with a passenger train in the summer of 1959.

THE CAMEL TRAIL

Wenford Bridge to Padstow

Following the closures of one of the oldest railways and one of the youngest railways in Cornwall, their combined trackbed has been given a new lease of life as one of Britain's most scenic family cycle trails.

Just 259¾ miles from London Waterloo, Padstow was a favourite destination for holidaymakers in the years before and after the Second World War. Much-loved by the poet John Betjeman, the final few miles alongside the Camel Estuary on board the 'Atlantic Coast Express' was the climax of a long and convoluted journey from the capital – the smell of the sea air, smoke, steam and musty seats mingling with the excited chatter of children clutching their buckets and spades. Sadly, as with many other former seaside destinations around the UK, this journey is no longer possible by rail and is now a fading memory for today's older generation.

▼ Introduced by the London & South Western Railway in 1874, the diminutive Class '0298' 2-4-0 well tanks were a common sight in the Wadebridge area until 1964. Here, No. 0298 waits to depart from Padstow with a local train for Wadebridge on 16 June 1926. The station building and platform at Padstow still survive.

▼ Seen here near the site of Grogley Halt between Wadebridge and Bodmin, the Camel Trail is popular with both cyclists and walkers as it meanders up the valley of the River Camel to Wenfordbridge.

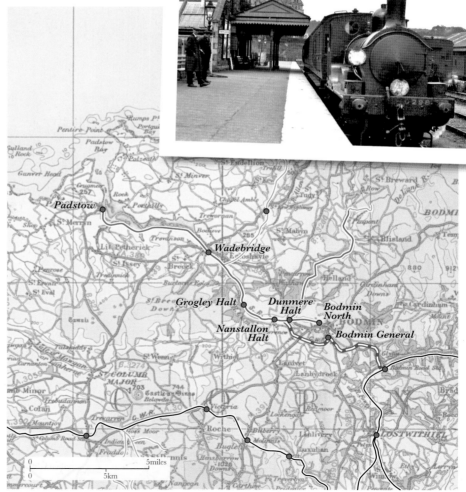

Railways first reached this part of North Cornwall in 1834 when the standard gauge Bodmin & Wadebridge Railway, Cornwall's first line to be operated by locomotives, opened from the quay at Wadebridge to Wenford Bridge with a branch to Bodmin. Mineral traffic, particularly sand and stone, was the *raison d'être* for the line and it remained isolated from the rest of the national railway system until 1888, when it was connected to the then recently opened line from Bodmin Road at Boscarne Junction.

The rest of North Cornwall slumbered on until the North Cornwall Railway (part of the mighty London & South Western Railway) finally completed its tortuous single-line route from Halwill Junction to Wadebridge in 1895. Apart from seasonal holiday traffic, this line also became vital for transporting vast quantities of slate from the giant quarry at Delabole. The final link in the chain, Padstow, was reached from Wadebridge in 1899 and it wasn't long before through trains from Waterloo brought ever-increasing numbers of holidaymakers to this once-sleepy fishing village. Under Southern

◀ ▲ The only major engineering structure on the Camel Trail, the three-span girder bridge half a mile east of Padstow crosses Little Petherick Creek. The bridge, which often featured in photographs and 1930s railway posters of the line, was completed by contractors shortly before the opening of the railway to Padstow in 1899.

▼ Apart from the track and the train, this scene has not changed much today. Ex-L&SWR 'T9' 4-4-0 No. 30712 runs alongside the Camel Estuary with a two-coach train of 'blood and custard' coaches bound for Padstow in 1957.

Railway ownership, Padstow's importance grew with the opening of a new fish market and the inauguration of the 'Atlantic Coast Express'. The latter departed from Waterloo with through carriages for Ilfracombe, Torrington, Bude and Padstow, and its popularity during the summer months led to a total of five such trains being run on Saturdays. The post-war years also saw the introduction of Bulleid's air-smoothed 'West Country' and 'Battle of Britain' light Pacifics on this route and it was quite common until the early 1960s to see one of these innovative locomotives pottering along the North Cornwall line with only a couple of carriages in tow. After the war, a 70ft turntable was installed at Padstow to turn these locomotives. Winding its way through woods up the narrowing valley of the River Camel, the Wenford Bridge branch was also the stamping ground for three of Beattie's veteran 2-4-0 well tanks

▼ Bodmin once had two stations – General was served by trains from the GWR main line at Bodmin Road, while North was served by SR trains from Wadebridge. General station is now the headquarters of the Bodmin & Wenford Railway, while a supermarket stands on the site of North. Here, ex-L&SWR Class '02' 0-4-4 tank No. 30236 is seen at North station with a train from Padstow in 1959.

(L&SWR Class 0298, BR Nos 30585-30587) until superseded by ex-GWR pannier tanks in 1962. The well tanks were based at the small two-road engine shed at nearby Wadebridge, which also boasted a 50ft turntable and was finally closed in 1964.

Sadly, by the early 1960s the end was in sight for the railways of North Cornwall; 1963 not only saw all former Southern Region lines west of Salisbury come under the control of the Western Region, but also the publication of the infamous Beeching Report. The last 'Atlantic Coast Express' ran in September 1964, the same month that

▼ Introduced in 1899, the ex-L&SWR 'T9' 4-4-0s were affectionately known as 'Greyhounds' due to their excellent steaming qualities and were a common sight on the North Cornwall lines until the early 1960s. Here, No. 30711, allocated to 72A Exmouth Junction shed, waits to depart from Wadebridge with a passenger train in the summer of 1959.

▲ Once a busy junction, Wadebridge station building has been restored as a day-care centre for elderly people. It is named after the poet John Betjeman, who immortalised the North Cornwall railway line in his famous 1960s BBC TV series.

WALKING AND CYCLING THE LINE

THE LINE TODAY

The entire route of the former railway line from Wenford Bridge to Padstow is now a popular and scenic traffic-free cycle trail used by nearly half a million people each year. Recent extensions have been added into the town of Bodmin and from Poley's Bridge to Wenford Bridge. Also popular with walkers and horse riders, the 17.3-mile Camel Trail is well equipped with car parking (at Padstow, Wadebridge, Bodmin, Hellandbridge and Poley's Bridge) and cycle-hire shops (at Padstow, Wadebridge and Bodmin). Managed and maintained by Cornwall Council, the Trail is said to generate several million pounds a year for the local economy.

Starting at Padstow, where the old station building is now a council office, café and cycle-hire centre, the Trail soon leaves the town behind to follow closely the south shore of the Camel Estuary for the next 5 miles to Wadebridge. A mile out of Padstow, the Trail crosses Little Petherick Creek on a three-span girder bridge that once featured often in posters and photographs of the old railway. Entering Wadebridge, where the restored station building, dating from 1895, has been renamed the Betjeman Centre, the Trail makes use of local roads until continuing its way up the winding river valley past the sites of Grogley Halt and Nanstallon Halt to Boscarne Junction. Here a connection can be made with the Bodmin & Wenford Railway to Bodmin General and Bodmin Parkway stations. Shortly after, a branch of the Trail heads into Bodmin town, while the main route continues its journey up through Dunmere Woods to Hellandbridge, where the level crossing track can still be seen in the road, the car park at Poley's Bridge and the final destination of Wenford Bridge, where the old clay dries can still be seen.

PLACES TO VISIT

HERITAGE RAILWAYS
Bodmin & Wenford Railway
General Station, Bodmin, Cornwall PL31 1AQ
Tel 0845 1259678/01208 73555
Website www.bodminandwenfordrailway.co.uk
Route Bodmin Parkway to Bodmin General and Boscarne Junction
Length 6½ miles

OTHER ATTRACTIONS
Llanhydrock House (NT)
Tel 01208 265950
Website www.nationaltrust.org.uk

Bodmin Jail
Tel 01208 76292
Website www.bodminjail.org

Pencarrow House & Gardens
Tel 01208 841369
Website www.pencarrow.co.uk

National Lobster Hatchery, Padstow
Tel 01841 533877
Website www.nationallobsterhatchery.co.uk

Padstow Museum
Tel 01841 532752
Website www.padstowmuseum.co.uk

Prideaux Place, Padstow
Tel 01841 532411
Website www.prideauxplace.co.uk

PRACTICAL INFORMATION

NEAREST RAILWAY STATION
Bodmin Parkway

TOURIST INFORMATION
Padstow Tourist Information Centre
Red Brick Building, North Quay, Padstow, Cornwall PL28 8AF
Tel 01841 533449
Website www.padstow-cornwall.co.uk

Wadebridge Tourist Information Centre
Wadebridge Town Hall, The Platt, Wadebridge, Cornwall PL27 7AQ
Tel 01208 813725

Bodmin Tourist Information Centre
Shire Hall, Mount Folly, Bodmin, Cornwall PL31 2DQ
Tel 01208 76616

OS MAPS
Landranger No. 200

CYCLE HIRE
Padstow Cycle Hire
South Quay, Padstow
Tel 01841 533533
Website www.padstowcyclehire.com

Bridge Bike Hire
The Camel Trail, Eddystone Road, Wadebridge, Cornwall PL27 7AL
Tel 01208 813050
Website www.bridgebikehire.co.uk

Bike Smart Cycle Hire
Eddystone Road, Wadebridge, Cornwall PL27 7AL
Tel 01208 814545

Bodmin Bikes & Cycle Hire
31 Hamley Court, Dennison Road, Bodmin PL31 2LL
Tel 01208 73192
Website www.bodminbikes.co.uk

▲ Today the Camel Trail follows the trackbed of the old railway up the picturesque valley of the River Camel to Wenfordbridge. With rails still embedded in the asphalt, this ungated level crossing at Hellandbridge recalls scenes of the past when heavily laden clay trains were waved across the road by a railway employee with a flag.

Padstow lost its freight service (the fish trains had disappeared in 1959), and other services on the North Cornwall line were downgraded, with passenger trains being replaced by ubiquitious diesel multiple units. The end for the North Cornwall line from Wadebridge to Halwill Junction and Okehampton came on 1 October 1966 and the remainder of passenger traffic in the region finally ceased on 30 January 1967. However, goods trains continued to operate for a while longer – freight to Wadebridge continued until 1978 and the Wenford Bridge branch soldiered on with 0-6-0 diesel shunters hauling china clay trains to Bodmin Road via Boscarne Junction until October 1983.

Fortunately for railway enthusiasts, the line between Bodmin Road (renamed Bodmin Parkway in 1984) and Bodmin General was reopened as the Bodmin & Wenford steam heritage railway in 1990 and was extended to Boscarne Junction 6 years later. The rest of the route between Wenford Bridge and Padstow via Wadebridge is now a well-used cycle and footpath known as the Camel Trail.

▲ The veteran Beattie 2-4-0 well tanks were a common sight hauling trains on the picturesque goods-only line from Wadebridge to Wenfordbridge. Introduced by the L&SWR in 1874, they were finally replaced by 0-6-0 diesel shunters in 1964. Here, No. 30585 is seen in Pencarrow Woods with a train for Wenfordbridge in 1960.

THE TARKA TRAIL
Braunton to Barnstaple and Meeth

Following in the footsteps of Henry Williamson's Tarka the Otter, *more than 30 miles of disused railways in North Devon are now a popular destination for cyclists and walkers*

Railways first came to North Devon in 1848 with the opening of a horse-drawn tramway between Barnstaple and Fremington Quay. By 1854 the North Devon Railway (later to become part of the London & South Western Railway) had opened its standard gauge single line from Crediton to Barnstaple (later known as Barnstaple Junction). The Fremington line became steam-hauled and was extended west to Bideford in 1855 and to Torrington in 1872.

Meanwhile the Great Western Railway had its sights on reaching Barnstaple and Ilfracombe. In 1873 the company opened its line from Taunton to Barnstaple (Victoria Road) via Dulverton. The following year the L&SWR opened its line from Barnstaple Junction to Ilfracombe, via a new bridge over the River Taw. A new station,

► Once a bustling station serving four different routes, Barnstaple Junction station is now a shadow of its former self. On 21 July 1925 (in happier Southern Railway days) Class 'N' 2-6-0 No. A861 is seen with an Ilfracombe to Waterloo train while 0-4-4 tank No. E628 is seen shunting on the right.

◄ A common sight in North Devon, the mixed-traffic Class 'N' 2-6-0 was originally introduced in 1917 by the South Eastern & Chatham Railway. Here ex-Southern Railway No. 31841 crosses the Taw Bridge at Barnstaple with a southbound freight from Ilfracombe in August 1952. In the background can be seen the old Regal Cinema and the Bell Hotel. The bridge was demolished after closure of the line in 1970.

► Introduced by the Southern Railway in 1927, the ten members of the Class 'E1/R' 0-6-2 tank locos were rebuilds of William Stroudley's Class 'E1' 0-6-0 tanks. Here No. 96 pauses at Bideford with a Barnstaple to Torrington train in the 1930s.

▲ Now used by the Tarka Trail, this old railway bridge over a creek at Fremington once saw the comings and goings of trains between Barnstaple, Bideford and Torrington. Nearby Fremington Quay was once a busy rail-connected transhipment point for outgoing clay from Marland and incoming coal from South Wales.

Barnstaple Quay, later renamed Barnstaple Town, was also opened on the opposite side of the river.

The final piece of Barnstaple's standard gauge jigsaw was put into place in 1885 when the GWR opened its link between Victoria Road and Junction stations. Through-running between Exeter, Taunton (and beyond) and Ilfracombe was now possible.

The next stage in the development of North Devon's railways was the opening of the narrow gauge (1ft 11½in) Lynton & Barnstaple Railway in 1898. Connecting with the Ilfracombe line at Barnstaple Town station, this wonderful scenic railway was never a financial success and although taken over by the Southern Railway in 1923 it had closed by 1935.

The final railway to be built in the region was the standard gauge

▶ A mile north of Torrington station the Tarka Trail crosses the meandering River Torridge on this stone-arched railway bridge built in the early 1870s.

▼ Complete with track, restored signalbox, platforms, station building and old BR Mark 1 coach, Bideford station today is a popular stopping-off point for refreshments on the Tarka Trail between Barnstaple and Torrington.

◄ Furnished with a platform, a short length of track, a few wagons and a coach, the old station building at Torrington is now the Puffing Billy public house. The adjacent goods shed is now a cycle-hire centre.

North Devon & Cornwall Junction Light Railway between Torrington and Halwill Junction. Partly replacing a 3ft-gauge tramway originally built in 1880 between Torrington and clay works at Marland, the line was opened in July 1925. Apart from the output from the clay works, which was transhipped at Fremington Quay, other traffic on this line, which ran through thinly populated countryside, was minimal, with most stations apart from Hatherleigh, miles from the town it purported to serve, being unstaffed halts.

Despite the opening of these railways, North Devon never developed to the extent of South Devon. The blame can be laid fairly and squarely on the shoulders of the L&SWR and its successor, the Southern Railway, who refused to double the existing single track from Crediton to Barnstaple or even lengthen the passing loops, with the consequence that Barnstaple and its connecting lines never received an adequate rail service.

Barnstaple and Ilfracombe continued to be served by both the Western and Southern Regions of British Railways after 1948, and Summer Saturdays in the 1950s and early 1960s saw through trains from both London Waterloo via Exeter (the latter including coaches from the 'Atlantic Coast Express') and from cities in the Midlands via Taunton. Clay from Marland and Meeth, coal from Fremington Quay and milk from the large creamery at Torrington also generated much railborne traffic, but the regional boundary changes of 1963 and the

▲ Looking in immaculate condition, ex-L&SWR Class '460' 4-4-0 No. 0476 waits at Torrington with a train for Barnstaple in the mid-1920s. Ten of these graceful locos were built by Robert Stephenson & Co. in 1884 but by the time this photograph was taken their days were numbered.

▼ Watergate, seen here on 28 September 1956, and its rudimentary Southern Railway-style concrete platform, was typical of many of the halts that served the isolated rural communities between Torrington and Halwill Junction. Apart from carrying clay from pits near Marland, this delightful railway, with its ungated crossings, saw little other traffic, as witnessed by the single wagon-load of coal waiting to be unloaded in the siding.

▲ Nature has encroached on the line since complete closure in 1983. Located on the Tarka Trail between Torrington and Meeth, the platform at Watergate Halt today is set in a delightful wooded glade.

Beeching Report soon brought this to an end. First to go was the Torrington to Halwill Junction line, which closed on 1 March 1965, although clay traffic from Meeth to Barnstaple continued to be carried until 1982; services from Barnstaple Junction to Torrington ceased on 4 October 1965, although creamery traffic continued until 1980; the Taunton to Barnstaple Junction line closed on 3 October 1966; Barnstaple Junction to Ilfracombe closed on 5 October 1970. All that was left was the single-track line from Exeter to Barnstaple with its service of diesel multiple units. Visitors to Barnstaple station today may catch glimpses of the railway ghosts of the past but the reality is that this thriving market town and capital of North Devon has been shunted by politicians into a long siding.

WALKING AND CYCLING THE LINE

THE LINE TODAY

Over 30 miles of closed railway lines centred on Barnstaple have been converted into a well-surfaced cycle and footpath to form part of the 180-mile-long Tarka Trail. The closed railway lines utilised also form part of the much longer Devon Coast-to-Coast Cycle Route (from Ilfracombe to Plymouth) and is also part of the National Cycle Network Route 27. The Trail starts at Braunton, on the former Ilfracombe line, and, apart from a short section through the streets of Barnstaple, is traffic-free and follows the old trackbed of the railway along the south shore of the Taw Estuary to Instow. Here it continues southwards along the wooded Torridge Valley through Bideford as far as Torrington, after which it meanders through attractive North Devon countryside to the village of Meeth. The trail is very accessible, with car parks, cycle-hire shops and cafés sited at strategic locations along the route.

This section of the Tarka Trail has much of interest. Apart from Barnstaple station, which is still open, many of the former stations and platforms have been preserved and have a new lease of life. Of note include Fremington Quay, now a café and cycle hire centre, Instow with its signalbox and level crossing, Bideford with its café in an old BR carriage and, last but not least, Torrington station, now the Puffing Billy pub (the adjacent goods shed is a cycle hire centre). South of Torrington, many small halts along the route of the North Devon & Cornwall Junction Light Railway are still in situ. Of note are those at Watergate – located in a wooded glade – and at the end of the Trail at Meeth. A café and bunkhouse are located at the site of Yarde Halt.

Old railway bridges abound: of note are those across the River Torridge at Pillmouth, just south of Bideford, and the attractive stone-arched bridge just north of Torrington. Even a short tunnel at Instow is utilised by cyclists and walkers.

PLACES TO VISIT

Braunton Museum
Bakehouse Centre, Caen Street,
Braunton EX33 1AA
Tel 01271 816688

Museum of Barnstaple & North Devon
The Square, Barnstaple EX32 8LN
Tel 01271 346747

Barnstaple Pannier Market
Butchers Row, Barnstaple EX31 1BW
Tel 01271 379084
Website www.barnstaplepanniermarket.co.uk

Burton Art Gallery & Museum
Kingsley Road, Bideford EX39 2QQ
Tel 01237 471455
Website www.burtonartgallery.co.uk

Dartington Crystal Visitor Centre
Torrington EX38 7AN
Tel 01805 626262
Website www.dartington.co.uk

RHS Garden Rosemoor
Great Torrington EX38 8PH
Tel 01805 626810
Website www.rhs.org.uk/Gardens/Rosemoor

PRACTICAL INFORMATION

NEAREST RAILWAY STATION
Barnstaple

TOURIST INFORMATION
Braunton Tourist Information Centre
Bakehouse Centre, Caen St, Braunton EX33 1AA
Tel 01271 816400

Barnstaple Tourist Information Centre
The Square, Barnstaple EX32 8LN
Tel 01271 375000
Website www.staynorthdevon.co.uk

Bideford Tourist Information Centre
Victoria Park, The Quay, Bideford EX39 2QQ
Tel 01237 477676

Great Torrington Tourist Information
Castle Hill, South Street Car Park, Great Torrington EX38 8AA
Tel 01805 626140
Website www.great-torrington.com

OS MAPS
Landranger Nos 180/191

CYCLE HIRE
Otter Cycle Hire
Station Road, Braunton EX33 2AQ
Tel 01271 813339

Tarka Trail Cycle Hire
Barnstaple Railway Station, Station Road, Sticklepath, Barnstaple EX31 2AU
Tel 01271 324202
Website www.tarkabikes.co.uk

Bideford Cycle, Surf & Kayak Hire
Torrington Street, East the Water, Bideford EX39 4DR
Tel 01237 424123
Website www.bidefordbicyclehire.co.uk

Torrington Cycle Hire
Unit 1 Station Yard, Torrington EX38 8JD
Tel 01805 622633
Website www.torringtoncyclehire.co.uk

▲ Ivatt Class 2 2-6-2 tank No. 41297 halts at Petrockstowe with the 4.37pm mixed train for Torrington on 5 July 1962, while a Halwill Junction-bound train waits in the passing loop.

DARTMOOR VISTA
Yelverton to Princetown

Set amid breathtaking Dartmoor granite scenery, this little line was an early victim of rail closures, but its trackbed is now a popular destination for serious walkers and mountain bike riders.

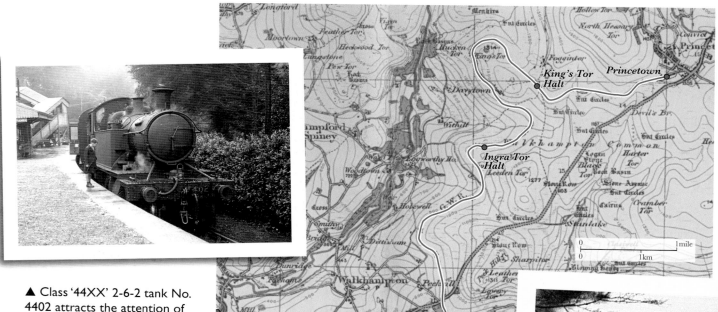

▲ Class '44XX' 2-6-2 tank No. 4402 attracts the attention of a young Richard Casserley at Yelverton before departing with the 2.50pm train for Princetown in 24 August 1945. Popular in the summer with walkers, this scenic but little-used line finally closed in 1956.

The first railway on Dartmoor, albeit horsedrawn, was the 4ft 6in-gauge Plymouth & Dartmoor Railway, completed between Sutton Pool in Plymouth and Princetown in 1826. Chiefly built to transport granite from a quarry at King's Tor, the line was never a financial success and the part of its route between Yelverton and Princetown was used during the building of the Princetown Railway, which opened in 1883.

Next on the Dartmoor railway scene was the South Devon Railway's broad gauge branch line to Launceston via Horrabridge and Tavistock, which opened throughout on 1 July 1865. Later a third rail was added between Marsh Mills and Lydford to enable London & South Western Railway 'standard gauge' trains to operate along the line.

▶ The Princetown branch is still easy to trace today. Between Dousland and Burrator Reservoir, the remains of an old stone cattle creep bisect the railway's embankment, with the rusting iron fence post adding yet more railway memories to the picture.

▼ Soon to disappear for ever, a wet but busy scene at Yelverton Junction on 20 December 1955. On the far left, Class '45XX' 2-6-2 tank No. 4568 has just arrived with the 12.08pm train from Princetown. In the centre, Class '14XX' 0-4-2 tank No. 1408 has also just arrived with a Tavistock to Plymouth train while on the right Class '55XX' 2-6-2 tank No. 5567 waits with a Plymouth to Launceston train.

Finally, in 1878, the Princetown Railway, a subsidiary of the Great Western Railway, obtained Parliamentary powers to build a 10-mile-long branch line from Yelverton, on the Launceston branch, to Princetown. Much of the route of this standard gauge line followed the meandering course of the now defunct Plymouth & Dartmoor Railway. With an intermediate station at Dousland, the line opened in 1883 but, until a new station was built at Yelverton in 1885, trains from Princetown proceeded to Horrabridge. Even when Yelverton station was opened there was no room for a run-round loop, so a spot of gravity shunting here was one of the quirky features of the line.

▲ At the highest point on the GWR – ex-GWR '45XX' 2-6-2 tank No. 4568 has just arrived at Princetown with its one-coach train from Yelverton on 20 December 1955. Only the houses behind still remain.

The Princetown branch was noted for its scenic route, climbing to a height of 1,300ft above sea level while winding its circuitous way around Ingra and King's Tors. As well as granite traffic from the quarry at King's Tor, the line also served the notorious Dartmoor Prison at Princetown and trains no doubt carried convicted prisoners on the last stage of their journey to incarceration in this gloomy granite pile. Traffic was never heavy, although a halt was opened at Burrator & Sheepstor Platform in 1924 for workmen building the nearby reservoir and dams. In the same year King's Tor Halt was opened for local quarry workers and, in 1936, Ingra Tor Halt was established for the same reason. These simple wooden platforms had no lighting and were served by trains only during daylight hours. After the war they became popular with walkers and, in the case of Ingra Tor Halt, there was even a famous sign warning about the dangers of snakes!

Services on the branch usually consisted of 5 or 6 passenger trains a day (no Sunday service) with a goods train running only on Mondays, Wednesdays and Fridays. Motive power to haul the single passenger coach usually consisted of a GWR '44XX' or '55XX' 'Prairie', which spent each night in the small single-road engine shed at Princetown.

Once in the hands of British Railways, the line's future looked bleak and closure was announced for September 1955. However, this did not take place and a second date set for Christmas Eve also slipped past until the inevitable happened on a typically foggy 3 March 1956. So many people turned out to see the 'last rites' performed that two engines and six coaches were required to convey them on the last journeys to and from England's highest station. By early 1957, the rails had been lifted and the scenic Princetown Railway had ceased to exist.

The Launceston branch lost its passenger service towards the end of 1962 and the section between Marsh Mills and Tavistock was closed completely on 31 December of that year. All that is left now is a ¾-mile heritage line at Marsh Mills known as the Plym Valley Railway.

◀ This remote granite bridge is a forceful reminder of the Princetown branch's *raison d'être*. Originally built as a tramway to carry granite from quarries in the area down to Plymouth, the trackbed is now a popular route for walkers and mountain bikers as it snakes around the slopes of Ingra Tor and King's Tor.

▼ On a fine day, the views across Dartmoor from the trackbed of the old Princetown branch are magnificent. Here the line wound its way up around the contours of Ingra Tor on its 10-mile journey to England's highest station at Princetown.

WALKING AND CYCLING THE LINE

THE LINE TODAY

In 1956 the railway preservation scene was in its infancy and the Princetown branch closure didn't even appear on the Richter Scale. If it had been saved by preservationists then this little line would now surely be one of the most delightful train journeys in the UK. Fortunately, most of the trackbed, from Dousland to Princetown, is today a popular rough cycle track and walkway offering the energetic, on a clear day, far-reaching vistas across Dartmoor. Climbing and winding its way up through deciduous woodland and round high Dartmoor tors, it is best reached either from the car park adjacent to Burrator Reservoir, near Dousland, or from Princetown. Between these two points there is little contact with the outside world as the clearly defined trackbed meanders around the contours of Ingra Tor and King's Tor and past granite quarries once famous for their stone used in many London buildings. The few granite bridges in place still add a railway flavour to the journey but there is little else left today of the wooden halts so favoured by walkers before closure. Dousland station building is now a holiday let and the station master's house has been named Crossing Cottage. In Princetown there is still a Station Road and Railway Inn but the old station, its buildings and platform, have disappeared for ever. Walkers are advised to take suitable footwear and clothing when walking this route as weather on Dartmoor can be very unpredictable and fast-changing. Mountain bikes are also essential equipment for cyclists on these exposed Dartmoor slopes.

PLACES TO VISIT

HERITAGE RAILWAYS
Plym Valley Railway
Marsh Mills Station, Coypool Road, Plympton, Plymouth PL7 4NW
Website www.btinternet.com/~plymvalleyrailway
Route Marsh Mills to Lee Moor Crossing
Length ¾ mile

OTHER ATTRACTIONS
Dartmoor National Park High Moorland Visitor Centre
Tavistock Road, Princetown, Devon PL20 6QF
Tel 01822 890414
Website www.dartmoor-npa.gov.uk

Dartmoor Prison Museum
HMP Dartmoor, Princetown, Devon PL20 6RR
Tel 01822 322130
Website www.dartmoor-prison.co.uk

Tavistock Museum
Court Gate, Guild Hall Square, Tavistock, Devon PL19 0EA
Tel 01822 612546
Website www.tavistockhistory.ik.com

Yelverton Paperweight Centre
Leg O' Mutton Road, Yelverton, Devon PL20 6AD
Tel 01822 854250
Website www.paperweightcentre.co.uk

Buckland Monachorum Garden
The Garden House, Buckland Monachorum, Yelverton, Devon PL20 7LQ
Tel 01822 854769
Website www.thegardenhouse.org.uk

PRACTICAL INFORMATION

NEAREST RAILWAY STATION
Plymouth

TOURIST INFORMATION
Tavistock Tourist Information Centre
Town Hall Building, Bedford Square, Tavistock PL19 0AE
Tel 01822 612938
Website www.tavistockonline.co.uk

Plymouth Tourist Information Centre
Plymouth Mayflower, 3–5 The Barbican, Plymouth PL1 2TR
Tel 01752 306330
Website www.plymouth.gov.uk

Dartmoor National Park High Moorland Visitor Centre
See above for address.
Website www.dartmoor-npa.gov.uk

OS MAPS
Landranger Nos.191/201/202

CYCLE HIRE
Tavistock Cycles
Paddons Row, Brook Street, Tavistock, Devon PL19 0HF
Tel 01822 617630
Website www.tavistockcycles.co.uk

Dartmoor Cycles
Dartmoor Cycles, Atlas House, Tavistock, Devon, PL19 9DP
Tel 01822 618178
Website www.dartmoorcycles.co.uk

Peak Hill Farm
Dousland, nr Yelverton PL20 6PD
Tel 01822 854808

WEST COUNTRY MILK TRAINS

▼ Unrebuilt 'Battle of Britain' Class 4-6-2 No. 34076 '41 Squadron' pulls into Andover Junction station with the 3.45pm milk empties from Clapham Junction to the West of England in the early 1960s. Milk trains on this route from Chard Junction ceased in March 1980.

During the 19th century, milk traffic became an important source of revenue for railway companies in Britain. Milk was then transported in metal churns from country stations all over Britain to the growing population of the cities. By the 1870s, milk distribution had become more organised with collection depots and creameries at strategic rural railheads and reception depots in the big cities.

Ventilated vans were also introduced to keep the milk cool in transit. By 1914, nearly 100 million gallons of milk per year was being carried by the railways to London, much of it from the West Country. Both milk production and consumption continued to rise and bottling plants for pasteurised milk were set up on the main railway routes into the capital – the main plant for Great Western Railway milk traffic from the West Country was at South Acton and for the Southern Railway at Vauxhall.

In 1933 the Milk Marketing Board was established to control all milk production and distribution in the UK. At this time, specially designed glass-lined or stainless steel six-wheel tank wagons holding 3,000 gallons of milk were introduced and the practice of collecting milk churns at individual stations soon became a thing of the past.

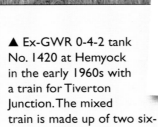

▼ The Wilts United Dairies creamery at Bason Bridge in Somerset was an important customer for the S&D Highbridge to Evercreech Junction line. Here, Ivatt Class 2 2-6-2 tank No. 41243 leaves Highbridge with a train of empty six-wheel milk tank wagons for Bason Bridge in the early 1960s. Despite closure of the S&D in March 1966, milk trains ran on the line's western section until 1972.

▲ Ex-GWR 0-4-2 tank No. 1420 at Hemyock in the early 1960s with a train for Tiverton Junction. The mixed train is made up of two six-wheel milk tank wagons from the nearby creamery and an ex-Barry Railway gas-lit coach for passengers. Passenger services ceased in 1963 but diesel-hauled milk trains continued to use the Culm Valley line from Hemyock until 1975.

After the Second World War, milk traffic from the West Country to London continued unabated with special trains running daily from creameries at St Erth, Camborne, Lostwithiel and Saltash in Cornwall, from Hemyock, Seaton Junction, Totnes, Lapford and Torrington in Devon and from Sherborne, Chard Junction and Bason Bridge in Somerset. They were so heavy that the milk trains from Cornwall were often double-headed over the South Devon Banks by two 'Castle' Class locomotives.

Despite the closure of many West Country branch lines to passenger traffic in the 1960s, some still remained open for the all-important milk traffic – one being the picturesque Culm Valley line from Tiverton Junction to Hemyock, which remained open for another 12 years following withdrawal of passenger services in 1963. Short stubs of the Somerset & Dorset Joint Railway at Bason Bridge and Bailey Gate also remained open for a few years after closure in 1966. The use of regular milk trains, such as those from Chard Junction and Totnes, ended in March 1980 and now all milk is transported by road.

THE STRAWBERRY LINE

Yatton to Witham via Cheddar

Named after the local produce that it used to convey to market, the first section of the Strawberry Line is fast becoming a popular traffic-free cycleway and footpath for families and keep-fit enthusiasts.

▲ Located between Winscombe and Axbridge, Shute Shelve Tunnel was the site of important Roman remains when excavated in 1855. Today, walkers and cyclists are guided through the tunnel by a line of innovative solar powered reflectors.

Railways first came to North Somerset in 1841 when the broad gauge Bristol & Exeter Railway, engineered by Isambard Kingdom Brunel, opened the first section of its route between Bristol and Bridgwater, with a branch line to Weston-super-Mare. By 1847 a short, also broad gauge, branch line from Yatton to Clevedon had been opened. The coming of the railway to these, then small, seaside villages soon led to their development as important health resorts.

Next on the scene in this part of Somerset was the opening, in 1859, of a branch line, initially broad gauge, from the Somerset Central's (soon to become the Somerset & Dorset Railway) main

▼ With only three weeks to go before closure of the Cheddar Valley line, this busy scene at Yatton station was soon to disappear. In the far platform, a single-unit diesel railcar waits to depart for Clevedon while in the foreground 0-6-0 pannier tank No. 3702 takes on water before departing with the 2.45pm train to Witham. On the far right, Class '2251' 0-6-0 No. 2298 stands in the cattle dock platform. The Strawberry Line path starts from the car park that was built on the site of these sidings.

line at Glastonbury to the small cathedral city of Wells. The first link in the chain that eventually came to be known affectionately as the Strawberry Line was the East Somerset Railway, a broad gauge concern that opened between Witham and Shepton Mallet in 1858 and to Wells in 1862. The second and final link of this route was the Cheddar Valley & Yatton Railway, also broad gauge, which opened throughout from Yatton to Wells in 1870.

Despite the building of the last two railways and their takeover by, first, the Bristol & Exeter, and, subsequently, the Great Western Railway, there was a little local problem at Wells, where just under 200yds of, by then standard gauge, track that separated them was owned by the Somerset & Dorset! Common sense finally prevailed and by 1875 both the East Somerset and Cheddar Valley lines were converted to standard gauge and through-running became possible. Both Cheddar, with its famous caves, and nearby Wookey Hole soon became popular destinations for excursion trains from Bristol. Local produce in the form of fruit, in particular strawberries, and milk also became important railborne traffic on the line until after the Second World War, when competition from road haulage led to its decline.

There were two short branch lines that tapped into the Cheddar Valley line; to the west a 6½-mile light railway was opened from Congresbury to Blagdon in 1901 but, its sparse traffic passenger services ceased in September 1931 and goods in 1950; a short branch to the east of Cranmore station was built to serve Merehead Quarry and this continues being used by giant stone-carrying trains with a main line connection at Witham.

Closures first started in 1951 when the Wells to Glastonbury branch ceased operation, but the main Cheddar Valley line carried on until 9 September 1963, when the passenger services – an early victim of the Beeching Report – also ceased to run. Goods trains continued to operate between Yatton and Cranmore until July 1964, but the

▲ Congresbury station, seen here on 8 July 1959, was once the junction for a 6½-mile light railway to Blagdon. Congresbury station building and platform still survive adjacent to the Strawberry Line footpath and cycleway.

▲ Access to the Strawberry Line and Millennium Green picnic site at Winscombe is via the old station approach road. Here the station platform has been preserved and the brick façade of the station buildings are now a one-dimensional sculpture.

◀ Immaculately turned out by Bristol Barrow Road shed, Class '2251' 0-6-0 No. 3218 is given a final polish at Wells Tucker Street while working the last day of passenger services on the Cheddar Valley line on 9 September 1963.

latter station, which was to become the HQ of David Shepherd's East Somerset Railway heritage line in 1973, was luckier with bitumen trains from Ellesmere Port continuing via Witham until 1985. Yatton at the other end of the Cheddar Valley line saw closure of the branch line to Clevedon in October 1966. Although Yatton station is still open on the Bristol to Exeter route, the only railway activity is located at the eastern end of the line at Cranmore, with the branch to Merehead Quarry and the East Somerset Railway both still in operation.

▲ 0-6-0 pannier tank No. 5757 arrives at Shepton Mallet High Street with the 3.28pm train from Witham to Yatton on 23 May 1957. Complete with a cattle wagon and cattle pens on the right, this scene has now totally disappeared and the site has now been redeveloped as yet another supermarket.

▼ BR Standard Class 3 2-6-2 tank No. 82039 stands at Cheddar with a Yatton to Witham train in February 1962. Following closure in 1963 the overall roof was demolished but the station building is now home to the stonemasons of Wells Cathedral.

WALKING AND CYCLING THE LINE

THE LINE TODAY

Luckily, 8 miles of the route of the Cheddar Valley line can now be explored on foot or on a cycle. Starting at the former GWR station at Yatton, the Strawberry Line, a mainly traffic-free path, follows the old trackbed through Congresbury, Sandford, Winscombe and Axbridge to Cheddar. Highlights of this section include the modern metal sculpture above the beginning of the route at Yatton, platforms and station buildings at Congresbury and Sandford and Banwell, the old station platform with its 'station building' sculpture at Winscombe and the straight and dank Shute Shelve Tunnel north of Axbridge – the path through the tunnel cleverly illuminated by a line of solar-powered reflectors. At Axbridge the route of the old railway is now a fast and dangerous stretch of the A371 bypass and the Strawberry Line takes a safer deviation through this attractive village. Located by the side of the bypass, the old Axbridge station building and goods shed can be seen clearly from a passing car but stopping to investigate is not recommended. After Axbridge, the path then continues as far as Cheddar.

West of Yatton, a feasibility study is being undertaken for a path along the Clevedon branch trackbed. The section from Haybridge to Wells is open to walkers and cyclists while planning is progressing with the remainder. Wells to Dulcote is already open, while a feasibility study is also being carried out on the section to Shepton Mallet and Cranmore. With continuing strong support from local community groups, councillors and politicians it is hoped to reopen the whole of the route between Clevedon and Cranmore within a few years.

Meanwhile, several old railway buildings can be seen, albeit with a different use – at Draycott where the station building is now a private house, at Westbury-sub-Mendip, where the old goods shed has been incorporated into a new industrial estate, and in Wells, where the GWR goods shed is now a vet's practice and pine shop. To the east of Shepton Mallet, the East Somerset Railway runs from Mendip Vale to Cranmore.

PLACES TO VISIT

HERITAGE RAILWAYS
East Somerset Railway
Cranmore Railway Station, Somerset BA4 4QP
Tel 01749 880417
Website www.eastsomersetrailway.com
Route Cranmore to Mendip Vale
Length 2¾ miles

OTHER ATTRACTIONS
Wookey Hole Caves
Wookey Hole, Wells, Somerset BA5 1BB
Tel 01749 672243
Website www.wookey.co.uk

Glastonbury Tor (National Trust)
Tel 01934 844518
Website www.nationaltrust.org.uk

Glastonbury Abbey
Magdalene Street, Glastonbury,
Somerset BA6 9EL
Tel 01458 832267
Website www.glastonburyabbey.com

Cheddar Gorge and Caves
North-east of Cheddar village,
Somerset BS27 3QF
Tel 01934 742343
Website www.cheddarcaves.co.uk

Wells Cathedral
Cathedral Green, Wells,
Somerset BA5 2UE
Tel 01749 674483
Website www.wellscathedral.org.uk

PRACTICAL INFORMATION

NEAREST RAILWAY STATION
Yatton

TOURIST INFORMATION
Wells Tourist Information Centre
Market Place, Wells, Somerset BA5 2RB
Tel 01749 672552
Website www.wellstourism.com

Cheddar Tourist Information Centre
The Gorge, Cheddar, Somerset BS27 3QE
Tel 01934 744071

Glastonbury Tourist Information Centre
9 High Street, Glastonbury, Somerset BA6 9DP
Tel 01458 832954
Website www.glastonburytic.co.uk

Shepton Mallet Tourist Information Centre
70 High Street, Shepton Mallet, Somerset
BA4 5AS
Tel 01749 345258
Website www.sheptonmallet-touristinfocentre.co.uk

OS MAPS
Landranger No. 200

CYCLE HIRE
Cheddar Cycle Store
1E Valley Line Industrial Park, Wedmore Road,
Cheddar, Somerset BS27 3EE
Tel 01934 741300
Website www.cheddarcyclestore.co.uk

ON THE LEVELS

Evercreech Junction to Burnham-on-Sea

Never fulfilling its Victorian promoters' dreams of linking ports on the Bristol Channel and the English Channel, this delightful rural line across the Somerset Levels spent its life as a quiet railway backwater.

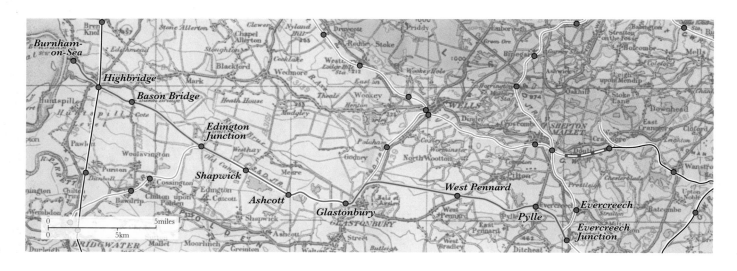

The closure of the Somerset & Dorset Joint Railway on 7 March 1966 led to an enormous outpouring of sadness among railway enthusiasts throughout the UK. The loss of this much-loved institution, faithfully recorded from the early 1950s by the railway photographer and film-maker Ivo Peters, created a void in the lives of the people of Somerset and Dorset. Fortunately John Betjeman's short film *Branch Line Railway*, made for the BBC in 1963, has granted immortality to the 'Slow & Dirty's' original main-line line from Evercreech Junction to Burnham-on-Sea.

History of the Somerset & Dorset Joint Railway

The S&D, as it became known, originated with the opening of the broad gauge Somerset Central Railway from Glastonbury to Highbridge in 1854. This was extended to Burnham-on-Sea

▼ Watched by two young trainspotters, Ivatt Class 2 2-6-2T No. 41304 enters Pylle station with the 5pm Evercreech Junction to Highbridge train on 19 August 1957. The road bridge, since demolished, carried the Fosse Way over the line. The S&D remained steam-hauled until the end.

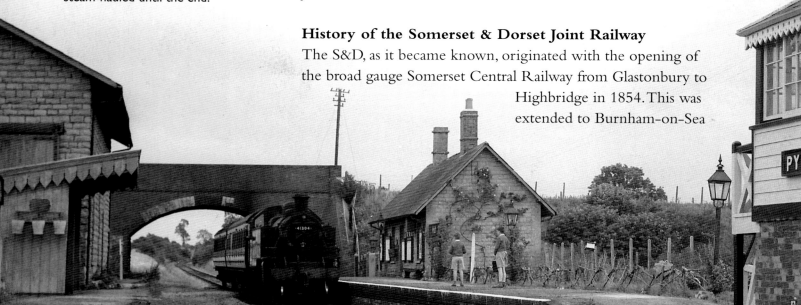

▲ In 1958 the S&D north of Templecombe fell into the hands of the Western Region and by 1959 ex-GWR locos were appearing at the head of local trains. Here a '2251' Class 0-6-0 departs from Evercreech Junction with a train for Highbridge on 1 September 1962.

▼ The S&D, as it became known, originated with the opening of the broad gauge Somerset Central Railway from Glastonbury to Highbridge in 1854. Dating from that period, this bridge now carries walkers and cyclists over the River Brue to the west of Glastonbury.

▼ Towards the end, Highbridge branch trains usually only consisted of one coach and a utility van. Seen here on a wet day in December 1965, Ivatt Class 2 2-6-2 tank No. 41296 pauses at West Pennard with a Highbridge to Evercreech Junction train.

in 1858 and a branch from Glastonbury to Wells was opened the following year. To further their ambitions to reach the South Coast and the English Channel ports, the SCR pushed eastwards to Cole in 1862 where it joined the standard gauge Dorset Central Railway from Wimborne – this latter line was operated by the London & South Western Railway. In the same year the SCR and the DCR were amalgamated as the Somerset & Dorset Railway. However, despite the building of a pier at Burnham and investing in a small fleet of ships, the optimistic hopes for traffic across the Bristol Channel to South Wales were never fully realised. In the early days of the S&D excursion, trains connected with steamers at Burnham for the crossing of the muddy waters of the Bristol Channel to Cardiff.

To the north the mighty Midland Railway had reached Bath in 1869 and the Somerset & Dorset was quick to realise that an extension across the Mendips through the North Somerset coalfield to the city would be most advantageous. Involving considerable engineering works with steep gradients, tunnels and viaducts, the Bath extension

▲ To the east of Ashcott station this refurbished railway bridge carries the trackbed over one of the many drainage channels that criss-cross the Somerset Levels. Once an area of feverish peat extraction, the old peat workings have been transformed into nature reserves.

▶ With less than five months to go before closure, Ivatt Class 2 2-6-2 tank No. 41296 pauses at Shapwick station on 13 October 1965 with a train for Evercreech Junction. Complete with S&DJR lower quadrant signal and photographer's bike leaning against the bridge, this evocative rural scene is now part of our long-vanished, and once proud, railway history.

from Evercreech was opened in July 1874. At the southern end, the line had just been extended to Bournemouth and soon through trains were running there via the S&DR from the Midlands and the North. Although traffic over the S&DR increased rapidly, the company was in a poor financial state caused by the heavy cost of building the extension. Unable to carry on, the S&DR agreed to lease the railway jointly to the L&SWR and the Midland Railway and on 13 July 1876 it became known as the Somerset & Dorset Joint Railway. An improved direct connection to Bournemouth was opened in 1886 but trains still had to reverse up to the L&SWR station at Templecombe – this antiquated operation continued until its closure in 1966.

With the opening of the through route between Bournemouth and Bath the original S&D main line across the Somerset Levels from Evercreech Junction to Highbridge and Burnham-on-Sea soon became a sleepy country byway. A 7¼-mile branch from Edington Junction to Bridgwater was opened in 1890 but this closed to passengers in 1952 and completely by 1954.

▼ To the west of Ashcott station, the Highbridge branch paralleled the South Drain across the Somerset peat moors towards Highbridge. Now a cycleway and footpath, the old trackbed runs for nearly 2 miles through Shapwick Heath National Nature Reserve.

Although the S&D's main workshop was at Highbridge, after joint ownership, locomotives for the railway were built at the Midland Railway's workshops in Derby – these included '2P' 4-4-0, '3F' 0-6-0 and 'Jinty' 0-6-0 tank. Derby also went on to build eleven powerful '7F' 2-8-0 tender locos specifically for use on the S&DJR main line, and many of these remained in service until the early 1960s. Until the regional boundary changes that took place in 1958, when the S&D lines north of Templecombe came under Western Region management, services on the Highbridge branch were usually in the hands of ancient Derby-built 0-4-4 tanks or 0-6-0 tender locos. However, by the early 1960s Swindon-built Collett 0-6-0 locos were making regular appearances on the line with, in the final years, more modern Ivatt 2-6-2 tanks handling the lightly loaded trains.

▲ Ivatt Class 2 2-6-2 tank No. 41296 stands at Highbridge with a train for Evercreech Junction on 13 October 1965. In the distance is the old S&D railway works, which closed in 1930 with the loss of 300 jobs. Trains for Burnham used the through line in the foreground, which crossed the GWR main line on the level.

▼ Burnham-on-Sea station on 8 September 1958 with '4F' 0-6-0 No. 44557 at the head of the 1.20pm train from Evercreech Junction. Although closed in 1951, excursion trains continued to use the station until 1962. This scene, complete with scout hut and an old S&D carriage body, has now disappeared for ever.

September 1962 saw the end of North–South through trains on the main line and from that date the S&DJR, or 'Slow & Dirty' as it was affectionately known, was doomed. Confirmed in 1965, closure was finally scheduled for 3 January 1966. Railway enthusiasts from far and wide came to witness the 'last rites' and special trains were run, but a local bus operator had the last laugh when he withdrew, at the last minute, his application to run an alternative bus service. For two more months the S&D struggled on with a skeleton service – only two return train trips a day ran on the Highbridge branch. The S&D was eventually put out of its misery when final closure came on 7 March 1966. R.I.P.

▲ Although closure of the S&D was scheduled for 3 January 1966, a local bus operator threw a spanner in the works at the last moment by withdrawing his application to run an alternative bus service. British Railways was then forced to run an emergency timetable on the line until final closure on 7 March.

WALKING AND CYCLING THE LINE

THE LINE TODAY
Despite the closure of the Somerset & Dorset Joint Railway in 1966, parts of the route of this delightful branch line across the Somerset Levels from Evercreech Junction to Burnham-on-Sea are still easy to trace. The site of Evercreech Junction station is now an industrial yard and some of the station buildings at Pylle and West Pennard still exist, albeit with a different use. The site of Glastonbury station is now a timber merchant's yard while the old island platform station canopy has been moved to St John's car park in the town. Replica level crossing gates have been erected at Dyehouse Lane crossing. Close by, the impressive former S&D headquarters' office building (1861–1877) is now the head office of a local timber company.

For 5 miles west of Glastonbury, the trackbed of the railway is now a well-surfaced cycleway and footpath. Running parallel to the old Glastonbury Canal, the trackbed to the site of Ashcott station crosses the River Brue on a railway bridge and then passes old peat workings along Ham Wall. In recent years these have been transformed into tranquil nature reserves, home to many species of rare birds and insects. Crossing yet another old railway bridge, the site of Ashcott station is reached. Here the old platform fencing is still visible alongside the trackbed, although the station building has been demolished to make way for a bungalow. Walkers, cyclists and birdwatchers can have refreshments at the nearby 'Railway Inn' free house before continuing along the trackbed, which now runs for nearly 2 miles through Shapwick Heath National Nature Reserve.

All traces of the former S&D works and station at Highbridge have long ago disappeared beneath a modern industrial estate. The end of the line at Burnham-on-Sea is today marked, rather appropriately, by the Somerset & Dorset public house.

PLACES TO VISIT

HERITAGE RAILWAYS
East Somerset Railway
Cranmore Station, Shepton Mallet, Somerset BA4 4QP
Tel 01749 880417/01749 880785
Website www.eastsomersetrailway.com
Route Cranmore to Mendip Vale
Length 2¾ miles

West Somerset Railway
The Railway Station, Minehead, Somerset TA24 5BG
Tel 01643 704996/01643 707650
Website www.west-somerset-railway.co.uk
Route Minehead to Bishop's Lydeard
Length 20 miles

OTHER ATTRACTIONS
Wookey Hole Caves
Wookey Hole, Wells, Somerset BA5 1BB
Tel 01749 672243
Website www.wookey.co.uk

Cheddar Gorge and Caves
Cheddar, Somerset BS27 3QF
Tel 01934 742343
Website: www.cheddarcaves.co.uk

Glastonbury Abbey
Magdalene Street, Glastonbury, Somerset BA6 9EL
Tel 01458 832267
Website www.glastonburyabbey.com

Somerset Rural Life Museum
Abbey Farm, Chilkwell Street, Glastonbury, Somerset BA6 8DB
Tel 01458 831197
Website www.somerset.gov.uk

Chalice Well
Chilkwell Street, Glastonbury, Somerset BA6 8DD
Tel 01458 831154
Website www.chalicewell.org.uk

PRACTICAL INFORMATION

NEAREST RAILWAY STATIONS
Highbridge, Castle Cary

TOURIST INFORMATION
Glastonbury Tourist Information Centre
9 High Street, Glastonbury, Somerset BA6 9DP
Tel 01458 832954
Website www.glastonburytic.co.uk

Burnham-on-Sea Tourist Information
South Esplanade, Burnham-on-Sea, Somerset TA8 1BU
Tel 01278 787852
Website www.visitsomerset.co.uk

OS MAPS
Landranger No. 182/183

CYCLE HIRE
On Your Bike
128a High Street, Street, Somerset BA16 0ER
Tel 01458 443048

Blue Bell Cycle Hire
Ye Olde Burtle Inn, Catcott Road, Burtle, Somerset TA7 8NG
Tel 01278 722123

See also www.glastonbury.co.uk

THE RODWELL TRAIL

Weymouth to the Isle of Portland

Built to serve the military installations, prisons and stone quarries on the Isle of Portland, part of this old railway line has since been converted into a popular cycleway and footpath.

Connected only by a bank of shingle to the mainland near Weymouth, the Isle of Portland has for centuries not only been home to several HM Prisons but has also been quarried for its vast quantities of sought-after limestone. Apart from a couple of horse-drawn tramways and an inclined plane railway from quarries down to Castletown Pier, the first railway to be built to Portland was the Weymouth & Portland Railway. Built to broad and standard gauge and operated jointly by the Great Western Railway and the London & South Western Railway, it opened between Weymouth, over Radipole Lake on a viaduct, and across the shingle embankment to Portland Victoria Square in 1865. Rodwell station, then the only intermediate station on the line, was opened in 1870 and the broad gauge third rail was removed in 1874.

The building of the extensive breakwater, which was completed by the end of the 19th century, had transformed Portland Harbour into one of the world's most important naval bases. To complete the building of this extensive stone structure, the Breakwater Railway came into use in 1878. A short section of it was later used to link another new railway, the

▶ Major improvements were made to the Weymouth & Portland Railway in 1909. These included opening new halts at Westham and Wyke Regis, a new station at Melcombe Regis and the rebuilding of this bridge across Radipole Lake. The main line station at Weymouth can just be seen in the distance.

▲ The Southern Railway concrete platform at Westham Halt still survives today and marks the northern end of the Rodwell Trail.

▲ A passing loop on the Weymouth & Portland Railway, Rodwell Station was seriously damaged by German bombs during the Second World War. Its platforms are approached through a short tunnel that forms part of the Rodwell Trail.

Easton & Church Hope Railway (owned by the GWR and L&SWR), which opened for passengers between Easton and Portland in 1902, and the existing Weymouth & Portland line.

The Weymouth & Portland had become strategically important even before the opening of the line to Easton as in 1891 the Whiteheads torpedo factory was opened at Wyke Regis, where sidings

▼ Although passenger services to Portland ceased in 1952, freight trains continued to operate until 1965. Here, ex-GWR 0-6-0 pannier tank No. 8799 departs from Portland with a freight from Easton to Weymouth in May 1959.

▶ The surviving halts on the Rodwell Trail are recognisable by their reproduction SR green totems. Sandsfoot Castle Halt was opened in 1932 to allow passengers access to the nearby ruins of Henry VIII's castle overlooking Weymouth Bay.

▼ The most scenic part of the old railway to Easton can be walked between Balaclava Bay and Church Ope Cove on the eastern side of Portland. Set on a high ledge beneath Grove Cliff, the trackbed here offers fine views across Weymouth Bay to the Dorset coastline.

▲ A rather striking view from ex-GWR 0-6-0 pannier tank No. 8799 (see also page 41) as it rattles down the line near Castletown with a train of Portland stone blocks from quarries near Easton in May 1959.

were installed. Other improvements arrived at the line in 1909 when an improved timetable came into operation, a new station was opened at Melcombe Regis and new halts were built at Westham and at Wyke Regis. The opening of Melcombe Regis station allowed a new push-pull service to operate from here to Portland and freed up platform space at nearby Weymouth station. For years Portland was well served by these trains with up to 18 return journeys on Mondays to Saturdays and seven on Sundays. Only five of these trains continued to the southern terminus at Easton with none on Sundays. In 1932, the tiny Sandsfoot Castle Halt was opened for visitors to the nearby ruin.

Not surprisingly the naval installations at Portland Harbour and Whiteheads torpedo factory became a prime target for the Luftwaffe during the Second World War. In several incidents between 1940 and 1941, Portland signalbox and Rodwell station were both destroyed in air raids. Passenger traffic was never heavy on this line and despite the

WALKING AND CYCLING THE LINE

THE LINE TODAY

Fortunately Weymouth & Portland Council had the foresight to purchase the trackbed of this line as far back as 1974 and the section from Westham (Abbotsbury Road) and Ferry Bridge soon became a popular but unofficial footpath for local residents. Although plans for a miniature railway along its length never materialised, funding was found by several local bodies to convert the 3½-mile trackbed into a walkway and cycleway. Named the Rodwell Trail, it officially opened in April 2000 and has since proved to be a popular traffic-free green route with local residents and visitors.

The Rodwell Trail also has much to interest lovers of old railways. The start of the Trail, in Abbotsbury Road, Weymouth, is marked by the standard mass-produced concrete Southern Railway platform of Westham Halt surmounted (as are other platforms on the line) by a reproduction SR green totem. Farther down the line a short tunnel leads to the two platforms of Rodwell station, set in a wooded cutting and once a passing loop on the line. After passing the diminutive wooden halt for Sandsfoot Castle, the Trail soon opens up with fine views across Portland Harbour to the Dorset coastline and the Isle of Portland. Continuing down the Trail, the concrete platform of Wyke Regis Halt is soon reached before the journey ends at Ferry Bridge. With the demolition of the viaduct over the Fleet in 1971, the rail link with Portland ceased to exist, but walkers can easily bypass this and continue along the old trackbed over the shingle bank to Portland.

Although not officially part of the Rodwell Trail, the most scenic part of the old railway to Easton can be walked between Balaclava Bay and Church Ope Cove on the eastern side of Portland. Set on a high ledge beneath Grove Cliff, the trackbed here offers fine views across Weymouth Bay to the Dorset coastline. From Church Ope Cove, the South West Coast Path offers walkers the chance to complete a circular walk around Portland.

PLACES TO VISIT

OTHER ATTRACTIONS

Portland Castle (English Heritage)
Castletown, Portland, Dorset DT5 1AZ
Tel 01305 820539
Website www.english-heritage.org.uk

Portland Museum
217 Wakeham, Portland, Dorset DT5 1HS
Tel 01305 821804
Website www.weymouth.gov.uk

Tout Quarry Sculpture Park
Portland, Dorset DT5 1BW
Tel 01305 826736
Website www.learningstone.org

Weymouth Sea Life Centre
Lodmoor Country Park, Weymouth, Dorset DT4 7SX
Tel 0871 4232110
Website www.sealife.co.uk

Weymouth Museum
Brewers Quay, Hope Square, Weymouth
Tel 01305 777622
Website www.weymouthmuseum.org.uk

Nothe Fort
Barrack Road, Weymouth, Dorset DT4 8UF
Tel 01305 766626
Website www.nothefort.org.uk

PRACTICAL INFORMATION

NEAREST RAILWAY STATION
Weymouth

TOURIST INFORMATION
Weymouth & Portland Tourist Information Centre
Kings Statue, The Esplanade, Weymouth, Dorset DT4 7AN
Tel 01305 785747
Website www.visitweymouth.co.uk

OS MAPS
Landranger No. 194

CYCLE HIRE
Weymouth Bike Hire
10 Bowleaze Coveway, Weymouth, Dorset DT3 6PU
Tel 01305 834951
Website www.weymouthbikehire.com

▼ The last passenger train to travel to Easton was an enthusiasts special which ran on 27 March 1965. Here it is seen under the cliffs on the east side of Portland, topped-and-tailed by Ivatt Class 2 2-6-2 tanks Nos. 41284 and 41324. The line closed completely a week later.

▶ Although passenger services ceased to run to Easton in 1952, the station was often visited by enthusiasts' specials. Here a two-coach auto train waits for the merry throng to embark for their return journey back to Weymouth on 7 June 1958.

rebuilding of Westham Halt and Wyke Regis Halt in 1946, regular passenger services ceased on 3 March 1952. The empty coaching stock of summer excursion trains to Weymouth continued to be stabled at Melcombe Regis station following closure of this line to passengers. Goods trains continued to serve Portland and Easton until complete closure of the line on 9 April 1965. Two weeks previously several special last passenger trains, packed with enthusiasts, had made the scenic return journey between Weymouth and Easton.

Despite total closure, the Portland branch slumbered on until August 1966, when the track was removed between Easton and Dockyard Junction. The rest of the branch between Portland and Weymouth was lifted in 1970 and the following year saw the demolition of the viaduct over the Fleet at Ferry Bridge. The final link with the past, the viaduct over Radipole Lake, was demolished in 1974.

SOUTHERN ENGLAND

◄ The Castleman's Corkscrew line between Brockenhurst and Hamworthy Junction was a useful Bournemouth-avoiding line for Weymouth trains in the summer months. Here, BR Standard Class 4 2-6-0 No. 76063 heads through West Moors with a Summer Saturday extra train for Weymouth in 1959.

CASTLEMAN'S CORKSCREW

Brockenhurst to Broadstone

Named after its promoter and its circuitous route, this redundant section of Castleman's Corkscrew is now a pleasant traffic-free route through Hampshire and Dorset heathland for walkers and cyclists.

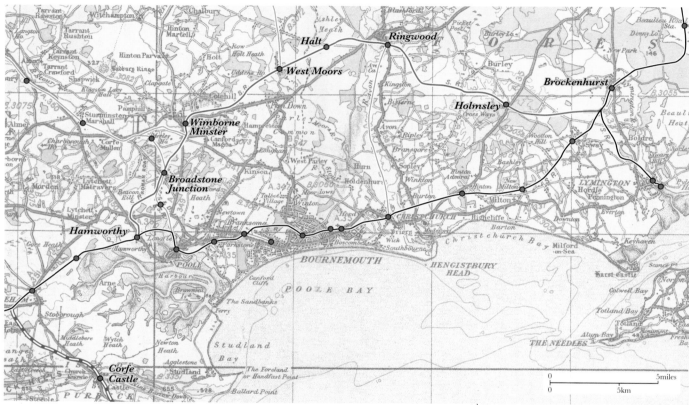

Promoted by a Wimborne solicitor by the name of Castleman, the Southampton & Dorchester Railway was an early scheme to build a main line from London Waterloo to Exeter and the West. By 1847 the single-track line to Dorchester was open across the New Forest via Brockenhurst, Ringwood, Wimborne and Broadstone. The following year the railway, known as Castleman's Corkscrew because of its roundabout route designed to serve as many centres of population as possible, was taken over by the London & South Western Railway. At this time, Christchurch and Bournemouth were only small hamlets but their rapid growth soon led to calls for a more direct coastal route.

▶ Unrebuilt 'West Country' Class 4-6-2 No. 34103 'Calstock' makes light work of a local train at Holmsley station on 18 September 1962. When the station opened in 1847, passengers for Christchurch were carried by horse-drawn bus from here (then named Christchurch Road but renamed in 1862).

▶ To the west of Lymington Junction near Brockenhurst, the trackbed of Castleman's Corkscrew passes through heathland of the New Forest National Park. Here, at Long Slade Bottom north of Sway, this fine brick arched road bridge spans the old railway, which is now popular with walkers, cyclists and horse riders.

◀ The westbound platform at Holmsley still survives as does the station building, which is now a tea room and restaurant. For about a mile east of Holmsley station, the route is now a minor road, its straightness providing a clue to the past.

▶ From Ringwood to Upton Park, near Hamworthy, the trackbed of the railway is now Castleman Trailway. About a mile west of Ringwood, the SR concrete platform of Ashley Heath Halt still survives along the side of the trail.

In the early days of the railway, passengers for Christchurch were conveyed by horse-drawn bus from Christchurch Road (later renamed Holmsley) station and for Bournemouth by a similar means from Hamworthy. The demand for a railway to serve these growing towns led to the Ringwood, Christchurch & Bournemouth Railway being opened, first to Christchurch in 1862 and then to Bournemouth in 1870. However, this circuitous route was slow and a new direct double–track main line from Lymington Junction, near Brockenhurst, via Sway and New Milton, to Christchurch, together with the doubling of the existing line thence to Bournemouth (later known as Central station) was opened in 1888. At the western end of Castleman's Corkscrew a line had already opened from Broadstone to Bournemouth West in 1874. At West Moors, the Corkscrew had been joined by the Salisbury & Dorset Junction Railway in 1867.

The opening of the new direct line from Waterloo to Bournemouth had an immediate effect on Castleman's Corkscrew west of Brockenhurst. The Ringwood to Christchurch line lost its importance and, although Weymouth-bound trains continued to use the old route, the opening of new cut–offs at Branksome and Holes Bay in 1893, led to its downgrading as a secondary route. The Ringwood to Christchurch line had succumbed in 1935 and, apart from local stopping services, the line between Brockenhurst and Broadstone came to life only on Summer Saturdays when Waterloo to Weymouth trains were diverted.

The end came on 4 May 1964 when remaining local passenger services from Bournemouth West to Brockenhurst via Wimborne and to Salisbury via West Moors were withdrawn. The majority of goods services to Ringwood and Wimborne ceased on 8 January 1967; only the western stub was worked by infrequent services until 1977. Thereafter the trackbed of Castleman's Corkscrew between Brockenhurst and Hamworthy Junction slowly reverted back to nature. The remaining two sections of the Castleman's Corkscrew that still see a rail service are between Southampton and Brockenhurst and between Hamworthy and Dorchester.

▶ Ex-Southern Railway Class 'Q' 0-6-0 No. 30538 heads a local train out of Ringwood station on 30 May 1963. Designed by Richard Maunsell, 20 of these freight locos were built at Eastleigh just before the Second World War. No. 30541 can be seen today on the Bluebell Railway.

◀ Apart from Weymouth-bound trains using the line on Summer Saturdays, the Brockenhurst to Hamworthy route saw the passing of local passenger services only. Motive power for these services could range from a Bulleid Light Pacific to a humble tank loco. Here, Class 'M7' 0-4-4 tank No. 30028, with utility van in tow, propels its push-pull train for Brockenhurst near Ringwood in 1960.

WALKING AND CYCLING THE LINE

THE LINE TODAY

Fortunately, much of the route of Castleman's Corkscrew between Brockenhurst and Hamworthy is now a cycleway, footpath and bridleway. Apart from a flooded cutting at Burbush Hill, the section between Lymington Junction, a mile south west of Brockenhurst, to the outskirts of Ringwood makes a very pleasant walk or ride through the heathlands of the New Forest National Park. Forestry Commission car parks and picnic sites abound and there are many opportunities to join or exit the route. There is still much to see for lovers of old railways including the long, straight embankment and graceful overbridge near Long Slade Bottom, the old platform and station building (the latter now an attractive tea room and restaurant) at Holmsley, a short section of level crossing rail still in situ in the road near Goatspen Plain and concrete level crossing posts at Crow, near Ringwood. About a mile of the route east of Holmsley station is now a minor road but its straightness belies its railway origins.

To the west of Ringwood the trackbed is now known as the Castleman Trailway, which, apart from a few diversions due to building or road development at West Moors and Wimborne since closure, makes a pleasant traffic-free route of 16½ miles through internationally important heathland for walkers and, on some sections, for cyclists and horse riders, to Upton Country Park near Hamworthy. Of railway interest on this section is the concrete platform with SR station totem at Ashley Heath Halt.

PLACES TO VISIT

HERITAGE RAILWAYS
Swanage Railway
Station House, Swanage, Dorset BH19 1HB
Tel 01929 425800
Website www.swanagerailway.co.uk
Route Swanage to Norden
Length 6 miles

OTHER ATTRACTIONS
Avon Heath Forest Park
Birch Road, St Ives, Ringwood, Hants BH24 2DA
Tel 01425 478470
Website www.dorsetforyou.com/avonheath

Walford Mill Crafts
Stone Lane, Wimborne, Dorset BH21 1NL
Tel 01202 841400
Website www.walfordmillcrafts.co.uk

Upton Country Park
Upton House, Poole, Dorset BH17 7BJ
Tel 01202 262748
Website www.uptoncountrypark.org

Moors Valley Country Park
Horton Road, Ashley Heath, Nr Ringwood, Dorset BH24 2ET
Tel 01425 470721
Website www.moors-valley.co.uk

PRACTICAL INFORMATION

NEAREST RAILWAY STATIONS
Brockenhurst, Hamworthy

TOURIST INFORMATION
Ringwood Tourist Information Centre
The Furlong, Ringwood, Hants BH24 1AZ
Tel 01425 470896
Website www.ringwood.gov.uk

Bournemouth Tourist Information Centre
Pavilion Theatre, Westover Road,
Bournemouth BH1 2BU
Tel 01202 451700
Website www.bournemouth.co.uk

Poole Tourist Information Centre
Welcome Centre, Enefco House, Poole,
Dorset BH15 1HJ
Tel 01202 253253
Website www.pooletourism.com

OS MAPS
Landranger No. 195/196

CYCLE HIRE
New Forest Cycle Hire
Downside Car Park, Brockenhurst Train Station, SO42 7TW
Tel 01590 623407/624204
Website www.newforestcyclehire.co.uk

New Forest Cycle Hire Centre
The Cross, Village Centre, Burley, Hants
BH24 4AB
Tel 01425 403584
Website www.forestleisurecycling.co.uk

In Shore Cycle Hire
Oakdene Holiday Park, St Leonards, Ringwood, Hampshire BH24 2RZ
Tel 01202 871222

THE RYE & CAMBER TRAMWAY

Rye to Camber Sands

*The eccentric 3ft-gauge Rye & Camber Tramway opened in 1895 to carry golfers to Rye Golf Club.
Closed at the start of the Second World War, much of its route can still be walked today.*

Railways first came to the hilltop town of Rye in 1851 when the South Eastern Railway opened a 26-mile line across Romney Marshes between Hastings and Ashford. A lucky escapee from the Beeching cuts, the line is still open and is known as the Marshlink Line. A short branch to Rye Harbour opened in 1854 but closed in 1962.

By the end of the 19th century, Victorian England was experiencing major social changes, many of them brought about by the coming of the railways and the subsequent ease of mass transport. Leisure time also increased for many people and the game of golf was increasing in popularity. At that time no golf club existed at Rye but this was soon rectified when Rye Golf Club opened in 1894 in the

▼ The Rye & Camber tramway was opened between Monkbretton Bridge at Rye and a terminus at Camber, later known as Golf Links Halt, on 13 July 1895. At that time services were handled by this small 2-4-0 tank loco 'Camber' hauling one passenger coach.

▲ To reduce operating costs this small rail tractor was introduced on the Rye & Camber in 1925. Its success led to the scrapping of one steam loco, 'Victoria', and the mothballing of the other, 'Camber'.

◀ Following requisition by the Admiralty in the Second World War, part of the Rye & Camber track was infilled with concrete to allow access to the construction site of a new jetty near Golf Links Halt. Today, about half a mile of 3ft-gauge track of this eccentric little line remains forever preserved in the concrete.

WALKING AND CYCLING THE LINE

THE LINE TODAY

Much of the route of this eccentric tramway can still be walked and, surprisingly, there is still much to interest lovers of old railways. Although the corrugated terminus building at Monkbretton Bridge has long since gone, the trackbed of the line from here is now a footpath as far as the Broadwater Bridge. The current footpath veers left here but a short distance farther on the trackbed can be rejoined along a concreted road that provides access to the harbourmaster's office and inshore rescue station. Formerly the route of the tramway, this stretch of road contains long sections of 3ft-gauge track that are preserved forever in the concrete that was added during the Second World War. Amazingly the corrugated structure of Golf Links Halt station building, which is now well over 100 years old, still stands in a very well-preserved state. From here a footpath follows the line of the 1908 extension of the tramway across the fairways of the golf club to Camber Sands. The wooden platform of the terminus has long since rotted away but those with keen eyes can spot its location, where ferns now grow.

▲With one year to go before the introduction of the petrol tractor, 2-4-0 tank 'Camber' and its crew pose for the camera at Camber Sands terminus in 1924. Behind the little station is the tea room that opened in the summer for day trippers on the railway. Both 'Camber' and sister engine 'Victoria' were built by the Stafford company of W. G. Bagnall.

PLACES TO VISIT

HERITAGE RAILWAYS
Romney, Hythe & Dymchurch Railway
New Romney Station, New Romney, Kent
TN28 8PL
Tel 01797 362353
Website www.rhdr.org.uk
Route Hythe to Dungeness
Length 13½ miles

OTHER ATTRACTIONS
Rye Castle Museum and Ypres Tower
3 East Street, Rye, East Sussex TN39 7JY
Tel 01797 226728
Website www.ryemuseum.co.uk

Rye Harbour Nature Reserve
Lime Kiln Cottage
Rye Harbour Road
Rye, East Sussex TN31 7TU
Tel 01797 227 784
Website www.wildrye.info

Old Dungeness Lighthouse
Dungeness, Romney Marsh,
Kent TN29 9NB
Tel: 01797 321300
Website: www.dungenesslighthouse.com

PRACTICAL INFORMATION

NEAREST RAILWAY STATION
Rye

TOURIST INFORMATION
Rye Tourist Information Centre
4/5 Lion Street, Rye, East Sussex TN31 7LB
Tel 01797 229049
Website www.visitrye.co.uk

OS MAP
Landranger No. 189

CYCLE HIRE
Rye Hire
1 Cyprus Place, Rye, East Sussex
TN31 7DR
Tel 01797 223033/227826

▲ The well-defined embankment of the 1908 extension from Golf Links Halt to Camber Sands is now a permissive footpath that bisects the links of Rye Golf Club. Walkers must beware of flying golf balls.

sand dunes of Camber Sands. Unfortunately, access to the site was poor so some local businessmen proposed building a tramway to convey golfers from Monkbretton Bridge, on the outskirts of Rye, to Rye Golf Club in Camber Sands.

Engineered by Colonel H. F. Stephens, the 3ft-gauge line opened on 13 July 1895 and was an immediate success. In 1908 the line was extended across the golf links to a new terminus at Camber Sands and the original terminus was renamed Golf Links Halt. Camber Sands soon became popular for day trippers and picknickers in the summer, but the little line struggled financially during the winter months, becoming dependent on subsidies from Rye Golf Club until 1924. To reduce running costs the two diminutive steam locos were replaced by a petrol rail tractor in 1925 and the little line struggled on until the outbreak of the Second World War in 1939. The line never reopened to passengers but the section between Rye and Golf Links Halt was requisitioned by the Admiralty to convey men and materials during the building of a large jetty on the Camber side of Rye Harbour. At the end of the war the tramway was handed back to its owners in a very dilapidated state and was never reopened.

▼ Happy days on the Rye & Camber! Hauled by the petrol tractor, all of the tramway's rolling stock is pressed into service on 12 July 1931. Laden with day trippers returning from their picnics on Camber Sands, the train is approaching Golf Links Halt on its journey back to Rye.

THE CUCKOO TRAIL

Eridge to Polegate

Running through the picturesque South Weald, the Cuckoo Line got its name from a legend that the first cuckoo of spring was heard every April at Heathfield Fair.

Affectionately known as the Cuckoo Line, the railway between Eridge and Polegate was built by the London Brighton & South Coast Railway in two sections. The southern section from Polegate, a junction on the main Eastbourne to London main line, to Hailsham opened on 14 May 1849. To the northwest the railway from East Grinstead to Tunbridge Wells via Groombridge opened in 1866 and from Uckfield to Groombridge via Eridge in 1868.

An early scheme to build a narrow gauge railway north of Hailsham failed to get off the ground and it was in 1876 that the LB&SCR obtained Parliamentary powers to build a second section of the Cuckoo Line, a standard gauge single-track line from Hailsham to Eridge. This opened throughout in September 1880 and the next year the junction arrangement at Polegate was rearranged to allow trains from the Cuckoo Line to continue on to Eastbourne. Following track improvements on the Uckfield line in 1894, the junction with the Cuckoo Line at Eridge was moved a mile south to a new location at Redgate Mill.

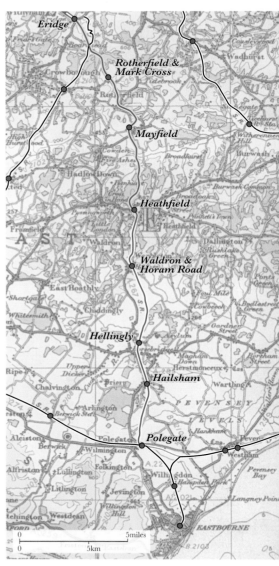

◀ To mark the closure of the Cuckoo Line as a through route, the Locomotive Club of Great Britain organised the Wealdsman Rail Tour on 13 June 1965. Here, Class 'U' 2-6-0 No. 31803 and Class 'N' 2-6-0 No. 31411 double-head the special as it approaches Mayfield.

▲ With its eerie sodium lighting, the railway tunnel at Heathfield has recently been reopened during daylight hours for walkers and cyclists on the Cuckoo Trail.

▶ Looking south on the Cuckoo Trail towards West Lane Bridge, between Heathfield and Horam. Nearly a quarter of a million people use the trail each year.

By the time of the 'Big Four Grouping' in 1923, train services on the line consisted of around seven trains each way every weekday between Tunbridge Wells and Eastbourne, of which three were through trains to and from London Victoria. Hailsham was better served with an additional seven a day to and from Eastbourne. Strangely, by the summer of 1963, when the Cuckoo Line had already been listed for closure in the Beeching Report, there was an even better service, although the through trains to and from Victoria had long ceased.

▲ Somewhat the worse for wear BR Standard Class 4 2-6-4 tank No. 80032 halts at Mayfield with a Cuckoo Line train in 1963.

As with the line's opening in the 19th century, closure of the Cuckoo Line also came in stages. In 1965, a survey showed that only 250 passengers each day were using the line, of which just 23 were season ticket holders. First to go were passenger services north of Hailsham which ceased on 13 June 1965. Heathfield continued to be served by goods trains until April 1968 and the final section from Polegate to Hailsham, then a fast-growing town, was closed completely on 8 September of that year.

▶ Four years after total closure, on 27 April 1972, the track has been lifted and Hellingly station waits for the next train that will never arrive. The view today is virtually unrecognisable – the Cuckoo Trail has brought the scene back to life and the station building has been beautifully restored as a private residence.

◄ The Cuckoo Trail takes walkers and cyclists past the restored station building at Hellingly. The only station on the Cuckoo Line with just one platform, it is certainly the best preserved and still retains its rear and front canopy. South of the station there was once an electric tramway serving Hellingly Mental Hospital.

▼ The sad remains of Hailsham station in April 1972 after the track had been lifted. The site has since been redeveloped but the nearby Terminus Inn recalls the early days of the railway, when Hailsham was the terminus of the line from Polegate.

WALKING AND CYCLING THE LINE

THE LINE TODAY
Much of the route of the closed Cuckoo Line south of Heathfield is now a footpath and cycleway known as the Cuckoo Trail, which terminates at Hampden Park north of Eastbourne. The trackbed of the railway south of Heathfield, a distance of about 13 miles, was purchased in 1981 by Wealden District Council and East Sussex County Council. In 1990 the route was improved by Sustrans and now forms part of National Cycle Network Route 21. It is estimated that nearly a quarter of a million people use the surfaced traffic-free route each year – a far cry from the 80,000 or so that used it each year when it was a railway line.

Of interest to lovers of old railways are the stations at Heathfield, now a cookware shop and café, and at Hellingly, now a private residence. There are brick arch bridges between Hellingly and Horam and the curving 250yd-long tunnel at Heathfield, lit by orange sodium lights, is also open for use during daylight hours only.

To the north of Heathfield the picture is very different. Until 1986 East Sussex County Council owned around 11 miles of the old trackbed but this has since been sold off. Efforts to extend the Cuckoo Trail northwards to link up with the Forest Way at Groombridge have so far faltered.

Car parks for Trail users are located at Heathfield, Horam, Hellingly, Hailsham, Polegate and Hampden Park. In recent years the Trail has been decorated by six wooden and steel sculptures that act as mileposts along the route.

PLACES TO VISIT

HERITAGE RAILWAYS
Spa Valley Railway
West Station,
Royal Tunbridge Wells,
Kent TN2 5QY
Tel 01892 537715
Website www.spavalleyrailway.co.uk
Route Tunbridge Wells West to Groombridge
Length 3½ miles

OTHER ATTRACTIONS
Groombridge Place Gardens
Groombridge, Tunbridge Wells,
Kent TN3 9QG
Tel 01892 861444
Website www.groombridge.co.uk

Eastbourne Miniature Steam Railway
Lottbridge Drove, Eastbourne,
East Sussex BN23 6QJ
Tel 01323 520229
Website www.emsr.co.uk

Michelham Priory
Upper Dicker, nr Hailsham,
East Sussex BN27 3QS
Tel 01323 844224
Website www.sussexpast.co.uk/michelham

Herstmonceux Castle
Hailsham, East Sussex BN27 1RN
Tel 01323 833816
Website www.herstmonceux-castle.com

Knockhatch Adventure Park
Hailsham Bypass, Hailsham,
East Sussex BN27 3GD
Tel 01323 442051
Website www.knockhatch.com

Hidden Spring Vineyard
Vines Cross Road, Horam, East Sussex
TN21 0HG
Tel 01435 812640
Website www.hiddenspring.co.uk

PRACTICAL INFORMATION

NEAREST RAILWAY STATIONS
Eridge, Polegate, Hampden Park

TOURIST INFORMATION
Eastbourne Tourist Information Centre
Cornfield Road, Eastbourne,
East Sussex BN21 4QL
Tel 0871 663 0031
Website www.visiteastbourne.com

Heathfield Visitor Information
Heathfield Leisure Centre,
Cade Street, Heathfield,
East Sussex TN21 8RJ
Tel 0845 803 5515

Tunbridge Wells Tourist Information Centre
The Old Fish Market, The Pantiles, Royal Tunbridge Wells, Kent TN2 5TN
Tel 01892 515675
Website www.visittunbridgewells.com

OS MAP
Landranger No. 199

CYCLE HIRE
Cycle Revival
Hailsham Road, Heathfield,
East Sussex TN21 8AA
Tel 01435 866118
Website www.cyclerevival.co.uk

THE FURZEBROOK RAILWAY

One of the principal deposits of ball clay for the UK pottery industry is on the Isle of Purbeck in Dorset. By the late 18th century, clay was being transported from here to the growing pottery business of Josiah Wedgwood in Etruria in Staffordshire. The clay was first carried by horse to Wareham where it was transhipped onto a barge, but increased demand soon led to a horse-drawn gravity tramway being built from the clay pits at Furzebrook to Ridge Wharf. Opened by the clay pit owners, William and John Pike, in 1830, the 4ft-gauge line allowed loaded clay wagons to run downhill to the wharf by gravity, with the empties being hauled back by horses.

The first steam locomotive, an 0-4-2 tank named 'Primus', was introduced in 1866 and at the same time the gauge was reduced to 2ft 8½in. The tramway was also extended to serve new clay pits at Povington, Cotness and Creech Grange and additional steam locomotives bought to handle the increased traffic. Between 1866 and 1930 seven steam locos were used on the line and

▲ Heavily laden wagons of ball clay at the Pike Brothers depot at Furzebrook in January 1956. Here, the clay was transhipped into standard gauge wagons for the long journey north to the Potteries.

▼ Although nearly at the end of its working life, 0-4-0 saddle tank 'Quintus' looks in fine fettle as it shunts clay wagons at Creech in January 1956. Built by Manning Wardle of Leeds in 1914, the loco was scrapped in 1958.

given Latin numeral names such as 'Secundus' (2), 'Tertius' (3) etc., ending in 'Septimus' (7).

With a route mileage of about 6 miles, the Furzebrook Railway continued its isolated existence until 1885 when a standard gauge branch line was opened by the London & South Western Railway from Wareham to Swanage. Despite passing over the clay line at Furzebrook, no transhipment sidings were built here until the early 20th century, when clay started to be shipped up to the Potteries via the main railway network. Further changes came during the Second World War when the line east of Furzebrook was closed by the War Department due to military activity on the surrounding heath.

The end came for the rest of the railway in 1956 when the line closed. Other narrow gauge clay lines on the Isle of Purbeck were the 3ft 9in-gauge tramways around Norden with the final section to Eldon, then worked by a small diesel, closing in 1969. Railway activity on the Isle ended when the Wareham to Swanage branch closed early in 1972. However, seven years later, a preservation group, known as the Swanage Railway, started operating steam trains and now this heritage line is open as far as Norden.

▼ Built by Bellis & Seeking in 1874, 0-6-0 well tank 'Secundus' was still at work on the Furzebrook Railway in August 1948. This historic loco has been preserved and is on display at the Swanage Railway Museum at Corfe Castle station.

▲ Seen here shunting on the Furzebrook Railway on 30 August 1948, 0-4-2 saddle tank 'Septimus' was built by Peckett & Sons of Bristol in 1930. After a relatively short working life, this diminutive little workhorse was finally scrapped in 1962.

WORTH WAY
Three Bridges to East Grinstead

Closed in 1967, the Three Bridges to East Grinstead line was yet another casualty of the Beeching Report, whose author lived nearby. It was reopened as a 7-mile footpath and cycleway in 1979.

▲ A view from the cab of Class 'M7' 0-4-4 tank No. 30053 as it approaches Rowfant with a train for East Grinstead High Level in the early 1960s. The line closed on 1 January 1967.

The opening of the London to Brighton main line by the London & Brighton Railway in 1840 brought the market town of East Grinstead within 7 miles of the nearest railway station on that line, Three Bridges. Fearing a loss of trade, East Grinstead's businessmen clamoured for a railway to be built to the town and in 1845 two schemes were put forward, one by the L&BR and the other by its arch rival, the South Eastern Railway. Nothing came of these due to the economic 'Panic of 1847', when British financial markets collapsed under the strain of financing the 1840s railway-building boom.

Despite this failure, a local firm, the East Grinstead Railway Company, was set up in 1852 to build a line from Three Bridges to the town. An arrangement was also made with the L&BR for them to lease and operate the line with an option to purchase it within ten years. Amid joyous celebrations in East Grinstead, the railway, with an intermediate station at Rowfant, opened on 9 July 1855. Another station, Grange Road, was opened in 1860. Leaving it to the last

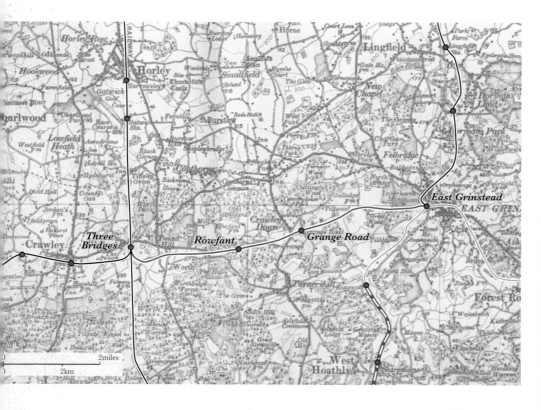

minute, the London Brighton & South Coast Railway, successor to the L&BR, went ahead with its option to purchase the East Grinstead Railway in 1865.

An extension to the East Grinstead Railway, known as the East Grinstead, Groombridge and Tunbridge Wells Railway Company, was authorised in 1862 and opened in 1866. The opening of the Lewes & East Grinstead Railway (part of which is now the Bluebell Railway) in 1882 led to a major rebuilding of East Grinstead station with the Three Bridges to Tunbridge Wells line platforms located at a higher level above the new line. The latter was extended northward in 1884 by the openings of the Croydon, Oxted & East Grinstead Railway. The two lines were linked by a spur built from St Margaret's Junction just north of East Grinstead station.

In an attempt to reduce running costs on the line, push–pull trains were introduced in 1905 and, under Southern Railway management, through trains from London Bridge and Victoria to Forest Row also began to run on the line. The period following the Second World War and nationalisation saw a rapid decline in services and the East Grinstead to Lewes line closed in 1955. Rowfant was one of the least-patronised stations in England and goods services were withdrawn from that station and Grange Road in 1961. The Three Bridges to Tunbridge Wells service

▲ Most of the station site at Rowfant, including the old station building, eastbound platform and stationmaster's house, is now occupied by a company manufacturing road-building materials. The Worth Way runs along the north side of the station building.

▼ Class 'M7' 0-4-4 tank No. 30109 leaves Rowfant station with a train for East Grinstead High Level in 1963. Rowfant once had the unenviable title of one of the least-used railway stations in England. For a period in the 1950s, its goods yard stored aviation fuel for the new Gatwick Airport.

saw the introduction of new diesel-electric multiple units in 1962, but even this modernisation failed to improve passenger numbers.

By 1963, when the Beeching Report was published (Beeching himself lived near East Grinstead), the writing was already on the wall for the loss-making line. Listed for closure in the report, the line struggled on with steam-haulage, ending in 1965. Despite fierce local objections, all services between Three Bridges, East Grinstead and Groombridge ceased on 1 January 1967. The section from Groombridge to Tunbridge Wells survived a while longer until it too closed in 1985. Today East Grinstead is the southern terminus of the electrified line from Oxted, while the line south to Sheffield Park is operated by the Bluebell Railway.

◀ Looking along the Worth Way towards East Grinstead at Crawley Down near the site of Grange Road station. Despite its name, the station actually served the village of Crawley Down.

▼ Fitted for push-pull operation, Class 'H' 0-4-4 tank No. 31263 stands at East Grinstead High Level station on 19 August 1962. To complete this evocative English scene, the two-tone double-decker bus waits patiently for connecting passengers to join it for the journey to Tunbridge Wells station.

WALKING AND CYCLING THE LINE

THE LINE TODAY

Opened in 1979, almost the entire length of the Three Bridges to East Grinstead railway is now a footpath and cycleway owned by West Sussex County Council and known as the Worth Way. There are diversions from the original trackbed due to development in the Crawley Down area and the building of the M23. The Worth Way was resurfaced in 1999 and now forms part of Route 21 of the National Cycle Network. Of interest to railway lovers is Rowfant station building, the stationmaster's house and part of the platform, which still stand.

At East Grinstead the Worth Way links with another footpath and bridleway known as the Forest Way, which runs for 9½ miles along the trackbed of the former railway to Groombridge. Owned by East Sussex County Council, the Forest Way is a linear country park set in the High Weald Area of Outstanding Natural Beauty. The station building and platform at Hartfield still exist.

PLACES TO VISIT

HERITAGE RAILWAYS
Bluebell Railway
Sheffield Park Station,
East Sussex TN22 3QL
Tel 01825 720800
Website www.bluebell-railway.co.uk
Route Sheffield Park to Kingscote
Length 9 miles

OTHER ATTRACTIONS
Ashdown Forest Centre
Wych Cross, Forest Row,
East Sussex RH18 5JP
Tel 01342 823583
Website www.ashdownforest.org

West Hoathly Priest House
North Lane, West Hoathly,
West Sussex RH19 4PP
Tel 01342 810479
Website www.sussexpast.co.uk/priesthouse

Hammerwood Park
East Grinstead, Sussex RH19 3QE
Tel 01342 850594
Website www.hammerwood.mistral.co.uk

Nymans Gardens (National Trust)
Handcross, nr Haywards Heath,
West Sussex RH17 6EB
Tel 01444 405250
Website www.nationaltrust.org.uk/nymans

PRACTICAL INFORMATION

NEAREST RAILWAY STATIONS
Three Bridges, East Grinstead, Tunbridge Wells

TOURIST INFORMATION
East Grinstead Tourist Information Centre
Library Buildings, West Street, East Grinstead,
West Sussex
Tel 01342 410121
Website www.eastgrinstead.gov.uk/tourism

Tunbridge Wells Tourist Information Centre
The Old Fish Market, The Pantiles, Royal
Tunbridge Wells, Kent TN2 5TN
Tel 01892 515675
Website www.visittunbridgewells.com

OS MAP
Landranger No. 187

CYCLE HIRE
Deers Leap Bikes
Saint Hill Green, East Grinstead, East Sussex
RH19 4NG
Tel 01342 325858
Website www.deersleapbikes.co.uk

◀ Having just exchanged the single-line tablet with the signalman, Fairburn Class 4 2-6-4 tank No. 42092 enters East Grinstead High Level station with the 9.06am train from Three Bridges on 31 March 1954. The track on the right leads down via St Margaret's Junction to the low-level station on the Oxted to Lewes line.

COLE GREEN WAY
Hertford to Welwyn Garden City

Originally part of a cross-country route between Dunstable and Ware, the Hertford to Welwyn branch fell into obscurity in the 1920s. Its trackbed is now a picturesque footpath and cycleway.

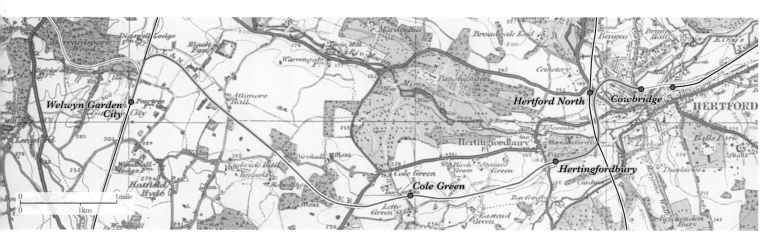

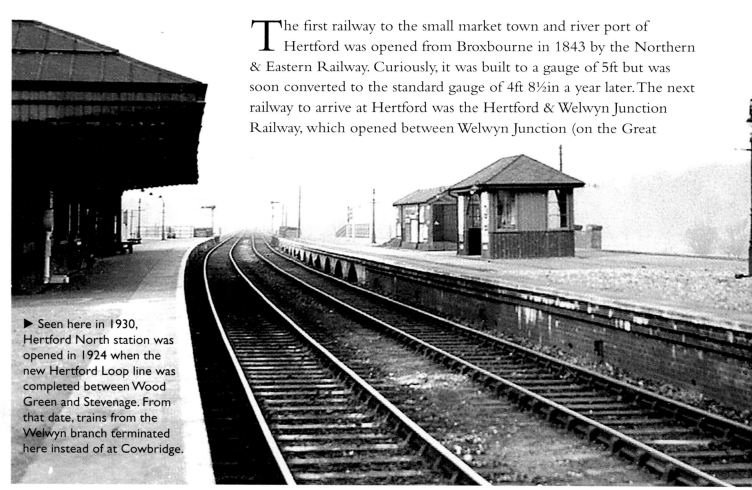

The first railway to the small market town and river port of Hertford was opened from Broxbourne in 1843 by the Northern & Eastern Railway. Curiously, it was built to a gauge of 5ft but was soon converted to the standard gauge of 4ft 8½in a year later. The next railway to arrive at Hertford was the Hertford & Welwyn Junction Railway, which opened between Welwyn Junction (on the Great

▶ Seen here in 1930, Hertford North station was opened in 1924 when the new Hertford Loop line was completed between Wood Green and Stevenage. From that date, trains from the Welwyn branch terminated here instead of at Cowbridge.

▶ Looking eastwards along Cole Green Way near Hertingfordbury station where the growth of vegetation and trees since closure in 1962 has turned the trackbed into a linear wildlife haven.

Hertford Station G. N. R.

▲ Opened in 1858, the first Great Northern Railway station in Hertford was at Cowbridge. Seen here in the early 20th century, the station was closed in 1924 when services from Welwyn were diverted to the North station on the newly opened Hertford Loop line.

Northern Railway's main line) and Hertford (Cowbridge) in 1858. In that year the H&WJR amalgamated with the Luton, Dunstable & Welwyn Junction Railway to become the Hertford, Luton & Dunstable Railway. The section from Luton to Welwyn opened in 1860 and, a year later, the HL&DR became part of the mighty GNR. By 1876 both the Luton and Hertford branches had been diverted into Hatfield station and, as all trains were required to reverse here, the route's life as a cross-country route was ended.

Traffic on the Hatfield to Hertford branch was never heavy and Hertford itself was better served by the Great Eastern line to Liverpool Street via Broxbourne. However, this situation changed in 1924 when the LNER's Hertford Loop from its main line at Wood Green to Stevenage via a new station at Hertford North came into full

▶ Several old railway bridges, such as this one near Birch Green, still survive along the route of Cole Green Way. It is a very popular traffic-free route for walkers, joggers, cyclists and horse riders.

WALKING AND CYCLING THE LINE

THE LINE TODAY

Almost the entire length of the old railway between Welwyn and Hertford is now a footpath and cycleway known as Cole Green Way. Also used as a bridleway, the picturesque 3½-mile-long traffic-free route starts at Cole Green Lane to the east of Welwyn and passes through the sites of Cole Green and Hertingfordbury stations before passing under the Hertford Loop viaduct to finish close to Hertford Football Ground. An extension to Cole Green Way continues along the towpath of the River Lea Navigation as far as Ware. At Cole Green, where there is a small car park and picnic site on the old station platform, refreshments can be taken at the refurbished Cowper Arms public house. Set alongside Cole Green Way, Hertingfordbury station building is now a private residence. Cowbridge station site is today an industrial estate.

PLACES TO VISIT

Hatfield House
Hatfield, Hertfordshire AL9 5NQ
Tel 01707 287010
Website www.hatfield-house.co.uk

Hertford Museum
18 Bull Plain, Hertford SG14 1DT
Tel 01992 582686
Website: www.hertfordmuseum.org

Hertford Castle
Hertford SG14 1HR
Tel 01992 552885
Website www.hertford.gov.uk

Knebworth House
Knebworth,
Hertfordshire SG3 6PY
Tel 01438 812661
Website www.knebworthhouse.com

Shaw Corner (National Trust)
Ayot St Lawrence, nr Welwyn,
Hertfordshire AL6 9BX
Tel 01438 829221
Website www.nationaltrust.org.uk

PRACTICAL INFORMATION

NEAREST RAILWAY STATIONS
Welwyn, Hertford North, Hertford East

OS MAP
Landranger No. 189

TOURIST INFORMATION
Hertford Tourist Information Centre
10 Market Place, Hertford SG14 1DF
Tel 01992 584322
Website www.hertford.gov.uk

▲ The edge of the eastbound platform can still be seen today at the site of Cole Green station. The station site is now a small car park and picnic spot for users of the Cole Green Way. The nearby Cowper Arms pub offers refreshments.

operation. The old H&WJR station at Cowbridge was closed and passenger trains from Hatfield were diverted into the new North station. Despite the introduction of short-lived rail-motor services in 1904 and 1905, and its route passing through the second garden city in England (founded in 1920), traffic remained light and the line was an early casualty of railway closures following nationalisation of the railways in 1948. Passenger services ceased on 18 June 1951 while goods trains continued to serve Cole Green and Hertingfordbury stations until 1962, when the whole line, apart from a short section at Welwyn, was closed. The latter section remained open until 1966 to serve a rubbish groundfill site at Holwell. To the west, passenger services ceased between Welwyn, Luton and Dunstable in 1965, although the section from Dunstable to the Midland main line at Luton remained open for freight until 1990.

▼ Hertingfordbury station, which closed to passengers in 1951 and to goods in 1962, is now a private residence. This view shows it in the years before total closure when the odd wagon load of coal was still delivered by rail for distribution in the nearby village.

NORTHERN HEIGHTS PARKLAND WALK

Finsbury Park to Alexandra Palace

Built to serve the grand Victorian edifice of Alexandra Palace, this short branch line through the suburbs of North London missed out on joining London's Underground system due to the Second World War.

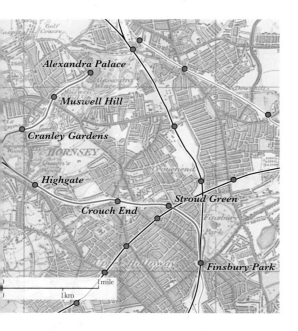

It must be hard to visualise it now, but in 1852 passengers on trains leaving the newly opened King's Cross station were treated to views of open countryside when they emerged from the smoky confines of Copenhagen Tunnel. Twenty years later, the middle-class suburbs had reached Finsbury Park and that is where the story begins. Despite frantic railway-building elsewhere, the villages of Highgate, Finchley and Edgware and the small town of Barnet still lacked a railway service. This situation was remedied when the rural and steeply graded Edgware, Highgate & London Railway (just before opening becoming part of the Great Northern Railway) opened from Finsbury Park on 22 August 1867.

In the meantime, plans were afoot to build Alexandra Palace, a Victorian pile set on high ground between Wood Green and Muswell Hill. To serve it, a short branch from the new line at Highgate was opened on 24 May 1873 – the official opening day of the Palace.

▶ Fitted with condensing apparatus for working Metropolitan Line trains to Moorgate, LNER Class 'N2' 0-6-2 tank No. 4727 bursts out of Highgate Tunnel with an Alexandra Palace to Finsbury Park train on 5 June 1937.

◀ In this wintry early 20th-century scene Great Northern Railway 0-4-4 tank No. 698 heads for Muswell Hill between Finsbury Park and Highgate with a long train of four-wheeled suburban stock.

▲ Wreathed in steam, ex-LNER Class 'N7' 0-6-2 tank No. 69694 heads away from Crouch End station with a train for Alexandra Palace in the early 1950s. Vestiges of the cancelled electrification of this line can still be seen alongside the track.

More than 124,000 people used the railway to visit the Palace over the next two weeks until it was badly damaged in a fire, only reopening again in 1875. Although operated throughout by the GNR, the final ¾ mile of the line was owned by the Muswell Hill Railway, a company that retained its independence until it was finally absorbed by the GNR in 1911.

By the early 20th century the opening of these railways to North London brought about a dramatic growth of the sprawling suburbs that we know today. By the 1930s, the existing railways were stretched to the limit and major changes were on the horizon. The deep-level Northern Line underground railway was extended from Archway to link with the existing steam-hauled line at East Finchley. Lines north of here to Barnet and Mill Hill were electrified in the early years of the Second World War while the service from Finsbury Park to Alexandra Palace continued to be steam-hauled. Plans to electrify the Mill Hill East to Edgware section and the Alexandra Palace branch were scrapped soon after the war.

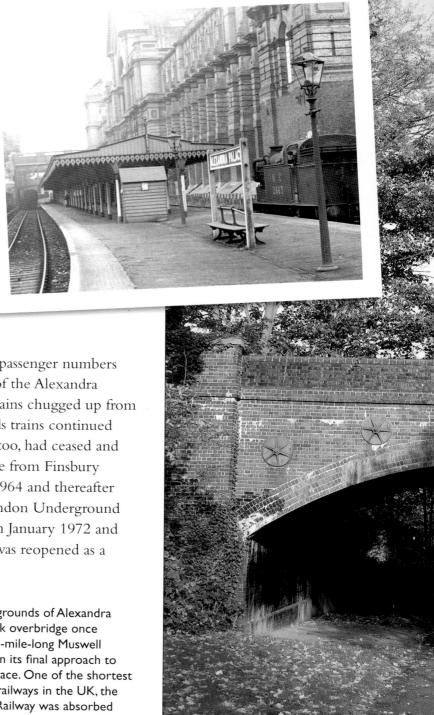

The scrapping of electrification plans, falling passenger numbers and shortages of coal all led to the early demise of the Alexandra Palace branch. The last steam-hauled passenger trains chugged up from Finsbury Park to Ally Pally on 3 July 1954. Goods trains continued to use the branch for a while but by 1957 these, too, had ceased and the line was soon lifted. The remainder of the line from Finsbury Park to Highgate continued to see freight until 1964 and thereafter remained in use for the occasional transfer of London Underground stock until September 1970. The line was lifted in January 1972 and the trackbed fell into disuse until 1984, when it was reopened as a linear green walkway.

▲ Fitted with condensing apparatus for working Metropolitan Line trains to Moorgate, LNER Class 'N2' 0-6-2 tank No. 2663 runs round its two-coach train at Alexandra Palace station on 11 August 1945. In 1873, only two weeks after opening, train services to the station were suspended for two years following a disastrous fire in the Palace.

▶ Set in the grounds of Alexandra Park, this brick overbridge once carried the ¾-mile-long Muswell Hill Railway on its final approach to Alexandra Palace. One of the shortest independent railways in the UK, the Muswell Hill Railway was absorbed finally by the Great Northern Railway in 1911.

WALKING AND CYCLING THE LINE

THE LINE TODAY

Known as the Parkland Walk, the resurfaced trackbed of the Finsbury Park to Alexandra Palace railway winds its way for 4½ miles through the suburbs of North London. The route is accessible for walkers only and a proposal to allow cyclists to use part of it led to much controversy.

With many bridges still intact and the overgrown platforms of Crouch End station extant today, the route retains much of its railway atmosphere. The site of Highgate station is approached along a cutting to the blocked-up twin tunnels where this section of the footpath ends. To continue to Alexandra Palace along the old railway line it is necessary to take a deviation along Muswell Hill Road to the road overbridge at the site of Cranley Gardens station. Here the Parkland Walk continues along the trackbed through what is now woodland before crossing a viaduct close to the site of Muswell Hill station, where the official footpath ends. There are extensive views across the rooftops of North London to the City from the top of the viaduct.

Alexandra Park is reached by continuing through a pedestrian tunnel under Muswell Hill. Although a school has been built on the trackbed here, there are still vestiges of the old railway, including an attractive bridge, on its final approach to the Palace. Refreshments can be taken at the Grove Café in the park where there is also a boating lake and a nine-hole pitch & putt golf course. The Palace itself, with its restored Palm Court, ice rink and Phoenix Bar, is also well worth a visit.

PLACES TO VISIT

OTHER ATTRACTIONS

Bruce Castle Museum
Lordship Lane, London N17 8NU
Tel 020 8808 8772
Website www.haringey.gov.uk

Kenwood House (English Heritage)
Hampstead Lane, London NW3 7JR
Tel 020 8348 1286
Website www.english-heritage.org.uk

Alexandra Palace,
Alexandra Palace Way
Wood Green, London N22 7AY
Tel 020 8365 2121
Website www.alexandrapalace.com

PRACTICAL INFORMATION

NEAREST RAILWAY STATIONS

Finsbury Park, Alexandra Palace, Highgate (Northern Line)

TOURIST INFORMATION

Britain and London Visitor Centre (BLVC)
1 Lower Regent Street, London SW1 4XT
Tel 08701 566 366
Website www.visitlondon.com

OS MAP

Landranger No. 176

CYCLE HIRE

Cycling is forbidden on the footpath

▲ Between Cranley Gardens and Muswell Hill, the Parkland Way crosses the 17-arch viaduct over St James's Lane. From here on a clear day there are panoramic views across the rooftops of North London to the City.

EASTERN ENGLAND

◀ Bardney, on the Lincoln to Boston line, was also the junction for a heavily graded single-track line over the Wolds to Louth. The line was never a financial success and it lost its passenger service in 1951. Apart from a few goods trains, which ran until 1956, the line was also occasionally visited by enthusiasts' specials. Here, the RCTS 'Lincolnshire Tour' has just arrived at Bardney before taking the train to Louth behind ex-GNR 0-6-0 No. 64199 on 16 May 1954.

THE MARRIOTT'S WAY

Norwich City to Melton Constable

Once an important cross-country route from the Midlands, the Midland & Great Northern Joint Railway became an early victim of railway rationalisation when it closed in 1959.

▲ During the final years of operation on the M&GNJR, motive power was usually in the hands of ex-LMS Ivatt Class 4 2-6-0s. Here, No. 43146 is seen arriving at Norwich City station with a train from Melton Constable on a snowy 10 January 1959, less than two months before closure.

The first railway to reach Norwich was opened from Colchester, where it formed an end–on junction with the Eastern Counties Railway from London (Bishopsgate), by the Eastern Union Railway in 1849. The two companies amalgamated in 1862 to form the Great Eastern Railway. At that time the GER terminus in Norwich was at Victoria station, but by 1914 this had fallen out of use, with all trains from London terminating at Thorpe station.

Before long the Great Eastern Railway had a virtual monopoly of railway lines in Norfolk until 1883 when the Eastern & Midlands

◄ This rare A-framed bridge once carried the M&GNJR over the River Wensum near Drayton. In its new life it carries walkers and cyclists along the 14-mile Marriott's Way from Hellesdon, near Norwich, to Reepham.

◄ Despite closing to passengers on 2 March 1959, the M&GN line from the Themelthorpe Curve to Norwich City remained open for freight until 1969. During this period the station was also visited by the occasional enthusiasts' special. Here veteran ex-GER Class 'J15' 0-6-0 No. 65469 awaits departure from City station on 21 May 1960 with the M&GNJR Preservation Society's Waveney Valley Special.

Railway was formed by the amalgamation of three independent companies – the Lynn & Fakenham, the Yarmouth Union and the Yarmouth & North Norfolk Railways. Its headquarters at Melton Constable, the new company soon opened two more lines – to Norwich (City) and to Cromer (Beach) – and absorbed the Midland & Eastern and the Peterborough, Wisbech & Sutton Bridge Railways. However, the Eastern & Midlands soon fell on hard times and it was taken over in 1893 by the Great Northern and the Midland Railways, who operated it as the Midland & Great Northern Joint Railway.

With a route mileage of 173 miles, the M&GNJR cut directly into Great Eastern territory and enabled the mighty Midland Railway access to the towns and ports of Norfolk. This was, by far, the largest

▲ Resplendent in its dark-brown livery, M&GNJR Beyer, Peacock 4-4-0 No. 80 awaits departure from Norwich City station on 26 June 1929 with the 5.20pm all stations to Melton Constable.

◀ The old M&GN station and goods yard at Whitwell & Reepham is currently being converted to a railway museum. To commemorate the 50th anniversary of closure of the M&GN, a Peckett 0-6-0 saddle tank operated on a short length of track here on 28 February 2009.

▶ The former GER station at Reepham is now a café and cycle-hire centre for users of Marriott's Way. A 7-mile footpath continues along the trackbed from here to Aylsham for connection with trains on the Bure Valley Railway to Wroxham.

▶ Within two months of this image being taken, the station at Attlebridge was closed to passengers on 2 March 1959. During the final years of operation, passenger traffic on the loss-making line from Norwich City to Melton Constable was fairly negligible, although its closure brought strong local protest. Attlebridge station is now a private residence alongside the Marriott's Way.

joint railway company in Britain, and was an important cross-country route linking the Midlands and the North with East Anglia. Although both goods traffic and through passenger traffic from the Midlands held up well until the Second World War, particularly during the summer months, it was severely disadvantaged by its long single-track sections.

The company owned 15 4-4-0s built by Beyer, Peacock between 1881 and 1888 for the former Lynn & Fakenham Railway and the later Eastern & Midlands Railway. The M&GN's locomotive livery was a light brown and burnt sienna colour until 1922, when a new dark-brown livery was introduced. In 1936, the LNER took over the

running of the railway and introduced Class 'K2' 2-6-0s and ex-GER 'Claud Hamilton' 4-4-0s to replace the ageing Beyer, Peacocks. Under British Railways the fairly new Ivatt 4MT 2-6-0s became the mainstay of motive power on the system until closure in 1959.

After the Second World War, the 'Muddle & Get Nowhere Railway', as it was affectionately known, saw its fortunes fade with competition from road transport and the changing habits of holidaymakers. In 1958, seeking to reduce mounting losses, the British Railways Committee recommended closure of the whole system – despite a huge local outcry the end came on 2 March 1959. The Sheringham to Melton Constable section escaped closure, but this, too, succumbed to the 'Beeching Axe' in 1964.

Goods traffic continued for a while between Melton Constable and Norwich City until 1960 when the sharpest radius curve on the entire BR network was laid at Themelthorpe, north of Whitwell & Reepham station. This enabled goods trains to run the 40 or so miles from Norwich Thorpe to Norwich City (geographically less than a mile apart!) via the former GER line from Wroxham and Aylsham while the M&GN section north to Melton Constable was completely closed. The goods traffic to Norwich City ceased in 1969 but trains continued to carry concrete products from a factory at Lenwade until 1982.

◀ Known as the 'Crewe of Norfolk', Melton Constable grew from rural obscurity into a railway village after the M&GNJR railway works were built there in 1883. With concrete pioneer William Marriott at the helm, the works went on to employ over 1,000 staff by the early 20th century. Once covering a site of 14 acres, most of the works closed in 1936 when the LNER took over operations. Today most of the site is an industrial estate but some buildings survive. The water tower is scheduled for listing as a historic building.

▼ To enable freight trains to reach Norwich City after closure of the M&GN, the infamous Themelthorpe Curve was laid in 1960 to link the branch with the ex-GER line to Aylsham and Wroxham. When laid the curve had the tightest radius of any BR line. It now forms part of the route of the Marriott's Way between Norwich and Reepham.

WALKING AND CYCLING THE LINE

THE LINE TODAY
The trackbed of the former M&GN line from Hellesdon, on the north-eastern outskirts of Norwich, to the Themelthorpe Curve and a short section of the former GER line to Reepham now forms the 14-mile Marriott's Way cycleway and footpath. Named after the long-serving Chief Engineer and Manager of the Midland & Great Northern Joint Railway, William Marriott, this level traffic-free route is now part of the National Cycle Network Route 1. Car parking along the route is available at Hellesdon, Freeland Corner, Attlebridge and Lenwade.

Although the Marriott's Way ends at Reepham, a footpath continues for another 7 miles along the old GER trackbed to Aylsham where connection can be made with the Bure Valley Railway to Wroxham. Here there is a main-line railway connection back to Norwich.

There is still much of interest along the route of Marriott's Way including the rare A-framed bridge that once carried the railway over the River Wensum at Drayton. Both Attlebridge and Lenwade stations are now private residences and the route near here is decorated with several concrete sculptures that are a reminder of the line's final years of operation. A short length of track has been relaid at Whitwell & Reepham station, which is now being restored as a railway museum. Here, the 50th anniversary of the line's closure was commemorated on 28 February 2009 by the steaming of a visiting Peckett 0-6-0 saddle tank.

The Marriott's Way continues to the Themelthorpe Curve where it makes a 180° turn to join the trackbed of the former GER line from County School to Wroxham as far as Reepham station. Here the old station building is now a tea room and cycle-hire centre.

PLACES TO VISIT

HERITAGE RAILWAYS
Bure Valley Railway
Aylsham Station, Norwich Road, Aylsham, Norfolk NR11 6BW
Tel 01263 733858
Website www.bvrw.co.uk
Route Aylsham to Wroxham
Length 9 miles

North Norfolk Railway
Sheringham Station, Station Approach, Sheringham, Norfolk NR26 8RA
Tel 01263 820800
Website www.nnrailway.co.uk
Route Sheringham to Holt
Length 5¼ miles

OTHER ATTRACTIONS
City of Norwich Aviation Museum
Old Norwich Road, Horsham St Faith, Norwich NR10 3JF
Tel 01603 893080
Website www.cnam.co.uk

Dinosaur Adventure Park
Weston Park, Lenwade, Norfolk NR9 5JW
Tel 01603 876310
Website www.dinosauradventure.co.uk

The Animal Ark
Fakenham Road
Great Witchingham, Norfolk NR9 5QS
Tel 01603 872274
Website www.theanimalark.org

Blickling Hall, Gardens and Park (NT)
Blickling, Norwich, Norfolk NR11 6NF
Tel 01263 738030
Website www.nationaltrust.org.uk

PRACTICAL INFORMATION

NEAREST RAILWAY STATIONS
Norwich, Aylsham (Bure Valley Railway)

TOURIST INFORMATION
Norwich Tourist Information Centre
The Forum, Millennium Plain, Norwich NR2 1TF
Tel 01603 213999
Website www.visitnorwich.co.uk

Broadland Tourist Information Centre
Bure Valley Railway, Norwich Road, Aylsham, Norfolk NR11 6BW
Tel 01263 733903

OS MAP
Landranger No. 133

CYCLE HIRE
Reepham Station Adventure Cycling
Station Road, Reepham, Norfolk NR10 4LJ
Tel 01603 871187

Huff and Puff Cycle Hire
Le Bonbon, 22 Red Lion Street, Aylsham, Norfolk NR1 6ER
Tel 01263 732935

BLYTH VALLEY WALK
Southwold to Halesworth

Despite a working life of only 50 years and closure more than 80 years ago, much of the route of this delightfully eccentric English narrow gauge railway can still be followed on foot today.

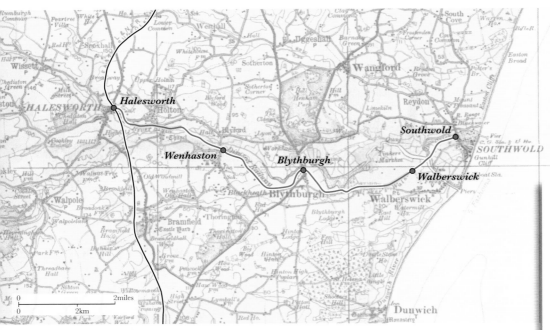

▼ A solitary lady passenger waits for the next train at Walberswick station in the late 19th century. The concrete base of the station still remains today, adorned by a seat provided by Southwold Railway Society.

Railways first arrived on the scene in East Suffolk with the opening of the East Suffolk Railway from Beccles to Halesworth in 1854. This line was extended south to Ipswich and north to Great Yarmouth in 1859 and the whole undertaking became part of the Great Eastern Railway in 1862. Despite the opening of this line, the small harbour town of Southwold was 9 miles from the nearest station at Halesworth and local residents were soon pressing for a railway of their own. A proposal to link the two towns with a narrow gauge railway found favour and in 1876 an Act of Parliament was passed that allowed for the building of a 3ft-gauge line. The Southwold Railway opened on 24 September 1879 with motive power in the form of three Sharp, Stewart 2-4-0 tank locos and passengers carried in six coaches – the latter having quirky ride qualities due to their unusual wheel arrangement of three two-wheeled bogies per coach.

The only major engineering work on the single-track line was a swing bridge across the River Blyth on the approach to Southwold. A new version replaced it in 1907 but was rarely used and last swung for shipping in 1914. A branch line to the harbour at Southwold was

▲ A mixed train from Southwold arrives at Halesworth on 11 September 1910. Passengers for Ipswich, London or Lowestoft could transfer to the nearby standard gauge station on the East Suffolk line. There was also a goods transfer shed here where shipments from the Southwold Railway were transferred by hand onto Great Eastern Railway wagons.

▼ The first station after Halesworth was at Wenhaston. This metal plaque, depicting Southwold Railway 0-6-2 tank locomotive 'Wenhaston', now marks the station site.

also opened in 1916 but the expected increase in fish traffic never materialised. Trains on this eccentric little line were of a mixed variety – carrying both passengers and goods – and this together with a 16mph speed restriction meant that the journey time for the 9 miles between Southwold and Halesworth was a painfully slow 35 minutes. Despite these shortcomings the Southwold Railway managed to stay profitable until the mid-1920s, when increasing competition from road transport marked a decline in its fortunes. The introduction of a regular motorbus service between Southwold and Halesworth was the final nail in the coffin and with only one week's notice the Southwold Railway abruptly closed on 11 April 1929.

Despite closure, the little railway took a long time to die – the track remained intact until 1941 when it was lifted for scrap and the railway's locomotives and rolling stock that had been stored at Halesworth were broken up in the same year. The Southwold Railway Company was not wound up until 1960 and an abandonment order was granted only in the 1990s.

▼ Seen here around the outbreak of the First World War, the second such locomotive on the Southwold Railway to carry the name 'Southwold' was 2-4-2 tank No.1, which was built by Sharp, Stewart in 1893. Not known for their riding qualities, the passenger carriages were of an unusual design, with the body carried on three two-wheeled bogies.

▼ The Southwold Railway published a series of colour postcards of the line in the early 20th century. This one depicts a mixed train passing through pine woodland between Blythburgh and Walberswick.

◄ The final approach to Southwold station was along this cutting that bisected the local golf club. A footbridge made out of second-hand rails was built in 1903 across the line to allow golfers access to the greens.

▼ The first railway swing bridge over the River Blyth at Southwold was replaced in 1907 by a wider version capable of carrying a standard gauge line. The plan to link the Southwold Railway with the national rail system never transpired and the bridge was demolished during the Second World War. The current modern Bailey bridge carries a footpath and pipeline.

WALKING AND CYCLING THE LINE

THE LINE TODAY

Despite closure more than 80 years ago, much of the route of this little railway can still be traced by walking. Known as the Blyth Valley Walk, a footpath starts at the site of the Halesworth terminus of the railway, now a housing estate. Within a short distance, the brick abutments of a road bridge, a brick arched bridge and the brick foundations of the former engine shed can all be discovered. Following various deviations from the route of the railway, the next railway relic can be found near Mells where Ball's Bridge is one of the few other structures that have remained intact.

Another reminder of the little railway can be found at the site of Wenhaston station, where an attractive steel plaque depicting locomotive No. 4 has been erected to mark the spot. The next station along the line was at Blythburgh, but little remains today apart from a timber coal house lurking in the undergrowth between the magnificent Holy Trinity Church and the River Blyth. Between Blythburgh and the next station, Walberswick, the trackbed passes through a

National Nature Reserve – however, half of this section is reserved for 'Horse Riders Only' and walkers have to use the B1387 near the Heronry before rejoining the trackbed west of Walberswick. The concrete base of Walberswick station still remains today and a seat has been provided by the Southwold Railway Society. Continuing along the trackbed we reach the site of the swing bridge over the River Blyth – here the original bridge was demolished in the Second World War and replaced by a modern Bailey Bridge, which carries the footpath and a pipeline across the river.

Very little remains of the Southwold Harbour branch except a small length of rusting track, which can be seen on the quay opposite the local sailing club. The final approach to the site of Southwold Station is across heathland and through a cutting that, until the 1970s, was crossed by a footbridge constructed of old railway lines. The site of Southwold Station has long disappeared and all that is left is a small brass plaque, fixed to the wall of the modern police station, commemorating the railway.

PLACES TO VISIT

HERITAGE RAILWAYS
Mid-Suffolk Light Railway
Brockford Station, Wetheringsett, Stowmarket, Suffolk IP14 5PW
Website www.mslr.org.uk
Route Brockford & Wetheringsett Station
Length ½ mile

OTHER ATTRACTIONS
Adnams Brewery
Sole Bay Brewery, East Green, Southwold, Suffolk IP18 6JW
Tel 01502 727225
Website www.brewerytours.adnams.co.uk

Southwold Lighthouse Visitor Centre
Tel 01502 722576
Website www.trinityhouse.co.uk

Southwold Museum
9–11 Victoria Street, Southwold, Suffolk IP18 6HZ
Tel 01502 726097
Website www.southwoldmuseum.org

Dunwich Museum
St James Street, Dunwich, Suffolk IP17 3DT
Tel 01728 648796
Website www.dunwichmuseum.org.uk

PRACTICAL INFORMATION

NEAREST RAILWAY STATION
Halesworth

TOURIST INFORMATION
Southwold Tourist Information Centre
69 High Street, Southwold, Suffolk IP18 6DS
Tel 01502 724729
Website www.visit-sunrisecoast.co.uk

OS MAP
Landranger No. 156

CYCLE HIRE
Southwold Town Garage
Station Road, Southwold IP18 6AX
Tel 01502 723140
Website www.southwold.biz/Services

▶ This jolly Edwardian scene depicts railway staff at Southwold posing in front of one of the Sharp, Stewart 2-4-0 tank locos that were built for the opening of the line.

▼ All trains on the Southwold Railway were of a mixed variety as seen in this photograph of Southwold station taken in the early 20th century. The carriage shed behind the locomotive was built with only one covered side to reduce construction costs while on the far left is the engine shed with one of the line's other locos. Today, the only reminder of the railway at Southwold is a brass plaque on the wall of the police station that now occupies this site.

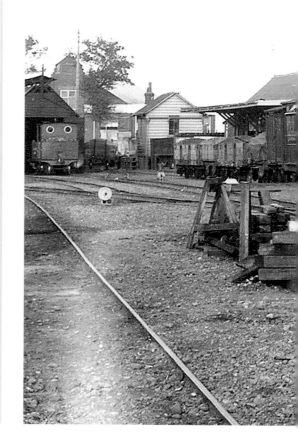

SOUTHWOLD RAILWAY STATION.

LINCOLNSHIRE'S POTATO RAILWAYS

▲ Extending to 11 miles, a 2ft-gauge light railway operated on the Dennis Estate at Deeping St Nicholas. Harvested potatoes were transported from the estate's fields to the Great Northern Railway's Peterborough to Spalding line at Littleworth station. Here the driver of one of the railway's paraffin-fired steam tractors stops at Littleworth for a chat with his GNR counterpart. The last section of the Dennis Estates railway closed in 1950.

The Fenlands of Lincolnshire, reclaimed from marshland by three centuries of drainage schemes, are one of the most important areas for growing arable crops. By the early 20th century, vast areas of this fertile land were being farmed for the all-important potato crop. Getting the crop to market was no mean feat – after harvesting by hand, the potatoes had to be transported in horsedrawn wagons along often muddy tracks to the nearest railway station, which might be miles away. During the peak of harvesting, special trains were run from the collection centres at Spalding and Boston to markets around England.

It wasn't long before a local potato grower hit on the idea of laying lightweight narrow gauge tracks so that horses could move the crop in wagons to the nearest standard gauge railhead. Opened around 1909, the first line at Weston was an immediate success and, over the next 20 years, many more were built, mainly in the southeast of the county, often using ex-War Department 60cm-gauge track and rolling stock previously employed in France during the First World War. By 1920 there were more than 35 narrow gauge systems totalling over 123 route-miles across the Fenlands. Many relied on horse power but some larger concerns also used diminutive locomotives.

The largest potato railway was the 23-mile network operated by W. Dennis & Sons on their 7,800-acre Nocton Estate. The main railhead was at Nocton & Dunston station on the LNER line between Lincoln and Sleaford and from here a large network of narrow gauge lines spread out like tentacles to the distant fields where potatoes, sugar beet and grain were grown; they even ran through the potato-chitting greenhouse, the piggeries and mill. Motive power on this network was provided by Simplex petrol-engined locomotives, although two steam engines did venture forth in the late 1920s but proved too heavy for the lightly laid lines. During the harvesting season gangs of female potato pickers were carried out to the fields on the railway, returning at the end of day sitting on sacks of potatoes loaded on the wagons.

The Nocton Estate was bought by Smith's Potato Crisps in 1936 and the line continued to operate until replaced by new farm roads and lorries in 1960. Some of the track and rolling stock was later used to create the Lincolnshire Coast Light Railway, now at Skegness.

▲ Built from ex-WD First World War 60cm-gauge track, the Nocton Estate railway ran through the piggeries at Halls Yard, Dunston, from where the muck was taken to be spread on the fields.

▼ The Nocton Estate's main customer was Smith's Potato Crisps, who bought the land in 1936. They used the railway for many years but by the late 1950s improved access to the fields and the introduction of tractors finally led to its demise.

SMITHS
have crispness in the bag!

Plain with salt · Hamburger
Cheese and Onion

◄ Probably the largest agricultural narrow gauge railway in Lincolnshire, the extensive narrow gauge system on the Nocton Estate railway even ran through this huge greenhouse, where potatoes were allowed to sprout before planting.

THE WATER RAIL WAY

Lincoln to Boston

The Lincoln to Boston railway line spent its working life serving the scattered villages and farming communities of central Lincolnshire and has recently been reborn as a footpath and cycleway.

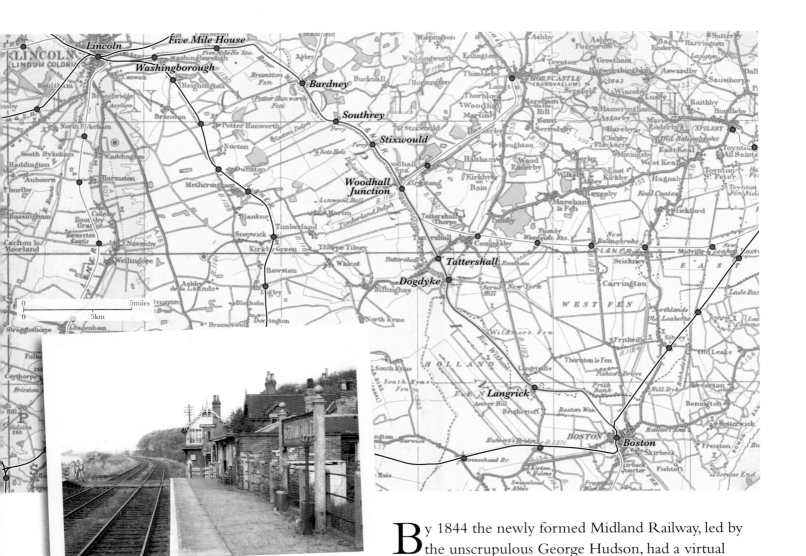

▲ Located on the east bank of the Witham Navigation and a mile from the village it served, deserted Stixwould station waits for the next train a few years before closure. Despite strong local protests, the station closed on 9 October 1970.

By 1844 the newly formed Midland Railway, led by the unscrupulous George Hudson, had a virtual stranglehold on railways from London to the Midlands, Derbyshire and Yorkshire. In the same year the London & York Railway put forward proposals for several new railways including a main line from London to York and a loop line from Peterborough to Bawtry via Spalding, Boston and Lincoln. In 1846, the London & York Railway became the Great Northern Railway and work commenced on the Lincolnshire Loop Line. Construction was rapid across the flat fenlands; between Boston and Lincoln the new railway closely followed the route of the Witham Navigation. The line opened on 17 October

1848 but the completion of the main line from London to York via Grantham in 1852, plus the opening in 1867 of a shorter route to Lincoln from the main line at Barkston via Honington, meant it soon had only secondary status.

Three other railways were also built that joined with the Lincoln to Boston line. The first was the independent Horncastle Railway, which opened between Woodhall Junction and Horncastle in 1855 (see pages 94–97). The second was the heavily graded Louth & Lincoln Railway, which opened from a junction at Bardney to Louth via Wragby in 1876. The final link in the chain was the building of a railway that provided a more direct and faster link between

▲ The setting sun leaves a golden glow on the Witham Navigation at Stixwould station, where the signalbox, station building and platforms still survive. The Water Rail Way passes through here on its 30-mile route from Lincoln to Woodhall Junction.

▼ The Water Rail Way now passes between the platforms at Southrey station, where excursion trains, filled with holidaymakers to Butlins at Skegness, once steamed through.

Lincoln and Skegness. Known as the New Line or the Kirkstead & Little Steeping line it opened in 1913 from a junction south of Woodhall Junction to Little Steeping on the Boston to Louth line. Although frequented by through excursion traffic during the summer, local traffic was light apart from the seasonal potato trains that once ran from Tumby Woodside.

Following the end of the Second World War and the nationalisation of the railways in 1948, the British Transport Commission's Branch Line Committee was given the task of weeding out loss-making lines. Eastern England generally was very badly hit and first to get the chop along the Lincoln to Boston route was the Bardney to Louth line, which closed to passengers in 1951 and to goods on 17 December 1956. Next came the Horncastle branch, which closed to passengers in 1954. Worse was to come as the Beeching Report of 1963 spelt the end for nearly all of Lincolnshire's rural railways. Closure of the Boston to Lincoln line came in two stages, with the section between Woodhall Junction and Boston going on 17 June 1963. Strong opposition from local councillors led to a stay of execution and the introduction of diesel multiple units (DMUs) for the Lincoln to Skegness via Woodhall Junction and Tumby Woodside services, but these, too, ceased on 5 October 1970. All that was left were goods trains from Lincoln to Horncastle via Woodhall Junction but even these ended a year later in April 1971.

▼ One of the largest station nameboards in Britain could once be found at Woodhall Junction. The Horncastle branch closed to passengers on 12 September 1954, while the Coningsby and Midville line struggled on until closure on 5 October 1970.

▲ Class 'B1' 4-6-0 No. 61281 pauses at Woodhall Junction with a Lincoln to Skegness train on 29 April 1954. This train would travel to the seaside town via the 1913-built cut-off line to Bellwater Junction via Tumby Woodside and Midville.

▲ The beautifully preserved station at Woodhall Junction is now a private residence. Before the opening of the branch line to Woodhall Spa and Horncastle in 1855, the station was named Kirkstead.

WALKING AND CYCLING THE LINE

THE LINE TODAY

Closely following the course of the Witham Navigation, a footpath and cycleway known as the Water Rail Way runs for much of its 30-mile route along the trackbed of the old Lincoln to Boston railway between Waterside South, near Lincoln station, to Boston Marina. Designated part of National Cycle Route 1, the recently completed Water Rail Way includes nearly 20 miles of traffic-free paths and features distinctive modern sculptures at strategic locations along the route. These include life-size sheep made from scrap metal, which can be found wandering across the path near Southrey.

There is still much of interest to lovers of old railways along the route. Starting from Lincoln, the first station was at Washingborough where the station building and platforms still survive. North of Bardney the route crosses the Lock into the Old River Witham by way of a long steel bridge and at Bardney itself there is much railway paraphernalia at the old station building that is now the Bardney Heritage Centre. At Southrey and Stixwould both platforms, surmounted by a station nameboard, the signalbox and station buildings, remain intact. At Woodhall Junction (formerly Kirkstead station) the station building, platforms and level crossing gate have all survived into private ownership. From here it is but a short walk to connect with the Spa Trail (see page 96) from Woodhall Spa to Horncastle. Farther south the rather splendid station building at Tattershall is now an art gallery. The next station, Dogdyke, is best remembered as being immortalised in the song Slow Train written by Flanders and Swann in 1963, which lamented the loss of our country railways under the axe of Beeching.

PLACES TO VISIT

HERITAGE RAILWAYS
Lincolnshire Coast Light Railway
Skegness Water Leisure Park, Walls Lane,
Ingoldmells, Skegness,
Lincolnshire PE25 1JF
Tel 01754 899400
Website www.skegnesswaterleisurepark.co.uk
Route Circular route at Skegness Leisure Park
Length approx. 1mile

OTHER ATTRACTIONS
Lincoln Cathedral
4 Priorygate, Lincoln LN2 1PL
Tel 01522 561600
Website www.lincolncathedral.com

**Lincoln Medieval Bishop's Palace
(English Heritage)**
Lincoln LN2 1PU
Tel 01522 527468
Website www.english-heritage.org.uk

Bardney Heritage Centre
Station Yard, Station Road, Bardney,
Lincolnshire LN3 5UF
Tel 01526 397299
Website www.lincsheritageforum.org.uk

Battle of Britain Memorial Flight
RAF Coningsby, Lincolnshire LN4 4SY
Tel 01522 782040
Website www.raf.mod.uk

Tattershall Castle (NT)
Sleaford Road, Tattershall,
Lincolnshire LN4 4LR
Tel 01526 342543
Website www.nationaltrust.org.uk

Dogdyke Steam Pumping Station
Bridge Farm, Tattershall, Lincolnshire LN4 4JG
Tel 01636 707642
Website www.dogdyke.com

PRACTICAL INFORMATION

NEAREST RAILWAY STATIONS
Lincoln, Boston

TOURIST INFORMATION
**Lincoln Castle Square Tourist Information
Centre**
9 Castle Hill, Lincoln LN1 3AA
Tel 01522 873213
Website: www.visitlincolnshire.com

Tattershall Tourist Information Centre
Butts Lane, Tattershall, Lincoln, Lincolnshire
LN4 4NL
Tel 01507 601111
Website www.visitlincolnshire.com

OS Maps
Landranger Nos 121/122/131

CYCLE HIRE
Bardney Heritage Centre
Station Yard, Station Road, Bardney, Lincs
LN3 5UF
Tel 01526 397299

Witham Cycle Hire
Boston Grand Sluice Lock, Boston, Lincs
Tel 07796 194095

THE SPA TRAIL
Woodhall Junction to Horncastle

Remaining independent until 1923, the Horncastle Railway was one of the only profitable lines in Lincolnshire. The section from Woodhall Spa to Horncastle now forms the Spa Trail footpath and cycleway.

▼ The only major engineering feature surviving along the Horncastle Railway, this brick-arched bridge carries the B1191 over the trackbed of the recently resurfaced Spa Trail between Woodhall Spa and Horncastle.

By the late 18th century the local merchants, farmers and landowners of Horncastle, supported by local celebrity Sir Joseph Banks, were clamouring for a canal to be built to their market town. Opened in 1802, the Horncastle Canal ran for 11 miles from the Witham Navigation at Dogdyke through Tattershall, Coningsby and Kirkby on Bain to wharves in Horncastle. Costing four times its original estimate, the canal was eventually profitable, bringing in coal and taking out wool and corn.

The canal's success was short-lived as the opening of the Great Northern Railway's loop line between Boston and Lincoln in 1848 soon saw local traders demanding their own railway. At that time the

▲ Former Great Central Railway Class 'A-5' 4-6-2 tank No. 69804 stands in the bay platform at Woodhall Junction with a train from Horncastle on 11 July 1954. The Horncastle branch closed to passengers two months later.

◄ Woodhall Spa was the only intermediate station on the Horncastle Railway. The station was rebuilt in 1896 in anticipation of an influx of visitors to this health resort. The station site is now a car park.

nearest station to Horncastle was 7 miles away at Kirkstead but by 1854 the Horncastle & Kirkstead Railway had been authorised to build a railway from a junction with the loop line at Kirkstead to Horncastle. With one intermediate station serving the village of Woodhall and no major engineering works, the line was opened on 26 September 1855. For the final 2 miles into Horncastle the railway closely followed the course of the Horncastle Canal that was soon, unsurprisingly, put out of business.

Unusually, although operated from the outset by the GNR, the Horncastle Railway was one of the few railways in Lincolnshire to be profitable and it remained independent until 1923 when it became part of the LNER. In the late 19th century, the village of Woodhall Spa had set its sights on becoming an important health resort and was making excessive claims about the healing nature of its waters – even the little station here was rebuilt in 1896 to reflect its so-called importance. The junction station at Kirkstead was also renamed Woodhall Junction in 1922 in an effort to encourage visitors to the spa, but the hoped-for influx never materialised.

Passenger traffic on the Horncastle branch was never heavy and the line became an early victim of the Branch Lines Committee's axe on 13 September 1954 when passenger services were withdrawn. Goods trains from Lincoln via Woodhall Junction lingered on until 6 April 1971 when the line was completely closed.

▲ Ex-GNR Class 'J6' 0-6-0 No. 64260 gets ready to leave Horncastle with the 8.55am train to Woodhall Junction on 29 April 1954. Because of its impending closure to passengers, in less than five months, the branch line became a mecca for railway photographers – one can just be seen in action on the right.

▼ Woodhall Spa station, looking towards Woodhall Junction on 29 April 1954. Less than five months later the Horncastle branch closed to passengers. Despite the coming of the railway, the anticipated growth of the village into a major health resort in the late 19th century never materialised.

WALKING AND CYCLING THE LINE

THE LINE TODAY

Now a private residence, the station building, platform and level crossing gates at Woodhall Junction station can be seen today from the Water Rail Way footpath and cycleway that follows the route of the loop line between Boston and Lincoln. Nothing much remains today of Woodhall Spa station, the site of which is now a car park. However, beyond Woodhall Spa golf course, the trackbed of the railway has recently been resurfaced as a 4-mile traffic-free footpath and cycleway to Horncastle, known as the Spa Trail. A car park for Trail users is located 1 mile south of Horncastle next to the old Horncastle Canal near Thornton Lodge Farm.

Nothing remains today of Horncastle station as the buildings were demolished to make way for a housing estate in the 1980s. Now converted into flats, the adjacent old granary at Horncastle is still a reminder of the railway's once-important role in carrying local agricultural produce.

PLACES TO VISIT

HERITAGE RAILWAYS
Lincolnshire Coast Light Railway
Skegness Water Leisure Park, Walls Lane,
Ingoldmells, Skegness, Lincs PE25 1JF
Tel 01754 899400
Website www.skegnesswaterleisurepark.co.uk
Route Circular route at Skegness Leisure Park
Length approx. 1 mile

OTHER ATTRACTIONS
Bolingbroke Castle
Old Bolingbroke, Moat Lane,
Old Bolingbroke, Lincolnshire
Tel 01529 461499
Website www.bolingbrokecastle.com

Cottage Museum
Iddesleigh Road, Woodhall Spa,
Lincolnshire LN10 6SH
Tel 01526 353775
Website www.woodhallspa-museum.co.uk

Lincolnshire Aviation Heritage Centre
East Kirkby Airfield, East Kirkby, Nr Spilsby,
Lincolnshire PE23 4DE
Tel 01790 763207
Website www.lincsaviation.co.uk

Stockwith Mill
Harrington Road, Hagworthingham, Spilsby,
Lincolnshire PE23 4NE
Tel 01507 588221
Website www.stockwithmill.co.uk

PRACTICAL INFORMATION

NEAREST RAILWAY STATION
Lincoln

ACCOMMODATION AND TOURIST INFORMATION
Horncastle Tourist Information Centre
14 Bull Ring, Horncastle, Lincs LN9 5HU
Tel 01507 526636
Website www.visitlincolnshire.com

Woodhall Spa Tourist Information Centre
Cottage Museum, Iddesleigh Road, Woodhall Spa,
Lincs LN10 6SH
Tel 01526 353775
Website www.poachercountry.co.uk

OS MAPS
Landranger Nos 121/122

CYCLE HIRE
None in Woodhall Spa or Horncastle. See Water Rail Way on page 93 for the nearest cycle hire.

▲ Visitors to Woodhall Spa today are greeted by this sign, which depicts a Great Northern Railway express in the early 20th century. In reality, services on the branch line to Horncastle would have seen more mundane locos hauling a couple of ancient carriages.

► Apart from this short length of track and a few old sleepers, nearly all traces of the railway in Horncastle have long ago disappeared.

CENTRAL ENGLAND

◀ Toddington is now the centre of operations for the Gloucestershire Warwickshire's 10½-mile heritage line to Cheltenham Racecourse station. A northward extension to Broadway is currently being completed. Here, ex-GWR 2-6-2 tank No. 5199 looks in fine fettle as it waits to depart with a train for Winchcombe in 2004.

FOREST OF DEAN
Lydney Junction to Coleford and Cinderford

Once criss-crossed by a network of tramways and railway lines serving numerous ironstone and coal mines, it is now hard to imagine that the beautiful Forest of Dean was once a hive of industrial activity.

From medieval times, the Forest of Dean had been an important source of iron ore and coal and by the early 19th century this relatively small area close to the Welsh border was experiencing its own industrial revolution. Railways came early to the Forest in the form of horsedrawn tramways, transporting the output of mines down to jetties on the Rivers Severn and Wye for shipment. The biggest of these operations was the Severn & Wye Railway & Canal Company, which opened in 1813 and eventually linked the Severn at Lydney with the Wye at Lydbrook. The opening of the broad gauge South Wales Railway

▲ Ex-GWR 0-6-0 pannier tank No. 2080 of Gloucester Horton Road shed has just arrived at Lydney Town with a short train from Junction station on 23 September 1950. On the right is an ex-GWR AEC railcar W7W, which had just arrived with an enthusiasts' special from Coleford. Passenger services north from Lydney Town had ceased in 1929.

◀ Beautifully restored 0-6-0 pannier tank No. 9681 departs from Norchard High Level, the headquarters of the Dean Forest Railway, with a train for Parkend in July 2009.

▼ Armed with notebooks and cameras, an excited throng of railway enthusiasts gather at Parkend after the arrival of the Railway Executive Committee 'Severn Venturer' railtour behind 0-6-0 pannier tank No. 1625 on 15 April 1956.

▼ Made up of three autocoaches packed with enthusiasts and propelled by 0-6-0 pannier tanks No. 6437 in the middle and No. 8701 at the rear, a Stephenson Locomotive Society trip is the last train ever to head up the 1 in 40 gradient to Serridge Junction on 13 May 1961. This section of the Severn & Wye Railway now forms part of the Forest of Dean Family Cycle Trail.

(later to become part of the GWR) along the west bank of the Severn in 1851 eventually led to major improvements on the S&W and in 1869 the ramshackled and steeply graded tramway from Lydney to Speech House Road was reopened as a broad gauge line using steam haulage. By 1874, the line had been relaid to standard gauge and extended from Serridge Junction to Lydbrook Junction where it met the recently opened Ross & Monmouth Railway. A year later, in September 1875, the Severn & Wye (S&W) was extended to the busy harbour at Lydney, where coal was transhipped onto sailing ships for distribution through southwest England. In the same year a 4-mile branch was also opened from Parkend to Coleford. A Mineral Loop

line from near Drybrook Road to Whitecroft had already been opened in 1872 to serve several important collieries in the Forest.

The Severn & Wye story was further complicated when the Severn Bridge Railway from Lydney to Sharpness and the Midland Railway branch from Sharpness to Berkeley Road opened throughout in 1879. In addition to providing an important link between the Forest of Dean and the Midland Railway's Bristol to Gloucester main line, the 22-span single-track bridge was also a useful diversionary route when the nearby Severn Tunnel was closed for maintenance.

In 1894 the Severn Bridge Railway and the Severn & Wye Railway had fallen on hard times and the GWR and the Midland Railway took them both over as a joint concern. In addition to the S&W, the Forest of Dean was also served by several other lines, all of which were eventually operated by the GWR, including Newnham to Mitcheldean

▲ Restored 0-6-0 pannier tank No. 9681 takes on water at Parkend after completing its trip on the Dean Forest Railway from Lydney Junction in July 2009.

Road (never opened throughout but with a link to Cinderford station at Bilson), Awre to Howbeach Colliery and Monmouth to Coleford.

The decline of the railways in the Forest of Dean was spread over many years and linked closely with the closures of collieries. Passenger traffic was always of secondary importance and the first to go were those from Monmouth to Coleford in 1917 (Coleford station closed on 1 January 1917) and Lydney Town to Coleford, Cinderford and Lydbrook Junction in 1929. The GWR branch from Newnham to Cinderford struggled on until 1958, when trains ceased to run through from Gloucester. The Lydney Town to Sharpness service was terminated abruptly in 1960 when the Severn Railway Bridge was closed permanently after it was hit by a petrol tanker travelling up-river. With the decline of collieries in the area, the Awre to Howbeach line closed in 1949, the Mineral Loop and Serridge Junction to Lydbrook Junction lines closed in 1956, as did the Lydney Docks branch in 1960. The last colliery, Northern United, closed in 1965 but stone output from Whitecliff Quarry on the Coleford branch continued until closure in 1967. Bitumen traffic for the Berry Wiggins depot at Whimsey also continued until 1967, when the ex-GWR line from Newnham was also closed. Fortunately for lovers of the Forest's railways the 4½-mile section of the Severn & Wye Railway from Lydney Junction to Parkend is now a heritage line.

◄ The trackbed of the Severn & Wye Railway from Cannop to Serridge Junction and Drybrook Junction now forms part of the Forest of Dean Family Cycle Trail. The site of Speech House Road station is marked by this nameboard.

▲ Now lined with trees, the final approach along the embankment of the Severn & Wye Railway from Drybrook Road to Cinderford is today a narrow pathway. A loop line at Bilson was opened in 1908 to allow GWR trains from Newnham to run into Cinderford station.

◄ Ex-GWR streamlined railcar W7W visited the freight-only Severn & Wye branch to Coleford with an enthusiasts' special on 23 September 1950. The station closed to passengers in 1929 but the line as far as Whitecliff Quarry continued to operate until 1967.

WALKING AND CYCLING THE LINE

THE LINE TODAY
Set in Britain's first National Forest Park, much of the old Severn & Wye Railway can still be followed today. For lovers of both steam and diesel railways, the Dean Forest Railway (see below), with its headquarters at Norchard, operates a heritage line from Lydney Junction to Parkend. From here the trackbed of the railway past Cannop Ponds and via the sites of Speech House Road station, Serridge Junction and the old Mineral Loop line via Dilke Bridge is now an attractive traffic-free circular footpath and cycleway, 11 miles in length, known as the Forest of Dean Family Cycle Trail. Managed by the Forestry Commission, the Trail starts at the Cycle Centre (formerly the site of Cannop Colliery) in the Cannop Valley, where there is a large car park, café and cycle-hire centre. The trail features station sites such as Cannop Wharf, Speech House Road and Drybrook Road, which are marked by reproduction station nameboards mounted on old railway sleepers.

From the site of Drybrook Road station, a sometimes muddy footpath follows the line of the railway through an avenue of closely growing trees into Cinderford. Nearby, the old Great Western Railways line from Bilson Green to Ruspidge, where the railway halt has been restored, is also now a footpath and cycleway known as the Cinderford Linear Park. At Ruspidge Halt a restored Berry Wiggins bitumen tank wagon stands on a short length of track in memory of the traffic that kept this line open until 1967. At Coleford the old S&W goods shed and signalbox is now a railway museum (see details below).

PLACES TO VISIT

HERITAGE RAILWAYS
Dean Forest Railway
Norchard, Forest Road, Lydney,
Gloucestershire GL15 4ET
Tel 01594 845840
Website www.deanforestrailway.co.uk
Route Lydney Junction to Parkend
Length 4½ miles

OTHER ATTRACTIONS
Great Western Railway Museum (Coleford)
The Old Railway Station, Railway Drive,
Coleford, Gloucestershire GL16 8RH
Tel 01594 833569
Website www.colefordgwr.150m.com

Clearwell Caves Ancient Iron Mines
Nr Coleford, Royal Forest of Dean,
Gloucestershire GL16 8JR
Tel 01594 832535
Website www.clearwellcaves.com

Puzzlewood
Perry Grove Road, Coleford,
Gloucestershire GL16 8QB
Tel 01594 833187
Website www.puzzlewood.net

Lydney Park Gardens
Lydney, Gloucestershire GL15 6BU
Tel 01594 842844/842922
Website www.lydneyparkestate.co.uk

Dean Heritage Centre
Camp Mill, Soudley,
Gloucestershire GL14 2UB
Tel 01594 822170
Website www.deanheritagemuseum.com

Perrygrove Railway
Perrygrove Farm, Perrygrove Road, Coleford,
Gloucestershire GL16 8QB
Tel 01594 834991
Website www.perrygrove.co.uk

PRACTICAL INFORMATION

NEAREST RAILWAY STATIONS
Lydney, Parkend (Dean Forest Railway)

TOURIST INFORMATION
Coleford Tourist Information Centre
High Street, Coleford,
Gloucestershire GL16 8HG
Tel 01594 812388
Website www.visitforestofdean.co.uk

OS MAP
Landranger No. 162

CYCLE HIRE
Pedalabikeaway Cycle Centre
Cannop Valley, Nr Coleford,
Gloucestershire GL16 7EH
Tel 01594 860065
Website www.pedalabikeaway.co.uk

WYE VALLEY
Chepstow to Monmouth

Despite passing through some of Britain's most beautiful scenery, the delightful Wye Valley line was never profitable. Sections of the former trackbed now form part of the Wye Valley Walk Long Distance Path.

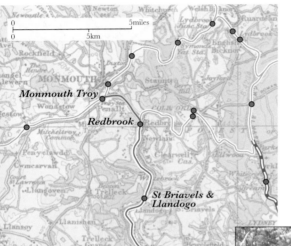

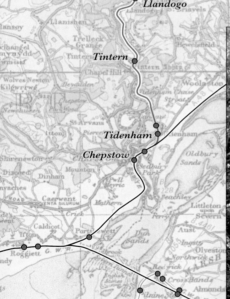

The first railway to reach Monmouth was opened by the Monmouth Railway as early as 1816. In reality a horsedrawn tramway, it ran from iron-ore mines in the Forest of Dean via Coleford and Redbrook to May Hill in Monmouth for onward river and canal transport to iron furnaces in South Wales. In 1857 the Coleford, Monmouth, Usk & Pontypool Railway opened its line from Little Mill Junction, near Pontypool Road, to Monmouth Troy station. The company remained independent until 1887 when it was absorbed by the GWR. The third railway to reach Monmouth was the Ross & Monmouth Railway, which opened to Monmouth May Hill station

▶ The southern portal of Tintern Tunnel, now home to a colony of bats, can be reached by way of a pedestrian bridge over the Wye at Tintern and along a footpath on the east bank of the river. The trackbed to the south of here is currently being evaluated as a possible cycleway by Sustrans.

in 1873 and was worked from the beginning by the GWR. A year later, the latter company built a short length of line to link the two stations in Monmouth.

The fourth railway to reach Monmouth was the Wye Valley Railway, which opened in 1876. Steeply graded and passing through picturesque scenery, the single-track line not only crossed and recrossed the River Wye at several locations but also passed through tunnels at Tintern and Tidenham before reaching Chepstow, where it formed a junction with the GWR's Cardiff to Gloucester main line. The final piece of the Monmouth railway jigsaw was put in place with the opening of the Coleford branch in 1883. Built by the Coleford Railway Company and worked by the GWR along the route of the former tramway (Monmouth Railway), the branch, which left the Wye Valley line at

▲ The last day of passenger services on the Wye Valley line. Ex-GWR 0-6-0 pannier tank pauses at Tintern station with the 11.50am Monmouth Troy to Severn Tunnel Junction train on 3 January 1959.

▼ An animated 'last day' scene at the east end of Monmouth Troy station on 3 January 1959 as the final 3.47pm train to Chepstow steams out behind ex-GWR 0-6-0 pannier tank No. 3726.

◀ The beautifully restored station at Tintern is now owned by Monmouthshire County Council. The site, with its own car park, camping and picnic site, includes a café in the station building, an arts and craft shop in the signalbox and a miniature railway. A gift shop operates in two old BR Mark I carriages, which stand on a short length of track next to the platform.

Wyesham Junction, had a short working life and, apart from a short section from Whitecliff Quarry to Coleford, was closed completely during the First World War.

Despite the attraction of the area's undoubted scenic beauty, the railways radiating out from Monmouth were lightly used and following nationalisation of the railways in 1948 their future looked decidedly bleak. By the early 1950s, the British Transport Commission's Branch Line Committee, given the task of weeding out unprofitable rural branch lines, had already started wielding its axe around Britain. Monmouth and the Wye Valley did not escape for long – first to go was the line from Monmouth to Usk and Pontypool, which closed to passengers in 1955. Passenger services on the remaining Wye Valley lines from Chepstow to Monmouth and from Monmouth to Ross-on-Wye were withdrawn in 1959. The line north to Lydbrook Junction was closed completely but goods trains on the southern section to Chepstow remained in operation until 1964. After that date only the section of this line from Chepstow to Dayhouse and Tidenham quarries remained open but even this has since been closed.

▶ The Wye Valley Walk crosses the River Wye at Redbrook along this footbridge attached to the side of the old railway bridge. The picturesque Boat Inn on the west bank of the river is a good place to stop for refreshments.

▼ Monmouth Troy station in the late 1950s as 0-4-2 tank No. 1455 waits to leave with a train for Ross-on-Wye. The station buildings have since been removed and rebuilt at Winchcombe, north of Cheltenham, on the Gloucester & Warwickshire Railway.

WALKING AND CYCLING THE LINE

THE LINE TODAY

Several sections of the Wye Valley line between Chepstow and Monmouth now form part of the Wye Valley Walk Long Distance Path. Although not walkable at the moment, the first 2½-mile section of the trackbed from Wye Valley Junction near Tutshill, on the eastern outskirts of Chepstow, through the long Tidenham Tunnel to Tintern Quarry, is attracting interest from Sustrans as a potential cycleway. The last train to the quarry ran through Tidenham Tunnel in 1981. Just north of the quarry, a footpath follows the trackbed as far as the southern portal of the boarded-up Tintern Tunnel. Walkers can cross the River Wye nearby on a footbridge into Tintern village. A footpath leads from here to the beautifully restored Old Tintern station, where the station building is now a café, the signalbox sells arts and crafts and several old BR coaches form a gift shop.

Two miles north of Tintern is the village of Llandogo. From here to Redbrook via Bigsweir Bridge the majority of the trackbed along the west bank of the Wye is now a footpath – in fact the section from Whitebrook to Redbrook also forms part of the Wye Valley Walk. The pretty Boat Inn on the west bank of the Wye is a handy place to stop for a break before crossing the river to Redbrook over the old railway bridge.

Although the trackbed between Redbrook and the outskirts of Monmouth is not a footpath there is still much to interest lovers of old railways on the eastern outskirts of this historic town. Here, at the confluence of the Rivers Monnow and Wye, are two fine structures – the truncated stone viaduct that once carried the railway over the Wye stands close to the girder bridge that formerlyt conveyed the railway northwards towards Ross-on-Wye. The latter structure now carries a footpath. Northwest of Monmouth, the Wye Valley Walk follows the trackbed of the old Ross & Monmouth Railway to Symonds Yat and on to the closed southern portal of the tunnel at Welsh Bicknor.

PLACES TO VISIT

HERITAGE RAILWAYS

Dean Forest Railway
Norchard, Forest Road, Lydney,
Gloucestershire GL15 4ET
Tel 01594 845840
Website www.deanforestrailway.co.uk
Route Lydney Junction to Parkend
Length 4½ miles

OTHER ATTRACTIONS

Chepstow Castle
Bridge Street, Chepstow,
Monmouthsire NP16 5EY
Tel 01291 624065
Website www.cadw.wales.gov.uk

Tintern Abbey
Tintern, Chepstow,
Monmouthshire NP16 6SE
Tel 01291 689251
Website www.cadw.wales.gov.uk

Old Tintern Station
Tintern, Chepstow,
Monmouthshire NP16 7NX
Tel 01633 644850
Website www.monmouthshire.gov.uk

The Kymin and Naval Temple (NT)
The Round House, Monmouth NP25 3SE
Tel 01600 719241
Website www.nationaltrust.org.uk

Monmouth Castle and Regimental Museum
Monmouth NP25 3BS
Tel 01600 772175
Website www.monmouthcastlemuseum.org.uk

PRACTICAL INFORMATION

NEAREST RAILWAY STATION
Chepstow

TOURIST INFORMATION
Chepstow Tourist Information Centre
Castle Car Park, Bridge Street, Chepstow,
Gwent NP16 5EY
Tel 01291 623772
Website www.visitwyevalley.com

Monmouth Tourist Information Centre
Market Hall, Priory Street, Monmouth
NP25 3XA
Tel 01600 713899
Website www.visitwyevalley.com

OS MAP
Landranger No. 162

CYCLE HIRE
Pedalabikeaway
The Cycle Centre, Hadnock Road,
Monmouth, NP25 3NG
Tel 01600 772821
Website www.pedalabikeaway.co.uk/monmouth.html

THE GREENWAY

Stratford-upon-Avon to Cheltenham

Opened throughout in 1908, the Stratford-upon-Avon to Cheltenham line was a belated attempt by the GWR to compete with the well-established Midland Railway route between Birmingham and Bristol.

▼ Single-unit diesel railcar W55009 and a Class 116 three car DMU head past Stratford-upon-Avon Racecourse station in 1964. Following diversion of north-south through trains via the Midland Railway route, the final passenger services between Stratford and Cheltenham were handled by single-unit diesel railcars until 1966.

By 1846 the mighty Midland Railway, through its acquisition of the Birmingham & Bristol Railway, had already pushed a tentacle deep into GWR territory. Surprisingly, the GWR did not consider building a similar route until more than 50 years later. During that time the Midland Railway had captured the majority of traffic between the two cities and, rather late in the day, the GWR decided to fight back. Opened in 1908, the GWR's Birmingham to Bristol route was a mixture of old and new – from the outskirts of Birmingham (Snow Hill) it went via the new Birmingham & North Warwickshire

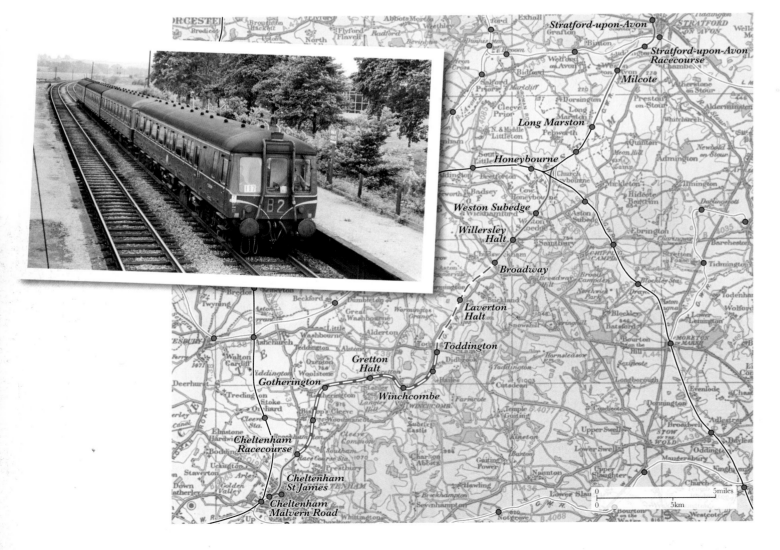

◀ Two old BR carriages now mark the start of the Greenway at Stratford-upon-Avon. Refreshments and cycle hire are available here.

▼ 'Modified Hall' Class 4-6-0 No. 7908 'Henshall Hall' heads into Stratford-upon-Avon from the south with a Ramblers Association special full of happy walkers in 1958.

line to Bearley where it joined the Stratford-upon-Avon Railway (opened 1860) line from Hatton into Stratford. From Stratford-upon-Avon to Honeybourne it used the route of the Oxford, Worcester & Wolverhampton Railway's branch line (opened 1859), while the line from Honeybourne to Cheltenham (Malvern Road) was newly built. The route then continued along existing GWR tracks via the Gloucester Avoiding Line to Standish Junction where it joined the Midland route as far as Westerleigh, then joined the newly opened GWR Badminton cut-off into Bristol via Filton.

Despite being longer than the MR line to Bristol, the Stratford-upon-Avon to Cheltenham line became an important north-south route for express passenger trains from Wolverhampton (Low Level)

and Birmingham (Snow Hill) not only to Bristol and the Southwest but also to South Wales via Gloucester. A streamlined diesel railcar express complete with buffet car was also introduced by the GWR between Birmingham and Cardiff in the 1930s and proved to be an outstanding success. After nationalisation the route continued to be well used, with the daily 'Cornishman' (introduced on this line in 1952) travelling over the line on its journey from Wolverhampton (Low Level) to Penzance. Express diesel multiple units (DMUs) were introduced in the early 1960s between Birmingham and Cardiff and, until 1965, the steam-hauled 'Summer Saturday' extra trains from the Midlands to various destinations in Devon and Cornwall were a highlight for every railway enthusiast. Freight traffic was also important and between 1960 and 1965 the line was heavily used by iron-ore trains bound for the blast furnaces of South Wales from Northamptonshire via the Stratford-upon-Avon & Midland Junction spur at Stratford Racecourse Junction.

▼ Now the headquarters of the Gloucestershire Warwickshire Railway, Toddington was one of the many stations and halts between Cheltenham and Honeybourne that lost its passenger service on 7 March 1960. Here ex-GWR 0-6-0 pannier tank No. 9727 calls at the station with the 1pm service from Cheltenham to Broadway on 27 February 1960. A week later, it had closed.

▲ The halfway point on the Greenway is at the site of Milcote station. It is hard to imagine now the 'Castle'-hauled 'Cornishman' passing through with a train of brown and cream coaches on its journey from Wolverhampton to Penzance in the 1950s. All that is left now is one of the platforms and a long line of fir trees.

▼ The rusting Stennals Bridge carries the Greenway over the River Avon south of Stratford. This section of the route as far as Honeybourne was originally opened as a branch line by the Oxford, Worcester & Wolverhampton Railway in 1859.

WALKING AND CYCLING THE LINE

THE LINE TODAY

Whether on foot or bicycle or by steam train, much of the route of this former GWR mainline can still be traced today. The 5 miles of trackbed from Seven Meadows Roundabout in Stratford-upon-Avon to Long Marston is now a dedicated footpath and cycleway known as the Greenway. It also forms part of National Cycle Network Route 5. Car parking is available at the start of the trail where two old BR carriages have been converted into a café and cycle-hire centre. A mile southwest of here the trail passes the site of Stratford-upon-Avon Racecourse station and crosses the River Avon on a fine girder bridge (Stennals Bridge) before reaching the site of Milcote station. Here the old platform still survives and there is also a small car park and a café in a converted BR carriage. From here the Greenway continues to Long Marston where it

ends at a car park on the northern perimeter of the large former MOD depot where the fledgling Stratford-upon-Avon & Broadway Railway has its base. The depot, which is still linked by rail to Honeybourne, is also used to store surplus diesel locomotives and rolling stock. The Stratford on Avon and Broadway Railway hope to reopen the line between the two towns to link up with the Gloucestershire Warwickshire Railway's northern extension to Broadway.

The 10½-mile southern section of the route from Toddington Station to Cheltenham Racecourse station is now a heritage line operated by the Gloucestershire Warwickshire Railway. Here, preserved former Great Western Railway locos haul trains below the Cotswold Escarpment through Winchcombe, Greet Tunnel and Gotherington.

PLACES TO VISIT

HERITAGE RAILWAYS

Gloucestershire Warwickshire Railway
The Railway Station, Toddington,
Gloucestershire GL54 5DT
Tel 01242 621405
Website www.gwsr.com
Route Toddington to Cheltenham Racecourse
Length 10½ miles

OTHER ATTRACTIONS

Anne Hathaway's Cottage
Cottage Lane, Shottery, Stratford-upon-Avon,
Warwickshire CV37 9HH
Tel 01789 292100
Website www.shakespeare.org.uk

Shakespeare's Birthplace
Henley Street, Stratford-upon-Avon,
Warwickshire CV37 6QW
Tel 01789 204016
Website www.shakespeare.org.uk

Domestic Fowl Trust
Station Road, Honeybourne, Evesham,
Worcestershire WR11 7QZ
Tel 01386 833083
Website www.domesticfowltrust.co.uk

Hailes Abbey (NT)
Nr Winchcombe, Cheltenham,
Gloucestershire GL54 5PB
Tel 01242 602398
Website www.nationaltrust.org.uk

Sudeley Castle
Winchcombe,
Gloucestershire GL54 5JD
Tel 01242 602308
Website www.sudeleycastle.co.uk

PRACTICAL INFORMATION

NEAREST RAILWAY STATIONS

Stratford-upon-Avon, Honeybourne,
Cheltenham Spa

TOURIST INFORMATION

Stratford-upon-Avon Tourist Information Centre
Bridgefoot Quay, Warwick Road,
Stratford-upon-Avon,
Warwickshire CV37 6GW
Tel 08780 1607930
Website www.shakespeare-country.co.uk

Cheltenham Spa Tourist Information Centre
77 Promenade, Cheltenham
Gloucestershire GL50 1PJ
Tel 01242 522878
Website www.visitcheltenham.com

OS MAPS

Landranger Nos 150/151/163

CYCLE HIRE

Stratford Bike Hire
Stratford Greenway Car Park, Seven Meadows
Road, Stratford-upon-Avon CV37 6GR
Tel 07711 776340
Website www.stratfordbikehire.com

▼ Railway photographers converged on the Stratford to Cheltenham line during the last summer of steam-haulage in 1965. Here, looking the worse for wear and without numberplates or nameplates, 'Grange' Class 4-6-0 No. 6855 'Saighton Grange' heads the 6.55am SO Wolverhampton Low Level to Penzance train away from Hunting Butts Tunnel near Cheltenham on 31 July.

Sadly this rosy picture was soon to end. First to go in March 1960 were the Cheltenham to Honeybourne auto trains that once called at the numerous halts along the line. After the summer timetable ended in September 1965, all of the Midlands to Bristol and Southwest services were diverted via the Midland main line and the only through passenger service left was a single diesel railcar running between Gloucester, Stratford-upon-Avon and Leamington Spa. Even this service ceased in January 1966 and thereafter the Stratford to Cheltenham section was freight-only. The end finally came in 1976 when a freight-train derailment north of Cheltenham closed the line. It never reopened as a through route.

▼ With water surging out of its full side tanks, ex-GWR 0-4-2 tank No. 1424 restarts the 1.17pm Honeybourne to Cheltenham auto train from Hayles Abbey Halt on 27 February 1960. Just over a week later the halt, along with the other stations on the line, was closed. No. 1424 continued its working life on the Gloucester to Chalford auto trains until late 1964.

▼ Looking rather neglected and without nameplates or numberplates, 'Modified Hall' Class 4-6-0 No. 7908 'Henshall Hall' heads a Summer Saturday train from the Southwest to Wolverhampton in 1965. By the end of that year steam had officially been ousted from the Western Region.

EAST MIDLAND'S IRONSTONE RAILWAYS

A lthough iron ore had been mined throughout the East Midlands from Roman times, it wasn't until increased demand during the Industrial Revolution in the mid–19th century that large-scale opencast quarrying operations began. The coming of the railways also allowed the iron ore to be transported some distance to iron and steelworks such as Scunthorpe, Corby, Stanton and Holwell. At first the iron ore was dug out by hand but by the early 20th century steam-powered mechanical excavators had taken over the task. The development of these machines, which by the 1930s were diesel-electric powered, led to the use of enormous quarry draglines such as the 1,675-ton 'Sundew' built by Ransomes & Rapier, which operated at an opencast mine in Rutland from 1957 until 1974.

▼ Standard gauge 0-6-0 saddle tank 'Carmarthen' at the lorry tipping dock at Stewarts & Lloyds Glendon Quarries, near Burton Latimer, Northamptonshire, on 18 April 1967. The end was nigh for steam with the imminent arrival of Rolls Royce Sentinel diesel locomotives.

▲ A general view of the giant Corby steelworks in September 1967 and some of Stewarts & Lloyds diesel locomotives that worked around the company's extensive railway network at that time.

Output from the quarries was carried by numerous private railways, both narrow and standard gauge, to exchange sidings on the nearest main railway line. Even by 1960 there were around 25 of these steam-hauled lines still operating in Oxfordshire, Northamptonshire and Rutland alone. Standard gauge motive power was usually supplied by powerful 0-6-0 saddle tanks from makers such as Andrew Barclay, Hunslet, Peckett and Hudswell Clarke.

The most famous and by far the largest ironstone railway system was operated by Stewarts & Lloyds around Corby, where there were around 60 steam locomotives still in use in the early 1960s. Steam was replaced by diesel in the 1960s and the system continued to operate until the by then nationalised Corby steelworks was closed in 1980. Another famous ironstone railway was at the Oxfordshire Ironstone quarries near Wroxton, which included a 3-mile long double-track section operating on Continental right-hand running. The quarries and the railway closed in 1967.

▲ The 3ft 3in-gauge system at Wellingborough Quarries was the last narrow gauge ironstone line to remain in use until closure in October 1966. Here, watched by passengers on a Bristol Lodekka bus, 0-6-0 saddle tank No. 87, built by Peckett in 1942, crosses a road with its loaded wagons of iron ore on its way from the quarries on 6 November 1963.

THE MONSAL TRAIL
Matlock to Buxton

Completed in 1867, the Midland Railway's scenic route to Manchester through the beautiful Peak District was not without its detractors. Chief among them were local landowners and the poet John Ruskin.

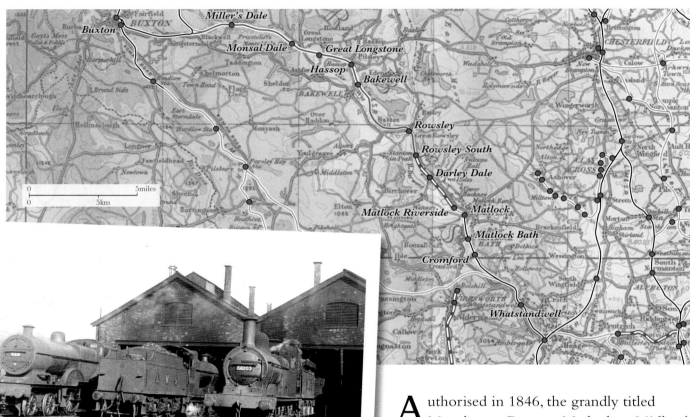

▲ The engine shed at Rowsley provided banking engines for heavy freight trains to the summit of the line at Peak Forest. Here, only nine months after nationalisation, products of the ex-Midland Railway's works at Derby line up at the shed on 19 September 1948. On the left is Class '2P' 4-4-0, still carrying its LMS No. 520; in the centre is '4F' 0-6-0 No. 4540; and on the right is the ancient Johnson '2F' 0-6-0 No. 58203.

Authorised in 1846, the grandly titled Manchester, Buxton, Matlock & Midlands Junction Railway (later to become part of the Midland Railway) was an ambitious and costly scheme to build a railway through the heart of the Peak District. The extensive engineering works on the route, including viaducts and tunnels, proved costly and, in 1849, only the section from Ambergate, where there was a junction with the Midland Railway, to Rowsley was completed. This undertaking, effectively a branch line, was leased jointly by the MR and LNWR. However, the Midland Railway, with ambitions to reach Manchester, was soon considering reviving the scheme as a through route. The first section from Rowsley to Millers Dale and Buxton was opened on 30 May 1863, the same day that the Stockport, Disley & Whaley Bridge Railway, backed by the London & North Western Railway, opened its own extension to Buxton, then an up-and-coming spa town.

In conjunction with the Manchester, Sheffield & Lincolnshire Railway's line from Manchester to New Mills, the Midland Railway completed its through route to Manchester via Millers Dale and Chinley in 1867. In 1871 the LNWR relinquished its joint lease on the Manchester, Buxton, Matlock & Midlands Junction Railway, which itself was then taken over by the Midland Railway. The mighty Midland now had a through route from London (St Pancras) to Manchester. Through trains also ran from London to Buxton.

Although reviled for its intrusion by the poet John Ruskin, the railway from Ambergate to Buxton was not only renowned for its scenic beauty but also for its many tall viaducts and tunnels – these attributes were not overlooked by the Midland Railway publicity department, who dubbed it 'Little Switzerland'. Local landed gentry, such as the Duke of Devonshire and Duke of Rutland,

▼ Closed in 1968, the section of line from Matlock to Rowsley has been reopened by Peak Rail as a heritage railway. Here, preserved ex-LNER Class 'J94' 0-6-0 saddle tank No. 68012 makes a vigorous start from the intermediate station at Darley Dale in October 2001.

▼ The stationmaster at Matlock Bath sees off a Buxton-bound train in the early 20th century. Next stop, via the tunnel under High Tor, was Matlock. The Swiss-style buildings along the line were inspired by the Midland Railway publicity department's notion that the resort was England's 'Little Switzerland'. The line from Ambergate to Matlock Bath and Matlock is still open.

even had their own private waiting rooms at their local stations, Rowsley and Bakewell respectively. When the line was being built, the Duke of Rutland had insisted that it passed out of sight through a tunnel under his estate at Haddon Hall.

Until the rationalisation of the railways in the 1960s, this through route to Manchester was heavily used, although freight trains often required banking assistance from Rowsley up to Peak Forest. In LMS and the early BR years, the principal express of the day was 'The Palatine', which ran between London (St Pancras) and Manchester (Central). Motive power was usually in the hands of 'Jubilee' or 'Royal Scot' 4-6-0s but in the latter steam years it also saw haulage by Longsight 'Britannia' Pacifics. By 1960, diesel haulage in the form of Type 4 'Peak' diesels and Blue Pullman expresses had ousted steam. Operating a daily return express service between Manchester and St Pancras, the Blue Pullmans were withdrawn in 1967, following completion of the West Coast Main Line electrification scheme the previous year. With closure already threatened in the Beeching Report, the end was near for this once-important route. Local passenger trains ceased to run between Matlock and Chinley and from Millers Dale to Buxton on 6 March 1967 and all other through services were diverted by the more northerly Hope Valley route on 1 July 1968.

▼ Returning after banking duties up the heavily graded line, ex-LMS Class '7F' 0-8-0 locomotive No. 49511 heads light-engine through Monsal Dale in August 1956. This section of the railway now forms part of the Monsal Trail footpath and cycle trail.

▲ Walkers along the Monsal Trail today enjoy fine views of the Wye Valley from the 72ft-high five-arch Headstone Viaduct across Monsal Dale. When built in the 1860s, it was criticised by John Ruskin, who said that, 'The valley is gone, and the gods with it.'

WALKING AND CYCLING THE LINE

THE LINE TODAY

Much of the line is still alive and kicking today – the Ambergate to Matlock section is still open for passenger services to and from Derby, the section from Matlock to Rowsley is now the Peak Rail heritage line and the section from Buxton to Chinley via the notorious Dove Holes Tunnel (nearly 2 miles long) is still used for stone traffic. The intervening section between Bakewell and Topley Pike is a footpath and cycleway known as the Monsal Trail. Buxton is still served by trains via the old LNWR route to Manchester.

The Monsal Trail runs for 8½ miles from Coombs Viaduct, 1 mile southeast of Bakewell, to the head of Chee Dale at Topley Pike.

Although closely following the route of the old railway, there are diversions in place around the many tunnels. Only the section from Bakewell to Little Longstone is suitable for cyclists; beyond here the route through Chee Dale is often hard going especially after heavy rain. The highlight of the Trail is the five-arch Headstone Viaduct that at 72ft provides spectacular views of the Wye Valley and Monsal Dale. Near here Great Longstone station survives as a private residence, while at Millers Dale, once the largest station on the line and the junction for Buxton, several of the five platforms and the station building still survive. Car parks allowing access to the Trail are located at Bakewell, Monsal Head, Tideswell Dale and Millers Dale.

PLACES TO VISIT

HERITAGE RAILWAYS
Peak Rail, Matlock Station
Matlock, Derbyshire DE4 3NA
Tel 01629 580381
Website www.peakrail.co.uk
Route Matlock Riverside to Rowsley
Length 4 miles

OTHER ATTRACTIONS
The Heights of Abraham
Matlock Bath,
Derbyshire DE4 3PD
Tel 01629 582365
Website www.heightsofabraham.com

Gulliver's Kingdom
Matlock, Derbyshire DE4 3PG
Tel 01925 444888
Website www.gulliversfun.co.uk

Haddon Hall
Bakewell, Derbyshire DE45 1LA
Tel 01629 812855
Website www.haddonhall.co.uk

Bakewell Old House Museum
Cunningham Place, Bakewell,
Derbyshire DE45 1DD
Tel 01629 813642
Website www.oldhousemuseum.org.uk

Chatsworth House
Bakewell, Derbyshire DE45 1PP
Tel 01246 565300
Website www.chatsworth.org

Buxton Pavilion Gardens
St John's Road, Buxton,
Derbyshire SK17 6XN
Tel 01298 23114
Website www.paviliongardens.co.uk

PRACTICAL INFORMATION

NEAREST RAILWAY STATIONS
Buxton, Matlock, Rowsley (Peak Rail)

TOURIST INFORMATION
Matlock Tourist Information Centre
Crown Square, Matlock,
Derbyshire DE4 3AT
Tel 01629 583388
Website www.visitpeakdistrict.com

Buxton Tourist Information Centre
Pavilion Gardens, St John's Road, Buxton
Derbyshire SK17 6XN
Tel 01298 25106
Website www.highpeak.gov.uk

OS MAP
Landranger No. 119

CYCLE HIRE
Peak Cycle Hire
Derbyshire County Council,
County Offices, Matlock,
Derbyshire DE4 3AG
Tel 01629 823204

Bike Active Cycle Hire
Old Coal Offices,
Station Yard, Station Road, Bakewell,
Derbyshire DE45 1GHE
Tel 01629 814004

THE HIGH PEAK TRAIL

Buxton to High Peak Junction via Parsley Hay

One of the oldest and highest railways in Britain, the Cromford & High Peak Railway crossed the Peak District by way of eight inclines to link two canals. Its trackbed now forms the 17-mile High Peak Trail.

▼ One of the engineering features on the C&HPR are massive dry-stone embankments such as this one near Minninglow. Today the well-surfaced level sections of the High Peak Trail are popular with both walkers and cyclists.

Incorporated as early as 1825, the Cromford & High Peak Railway was one of the earliest railways in Britain. Built in the years when canals were still seen as the primary form of long-distance transport, the C&HPR opened throughout between Peak Forest Canal at Whaley Bridge and the Cromford Canal at Cromford Wharf in 1831. The 33-mile line included eight inclines, the steepest being Bunsall Incline with a gradient of 1 in 7, and reached a height of 1,266ft above sea level at Ladmanlow, making it one of the highest railway lines ever built in Britain. Unlike modern railways, the standard gauge fishbelly rail was laid on stone blocks and the level sections between inclines were horse-powered. Stationary steam engines winched wagons up and down the inclines and it took two days for wagons to complete the journey over the line. Although designed as a freight-only line, it

▼ A Stephenson Locomotive Society brake van special on 30 April 1967 was among the last workings on the C&HPR before closure. Here the special has arrived at Parsley Hay behind Class 'J94' 0-6-0 saddle tanks Nos 68012 and 68006.

▼ Not on the High Peak Trail, the original northern section of the C&HPR between Ladmanlow and Whaley Bridge, including three inclines, was closed in 1892 when the LNWR opened a new connection from Buxton. The trackbed of the old line can still be seen below Burbage Edge as it makes its way down to the Goyt Valley. A road now runs down the length of Bunsall Incline towards Fernilee Reservoir.

► Introduced in 1879, several ex-North London Railway 0-6-0 tanks found their way to Derbyshire to work on the Cromford & High Peak Railway. Here, LMS No. 7527 makes a fine sight as it struggles up the Hopton Incline with a short freight on 4 May 1934.

▼ Ex-LNWR 0-8-0 No. 49406 climbs tender-first out of Buxton with a southbound freight for the Ashbourne line on 23 September 1961. This section of line from Buxton to Harpur Hill was opened in 1892, which meant trains were able to avoid the inclines at Whaley Bridge, Shallcross and Bunsall.

▲ Now preserved as an Ancient Monument, the engine house at Middleton Top can again be seen in action hauling and lowering wagons up and down the incline on certain days during the summer. Originally steam-powered, the engine house now operates by compressed air.

carried passengers from 1855 until 1877 when a fatality ended the service.

The opening of the Manchester, Buxton, Matlock & Midland Junction Railway to Matlock in 1849 (see pages 118–121) left the C&HPR isolated from the main railway system, but in 1853 this was remedied by a short extension to High Peak Junction near Cromford. With its sights set on a potential direct route from Buxton to London, the London & North Western Railway took over the C&HPR in 1887 and in 1892 opened a new line from Buxton to Harpur Hill, thus avoiding the inclines at Whaley Bridge, Shallcross and Bunsall, which were then abandoned. From a new junction at Parsley

▲ Each of the eight inclines on the original Cromford & High Peak Railway was equipped with a stationary steam engine to haul and lower wagons. Closed in 1963, the engine house at the top of the Middleton Incline is seen here on 4 May 1934.

Hay, the LNWR then built a new line to Ashbourne where, in 1899, it connected with the North Staffordshire Railway's line from Uttoxeter. By using this route the LNWR were able to operate a through service from Euston to Buxton until 1914, when it ceased on the outbreak of the First World War.

The first closures came in 1954 when passenger trains between Buxton, Parsley Hay and Ashbourne ceased. However, stone traffic from local quarries kept the line open until 1963, when it closed completely south of the stone quarries near Hindlow. For years serving many private quarry sidings, the Parsley Hay to Cromford section of the C&HPR was cut back progressively until its complete closure in 1967. Steam-operated until the end, this section of line not only featured the 1 in 14 Hopton Incline, the steepest adhesion-worked railway line in the UK, but also Gotham Curve – with its 165ft radius it was the sharpest standard gauge curve in the UK.

▼ Double-headed by Class 'J94' 0-6-0 saddle tanks Nos 68006 and 68012 and filled to capacity with enthusiasts, the SLS brake van special returns to Longcliffe from Parsley Hay on 30 April 1967. The massive stone embankments were a feature of the line, which opened in 1831.

▲ The 711yd 1 in 8 Sheep Pasture Incline was combined with the 580yd 1 in 9 Cromford Incline in 1957. Here, a locomotive driver and his bike hitch a lift on a water tender as it is hauled up the incline in May 1934.

▲ This fine stone-arched bridge on the Hopton Incline now carries walkers and cyclists on the High Peak Trail.

◄ With gradients ranging from 1 in 20 to 1 in 14, the Hopton Incline was the steepest adhesion-worked incline in Britain. Today, with the sounds of steam engines struggling uphill a fading memory, the incline witnesses the exertions of cyclists and walkers traversing the High Peak Trail instead.

WALKING AND CYCLING THE LINE

THE LINE TODAY

The trackbed of the Cromford & High Peak Railway between Dowlow, south of Buxton, and Cromford Wharf is now 17 miles of traffic-free footpath and cycle trail managed jointly by Derbyshire County Council and the Peak District National Park. The Trail is liberally supplied with car parks and picnic sites at Hurdlow, Parsley Hay, Friden and Minninglow and cycle-hire facilities are available at Parsley Hay and Middleton Top, where there is also a visitor centre; there is also a visitor centre at High Peak Junction. The northerly section of the Trail from Dowlow to Parsley Hay, where it joins the Tissington Trail (see pages 128–131) forms part of National Cycle Network Route 68.

Close to the summit of the original line at Ladmanlow, the High Peak Trail winds its way down through rugged Peak District scenery from Dowlow to Parsley Hay. Here, at the site of the former junction for the Ashbourne line (now the Tissington Trail), there is a visitor centre, picnic site, car park and cycle-hire centre. Past Parsley Hay, the trail soon reaches Newhaven Tunnel followed by the sites of Friden, Minninglow and Longcliffe goods yards. The 1 in 14 descent down the Hopton Incline follows to Hopton Tunnel and Middleton Top Engine House. From here the ½-mile 1 in 8½ Middleton Incline leads down to Steeple House where the 18in-gauge Steeple Grange Light Railway heads off for its ½-mile journey up the former Killer's Branch towards Middleton Quarry. The National Stone Centre and the Ecclesbourne Valley Railway are also located near here. The Trail continues its downhill route via the ¾-mile 1 in 8 Sheep Pasture incline before terminating at the Cromford Canal and High Peak Junction. Here, set within the Derwent Valley Mills World Heritage Site, the majority of the original C&HPR buildings have been preserved. Parking is provided at nearby Lea Bridge and from here High Peak Junction is reached via a footbridge across the River Derwent, Cromford Canal and main railway line.

PLACES TO VISIT

HERITAGE RAILWAYS
Ecclesbourne Valley Railway
Wirksworth Station, Station Road, Coldwell Street, Wirksworth, Derbyshire DE4 4FB
Tel 01629 823076
Website www.e-v-r.com
Route Idridgehay to Wirksworth and Ravenstor
Length 8½ miles

OTHER ATTRACTIONS
Steeple Grange Light Railway
(between Cromford and Wirksworth), Derbyshire DE4 4LS
Tel 01246 205542/07769 802587
Website www.steeplegrange.co.uk

National Tramway Museum
Crich Tramway Village, Nr Matlock, Derbyshire DE4 5DP
Tel 01773 854321
Website www.tramway.co.uk

Middleton Top Visitor Centre
Middleton By Wirksworth, Derbyshire DE4 4LS
Tel 01629 823204
Website www.middleton-leawood.org.uk

Cromford Canal Wharf
Cromford Mill, Cromford, Derbyshire DE4 3RQ
Tel 01629 823204/825336
Website www.derwentvalleymills.org

National Stone Centre
Porter Lane, Middleton by Wirksworth, Derbyshire DE4 4LS
Tel 01629 824833
Website www.nationalstonecentre.org.uk

Wirksworth Heritage Centre
Crown Yard, Market Place, Wirksworth, Matlock, Derbyshire DE4 4ET
Tel 01629 825225
Website www.storyofwirksworth.co.uk

PRACTICAL INFORMATION

NEAREST RAILWAY STATIONS
Buxton, Cromford

TOURIST INFORMATION
Matlock Tourist Information Centre
Crown Square, Matlock, Derbyshire DE4 3AT
Tel 01629 583388
Website www.visitpeakdistrict.com

Buxton Tourist Information Centre
Pavilion Gardens, St John's Road, Buxton SK17 6XN
Tel 01298 25106
Website www.highpeak.gov.uk

OS MAP
Landranger No. 119

CYCLE HIRE
Middleton Top Cycle Hire
Visitor Centre, Middleton By Wirksworth, Derbyshire DE4 4LS
Tel 01629 823204
Website www.derbyshire.gov.uk

Peak Cycle Hire
Parsley Hay, Buxton, Derbyshire SK17 0DG
Tel 01298 84493
Website www.peakdistrict.gov.uk

THE TISSINGTON TRAIL
Ashbourne to Parsley Hay

Although now sadly missed by ramblers, the closed railway from Ashbourne to Parsley Hay was one of the earliest schemes for a traffic-free footpath and cycleway when it opened as the Tissington Trail in 1971.

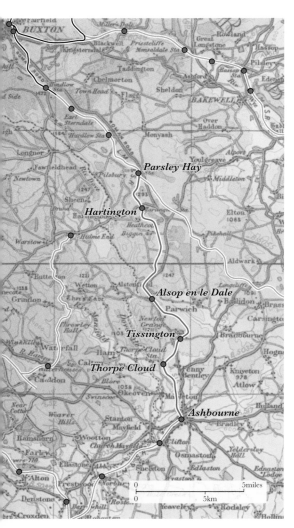

The history of the Ashbourne to Parsley Hay line is closely interwoven with that of the adjoining Cromford & High Peak Railway (see pages 122–127). However, the first railway to reach Ashbourne was the North Staffordshire Railway's branch from Rocester, which opened in 1852. Ashbourne remained at the end of a branch line for 47 more years until the London & North Western Railway opened a new line to the town in 1899 from a junction with the modernised C&HPR at Parsley Hay. At the same time a new LNWR/NSR joint station was built in Ashbourne. With the link to the North Staffs at Ashbourne, the LNWR effectively opened up a new through route from the south to Buxton and Manchester but, apart from a through service between London Euston and Buxton, which ceased in the First World War, passenger traffic was light. Except

▶ The beautifully restored LNWR signalbox at Hartington is now an information centre and café for users of the Tissington Trail. In common with many rural railways, the station was about 2 miles away from the village it purported to serve but, despite this shortcoming, was a popular destination for ramblers during the interwar years.

▲ Stone traffic was the lifeblood of the line between Buxton and Ashbourne. Here, ex-LNWR 0-8-0 No. 49281 arrives at Ashbourne with a stone train from Buxton on 26 October 1959.

▼ LMS 0-6-2 tank No. 2264 waits to leave Ashbourne with the 5.53pm Buxton to Uttoxeter train on 3 May 1934. The loco was one of a batch built by the North Staffordshire Railway at their Stoke Works just prior to the 1923 Big Four Grouping. The joint station at Ashbourne was opened in 1899 when the LNWR completed its line from Buxton – note its wooden platforms, which could be treacherous in rain.

for a daily milk train to London, the lifeblood of the line was stone traffic from the many quarries in the area, and ex-LNWR 0-8-0 heavy goods locos were a common sight at the head of these trains along the line until the early 1960s.

The end came for passenger services between Buxton and Ashbourne and the ex-NSR line from there to Rocester on 1 November 1954. But this was not the end for the line just yet as stone trains continued to use it along with ramblers' specials in the summer. An emergency passenger service also ran during exceptional snowfall in the winter when local roads were blocked. Despite its year-round usefulness, time eventually ran out for the line and it was closed completely on 7 October 1963.

▶ The junction of the line from Ashbourne and the Cromford & High Peak Railway was at Parsley Hay station. Today, it is the junction of the High Peak Trail from Dowlow to Cromford and the Tissington Trail, the latter seen disappearing into the cutting on the right.

▼ With less than five months to go before closure of the Ashbourne line, ex-LNER 'B1' 4-6-0 No. 61360 heads into Parsley Hay with a special from Buxton on 11 May 1963. The shriek of steam whistles has been replaced by the sound of skylarks twittering.

▲ Popular with ramblers, the station at Alsop-en-le-Dale, see here on 3 August 1959, was but a short walk from the scenic beauty of Dovedale and Milldale. Despite closing to regular passenger trains in 1954, stations on the line continued to see emergency services run during the winter when heavy snowfalls blocked local roads.

▼ Built to accommodate a double track, the deep cutting at Heathcote forms part of the Tissington Trail between Hartington and Parsley Hay.

◄ Both the Tissington Trail and the High Peak Trail (pages 122–127) feature excellent illustrated information panels placed at strategic distances along each route. This one, at Parsley Hay, the junction of the two trails, illustrates the station before it closed.

WALKING AND CYCLING THE LINE

THE LINE TODAY

The 13-mile trackbed of the old railway between Ashbourne and Parsley Hay is now a traffic-free footpath, cycleway and bridleway know as the Tissington Trail. It was one of the first such schemes in the country when it opened in 1971 and its accessibility and wonderful scenery have ensured its popularity ever since.

The Trail, which also forms part of National Cycle Network Route 68, starts at Mapleton Lane in Ashbourne, where there is a car park and cycle-hire centre. Just north of here, the former viaduct has been demolished but the Trail soon rejoins the trackbed and continues on to the site of Thorpe station, where there is a car park. From here it is but a short diversion to the beauty of Dovedale and Milldale. The next 'station stop' along the Trail is at the pretty village of Tissington, where there is a large car park and picnic site alongside the old platform. Of note along the route are several stone overbridges that were built at the end of the 19th century to accommodate a double track, but in reality the line was single as far as Parsley Hay with passing loops at the stations. The trail continues on through Alsop-en-le-Dale (where there is another car park) to Hartington, where the restored signalbox is now an information centre. From here the final stretch of the Tissington Trail continues through the deep Heathcote Cutting to end at Parsley Hay where it meets the High Peak Trail (see pages 122–127). Here there is a large car park, picnic site and cycle-hire centre.

PLACES TO VISIT

HERITAGE RAILWAYS
Ecclesbourne Valley Railway
Wirksworth Station, Station Road, Coldwell Street, Wirksworth, Derbyshire DE4 4FB
Tel 01629 823076
Website www.e-v-r.com
Route Idridgehay to Wirksworth and Ravenstor
Length 8½ miles

OTHER ATTRACTIONS
Alton Towers Resort
Alton, Staffordshire ST10 4DB
Tel 0871 222 3330
Website www.altontowers.com

Ilam Country Park and South Peak Estate (NT)
2 miles west of Thorpe,
DE6 2AZ
Website www.derbyshire-peakdistrict.co.uk

Dovedale (NT)
north of Ashbourne
Website www.nationaltrust.org.uk

Tissington Hall
Tissington, Ashbourne, Derbyshire DE6 1RA
Tel 01335 352200
Website www.tissington-hall.com

PRACTICAL INFORMATION

NEAREST RAILWAY STATIONS
Buxton, Uttoxeter

TOURIST INFORMATION
Ashbourne Tourist Information Centre
13 Market Place, Ashbourne, Derbyshire DE6 1EU
Tel 01335 343666
Website www.visitpeakdistrict.com

OS MAP
Landranger No. 119

CYCLE HIRE
Peak Cycle Hire
Mapleton Lane, Ashbourne, Derbyshire DE6 2AA
Tel 01335 343156
Website: www.peakdistrict.gov.uk

Peak Cycle Hire
Parsley Hay, Buxton, Derbyshire SK17 0DG
Tel 01298 84493
Website: www.peakdistrict.gov.uk

CHURNET VALLEY
North Rode to Rocester

One of the most scenic routes of the old North Staffordshire Railway, much of the Churnet Valley line can be explored today either by walking or cycling or on miniature and standard gauge steam trains.

By the early 20th century the North Staffordshire Railway, one of the most successful and independent pre-Grouping railway companies in Britain, had succeeded in spreading its tentacles throughout the industrialised region of the Potteries and beyond. With more than 200 route-miles of railway, the company also owned 130 miles of canals, mainly the Trent & Mersey Canal. The company's independence was also enhanced by the opening of its own carriage and wagon works at its headquarters in Stoke in 1849. Locomotives were also built here from 1868 until 1923.

▼ Carrying LMS No. 1431, an ex-North Staffordshire Railway 0-4-4 tank waits to depart from Leek with the 5.18pm Saturdays-only train for Rushton on 28 June 1933. The main station on the Churnet Valley line, Leek was also once served by special trains on market days.

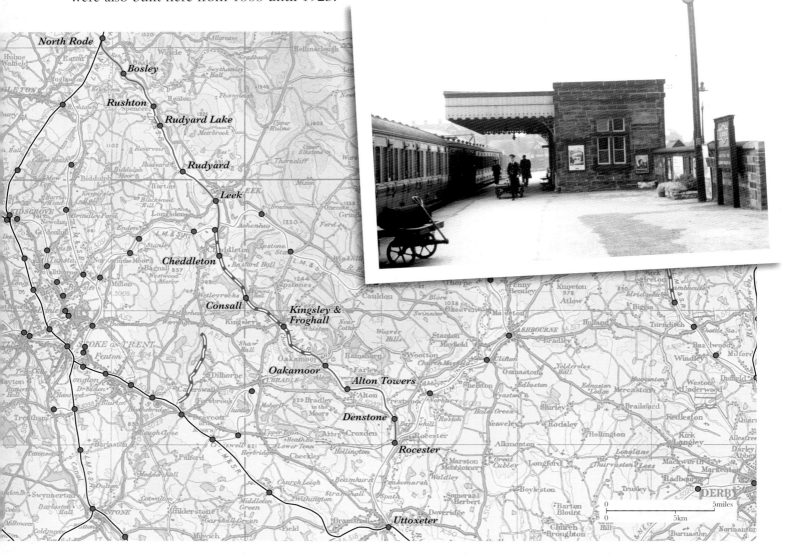

▼ Cheddleton station, now Grade II listed, exudes the grand pseudo architectural style so beloved by the North Staffordshire Railway. Today, the best example of this style, known as 'robust Jacobean manor house', can be seen at Stoke-on-Trent station. Meanwhile, Cheddleton station is now the headquarters of the 5½-mile Churnet Valley Railway.

▶ Another visitor to the Churnet Valley Railway, 'Manor' Class 4-6-0 No. 7821 'Ditcheat Manor' makes a fine sight near the southern end of the railway at Kingsley & Froghall. A new venture, called the Moorland & City Railways, has recently been announced that it will reopen the line from Stoke-on-Trent to Cauldon Low via the CVR at Leek Brook Junction.

▼ Despite the ending of passenger services north of Leek in 1960, the town was still served by trains to Uttoxeter until 1965. Here, ex-LMS Stanier 2-cylinder 2-6-4 tank No. 42603 waits to depart in 1962.

The NSR was not only independent but also individualistic. The company's trademark was the Staffordshire Knot and this gave rise locally to the endearing nickname of 'Knotty'. The company's livery, applied to its locomotives and carriages, was a striking brown with gold and blue lining and the knot appeared on everything from locomotives and rolling stock to porters' uniforms and hotel menus.

While the majority of the Knotty's lines served collieries, iron and steelworks and growing areas in the Potteries themselves, a few of the NSR routes were also famed for their scenic beauty. One of these was the double-track Churnet Valley line, which, at 27¾ miles, opened from North Rode to Uttoxeter on 13 July 1849. By the late 19th century, the line was promoted heavily by the NSR for tourism, even building its own hotels at Leek and Rudyard. The latter, alongside

Rudyard Lake (also NSR–owned), was marketed as a leisure resort complete with golf course.

In addition to excursion traffic to Rudyard Lake, Alton Towers and Uttoxeter Racecourse, the Churnet Valley line was also a useful diversionary route for north-south freight trains avoiding the congestion around Stoke. Special trains were also run to Leek, the principal station on the line, where the twice-weekly agricultural and livestock market brought in much business for the railway.

◀ Beyond Oakamoor, the trackbed of the Churnet Valley line is now a footpath and cycleway, which is seen here passing beside the restored Alton Towers station.

▼ The visiting preserved ex-LNER Class 'V2' 2-6-2 makes a fine sight on the Churnet Valley Railway as it crosses the Caldon Canal near the Black Lion pub. Completed in 1779, the canal was built by the Trent & Mersey Canal, which was itself taken over by the North Staffordshire Railway. In recent years the canal, with its 17 locks and one tunnel, has been restored to its southern terminus at Froghall. Close to Consall station on the CVR, the popular Black Lion pub is reached on foot across the canal and the railway.

WALKING AND CYCLING THE LINE

THE LINE TODAY

Several sections of the Churnet Valley line are now open either as a footpath or a cycleway. At the northern end of the line the trackbed from north of Rushton Spencer to the northern end of Rudyard Lake forms part of the Staffordshire Way Long Distance Path. There are car parks at both of these points. The trackbed of the railway, which can be followed on foot, then runs along the eastern shore of Rudyard Lake to the B5331 near the village of Rudyard, where there is another car park. Here the 10¼in-gauge Rudyard Lake Steam Railway follows the trackbed of the Churnet Valley line northwards for a distance of about 1½ miles. Trains usually operate on Saturdays and daily in school holidays (see below for details). From the car park at Rudyard Lake station a footpath follows the trackbed of the Churnet Valley line across the River Churnet to the outskirts of Leek. South of Leek the Churnet Valley Railway now operates regular services from Cheddleton to Consall and Kingsley & Froghall. From here the railway continues for another 2 miles along the Churnet Valley to the outskirts of Oakamoor, where there is a run-round loop but, at present, no station facilities. From Oakamoor to Denstone, near Rocester, the trackbed of the Churnet Valley line is now a footpath and cycleway. Forming part of National Cycle Network Route 54, this 5-mile route passes close to the delights of Alton Towers Resort and past the beautifully restored Italianate-style Alton Towers station.

PLACES TO VISIT

HERITAGE RAILWAYS

Churnet Valley Railway
Cheddleton Station, Station Road, Cheddleton, Staffordshire ST13 7EE
Tel 01538 361848
Website www.churnet-valley-railway.co.uk
Route Leekbrook to Kingsley & Froghall
Length 5½ miles

Foxfield Railway
Caverswall Road Station, Blythe Bridge, Stoke-on-Trent, Staffordshire ST4 8YT
Tel 01782 396210/259667
Website www.foxfieldrailway.co.uk
Route Blythe Bridge to Dilhorne Park
Length 2¾ miles

OTHER ATTRACTIONS

Rudyard Lake Miniature Railway
Rudyard, Staffordshire ST13 8PF
Tel 01538 306704
Website http://web.ukonline.co.uk/hanson.mike

Brindley Mill
Mill Street, Leek, Staffordshire ST13 8FA
Website www.brindleymill.net

Alton Towers Resort
Alton, Staffordshire ST10 4DB
Tel 0871 222 3330
Website www.altontowers.com

PRACTICAL INFORMATION

NEAREST RAILWAY STATIONS
Stoke-on-Trent, Uttoxeter

OS MAPS
Landranger Nos 118/128

TOURIST INFORMATION
Leek Tourist Information Centre
1 Market Place, Leek, Staffordshire ST13 5HH
Tel 01538 483741
Website www.staffsmoorlands.gov.uk

By the 1930s, the Knotty had become part of the newly formed LMS, and competition from road transport had already taken away much traffic from the Churnet Valley line by the war. Under British Railways, the line's future looked uncertain and closures, even pre-Beeching, soon followed. First to go were through passenger services between Macclesfield and Uttoxeter, which ceased on 7 November 1960. Despite this there was still a minimal service of workmen's trains between Leek and Uttoxeter until they too stopped running on 4 January 1965. Leek station was closed to goods in 1970 but the now single-line section from Oakamoor northwards to Leekbrook Junction (and thence to Stoke) was open until 1988 for industrial sand traffic to Pilkington's glassworks in St Helens. However, waiting in the wings at Cheddleton station, which they had purchased in 1976, was the North Staffordshire Railway Society. Later to become the Churnet Valley Railway, this preservation group has since reopened 5½ miles of the line from Leekbrook Junction to Kingsley & Froghall.

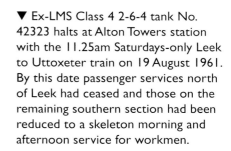

▼ Ex-LMS Class 4 2-6-4 tank No. 42323 halts at Alton Towers station with the 11.25am Saturdays-only Leek to Uttoxeter train on 19 August 1961. By this date passenger services north of Leek had ceased and those on the remaining southern section had been reduced to a skeleton morning and afternoon service for workmen.

WALES

◀ Ex-GWR 2-6-0 No. 7341 leaves Penmaenpool with a Ruabon to Barmouth train, c.1960. The line closed after flooding in December 1964 and now the section from Dolgellau to Morfa Mawddach, alongside the Mawddach Estuary, is a popular traffic-free cycle trail and footpath.

LÔN LAS OGWEN

Port Penrhyn to Bethesda

Once home to one of the oldest railways in Britain and the largest slate quarry in the world, the village of Bethesda in North Wales was also served for a while by a short standard gauge branch line from Bangor.

▲ An interesting track layout at Port Penrhyn on 25 June 1956. On the left is the track of the 1ft 10¾in-gauge Penrhyn Railway while on the right are the standard gauge sidings. In the foreground the Penrhyn Railway track crosses the standard gauge on a fairly novel level crossing.

Nearly 1 mile long and 1,200ft deep, the Penryhn Quarry at Bethesda in North Wales is probably the largest slate quarry in the world. It was developed in the late 18th century by slave owner, landowner, MP and Irish peer Richard Pennant, 1st Baron Penrhyn. Initially the slate was carried on horses for the 6-mile journey down to Port Penrhyn where it was then loaded onto ships. In 1801, a horsedrawn tramway with inclined planes – one of the earliest railways in Britain - was opened between the quarry and the port. With a gauge of 1ft 10¾in, the line continued to operate in this fashion until 1877, when it was realigned to avoid the inclines and to allow the operation of steam locomotives. However, apart from workmen who would often perch on the slate wagons, the little line did not carry passengers.

This state of affairs led to demands from the people of Bethesda for a standard gauge passenger-carrying line and in 1884 the London

◄ Built by Hunslet in 1893, Penryhn Railway 0-4-0 saddle tank 'Blanche' leaves Port Penrhyn for Bethesda with a train of empty slate wagons on 11 August 1953. Upon closure of the railway in 1962, 'Blanche' and sister loco 'Linda' were bought by the Ffestiniog Railway where they were converted to 2-4-0 saddle tanks.

▲ Felin Hen was the first intermediate station on the LNWR Bangor to Bethesda standard gauge branch. Despite serving scattered farming communities, the station was important enough to have a booking office, waiting room and ladies and gents toilets. Today the trackbed here is part of the Lôn Las Ogwen cycleway and footpath.

◄ Leaving Port Penrhyn, the narrow gauge and standard gauge lines passed through separate arches before climbing up the valley towards Bethesda. The trackbed is now used by walkers and cyclists. Several buildings of the old railway, including the engine shed and head office, can still be seen at the port.

WALKING AND CYCLING THE LINE

THE LINE TODAY

Much of the route of both the narrow gauge Penrhyn Railway and the adjacent ex-LNWR standard gauge branch to Bethesda can be explored today. Known as Lôn Las Ogwen, the trackbed of the standard gauge line from Port Penrhyn as far as Tregarth is now a footpath and cycleway. An extension along the line to Bethesda is planned for the future.

There is still much to interest lovers of old railways along the route including the stone wharfs and short tunnel at Port Penrhyn and the seven-arch viaduct over the Afon Cegin at Glasinfryn. While the cycleway and footpath currently terminates at the site of Tregarth station, further investigation up the route of the line to Bethesda reveals a vast amount of railway infrastructure including Penrhyn Railway bridges, the standard gauge Tregarth Tunnel and the five-arch viaduct over the Afon Ogwen. The LNWR station site at Bethesda has long since disappeared beneath a sports ground. Dwarfing Bethesda, the flooded Penryhn Quarry, in its heyday the workplace of 3,000 men, has fallen silent after nearly 200 years of slate extraction. The Lôn Las Ogwen cycleway continues for a further 5 miles via roads, lanes and tracks up the dramatic Ogwen valley as far as Llyn Ogwen.

PLACES TO VISIT

HERITAGE RAILWAYS
Llanberis Lake Railway
Gilfach Ddu, Llanberis, Caernarfon,
Gwynedd LL55 4TY
Tel 01286 870549
Website www.lake-railway.co.uk
Route Gilfach Ddu to Llanberis and Cei Llydan
Length 2½ miles

Snowdon Mountain Railway
Llanberis, Gwynedd LL55 4TY
Tel 0844 493 8120
Website www.snowdonrailway.co.uk
Route Llanberis to Snowdon Summit
Length 4¾ miles

OTHER ATTRACTIONS
Gwynedd Museum and Art Gallery
Ffordd Gwynedd, Bangor, Gwynedd LL57 1DT
Tel 01248 353368
Website www.gwynedd.gov.uk

Penrhyn Castle (NT)
Bangor, Gwynedd LL57 4HN
Tel 01248 371337
Website www.nationaltrust.org.uk

Electric Mountain Centre
Llanberis, Gwynedd LL55 4UR
Tel 01286 870636
Website www.fhc.co.uk

National Slate Museum
Llanberis, Gwynedd LL55 4TY
Tel 01286 870630
Website www.museumwales.ac.uk

PRACTICAL INFORMATION

NEAREST RAILWAY STATION
Bangor

TOURIST INFORMATION
Bangor Tourist Information Centre
Town Hall, Ffordd Deiniol, Bangor, Gwynedd LL57 2RE
Tel 01248 352786

Llanberis Tourist Information Centre
41b High Street, Llanberis, Gwynedd LL55 4EU
Tel 012286 870765

OS MAP
Landranger No. 115

▲ The Lôn Las Ogwen cycleway along the standard gauge trackbed from Port Penrhyn currently ends at the site of Tregarth station. It is hoped that the cycleway will be extended through Tregarth Tunnel and across the Ogwen Viaduct into Bethesda.

◀ Although passenger services to Bethesda had ceased on 3 December 1951, the neglected station building and platform, seen here on 19 July 1963, survived the complete closure of the line. Bethesda Rugby Club is now located on the station yard site.

◀ East of Tregarth the trackbed of the standard gauge line passes through the short Tregarth Tunnel before emerging on to the five-arched Ogwen Viaduct. The overbridge in the foreground once carried the narrow gauge Penrhyn Railway.

& North Western Railway opened a 4½-mile branch from their main line at Bangor. The steeply graded line, closely following, crossing over and passing under the route of the existing Penrhyn Railway, included two viaducts and a tunnel. Intermediate stations were at Felin Hen and Tregarth and by the early 20th century an intensive passenger service was being handled by LNWR steam railmotors. This happy state of affairs continued until the outbreak of the Second World War, when services became severely restricted. After the war the line never fully recovered and, under a British Railways management looking to cut mounting losses, passenger services ceased on 3 December 1951. Goods and excursion traffic continued until 7 October 1963.

Meanwhile, the narrow gauge Penrhyn Railway was experiencing a serious drop in traffic from the quarry and the little line, with its veteran steam locomotives, closed completely in July 1962. By that date the Penrhyn Estate, centred around the Pennant family's early 19th-century castle, had already been given to the National Trust in lieu of death duties. Today the castle houses an industrial railway museum, and includes two locomotives that once worked on the Penrhyn Railway.

▼ Two weeks after official closure to freight, a final enthusiasts' special was run over the Bangor to Bethesda branch on 20 October 1963. Here beautifully turned-out Ivatt Class 2 2-6-2 tank No. 41234 waits to depart from Bethesda on the last journey down to Bangor.

LÔN EIFION

Caernarfon to Afon Wen

By 1870, the mighty London & North Western Railway had acquired a route that penetrated deep into Caernarfonshire. Sadly, even a post-war revival of holiday traffic failed to halt its axe under Beeching.

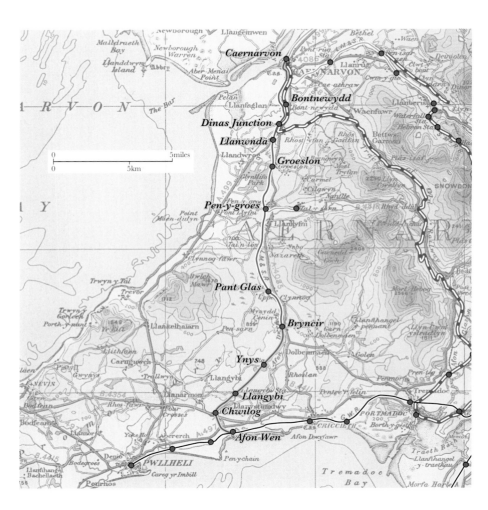

The first railway to reach Caernarfon was the horsedrawn 3ft 6in-gauge Nantlle Railway that opened in 1828 and ran from slate and copper quarries at Nantlle Vale to the harbour below Caernarfon Castle, a distance of 9 miles via Pen-y-groes. The first standard gauge railway to reach Caernarfon was the 8½-mile Bangor & Carnarvon Railway that opened from a junction with the Chester & Holyhead Railway (later the LNWR) at Menai Bridge in 1852.

Next on the scene was the Carnarvonshire Railway, which was authorised in 1862 to build a standard gauge line from Caernarfon to Porthmadog via Afon Wen. The first part of this line from Caernarfon to Pen-y-groes entailed building over the existing narrow gauge

▶ Separated from the Welsh Highland Railway by a fence, the Lôn Eifion cycleway, part of National Cycle Network Route 8, passes the request halt at Bontnewydd, north of Dinas. Refreshments are available in the nearby village.

▲ Despite the passage of more than 70 years, the scene at Dinas Junction is very similar today. The differences are a smartened-up station building and narrow gauge track instead of standard gauge.

◀ The starting point of the Lôn Eifion cycleway and the Welsh Highland Railway is close to the World Heritage Site of Caernarfon Castle. From here they both share the trackbed of the Caernarfon to Afon Wen line as far as Dinas.

Nantlle Railway. The latter section was completed by 1866 but serious financial problems delayed its opening throughout until September 1867 by which time the Cambrian Railways, who by then owned the Afon Wen to Porthmadog section, were given running powers to Caernarfon. Two years later the Euston-based LNWR, who already owned the line from Bangor to Caernarfon, opened a branch line from Caernarfon to Llanberis and, in 1870, completed its stranglehold on this part of North Wales by absorbing the Carnarvonshire Railway to Afon Wen. In the same year the remaining southern section of the narrow gauge Nantlle Railway from Pen-y-groes to Nantlle was converted to standard gauge.

The final railway to connect with the Caernarfon to Afon Wen line was the North Wales Narrow Gauge Railway that opened from Dinas Junction to Bryngwyn in 1877. Later to become the Welsh Highland Railway, the extension to Porthmadog via Beddgelert was not completed until 1923. The whole undertaking was later leased by

▲ North of Pant Glas the asphalted section of the Lôn Eifion cycleway near Graianog Crossing was once used by lorries serving a nearby quarry. Today it is easy going for the many cyclists that use this level, traffic-free trail.

▼ At Afon Wen the line from Caernarfon formed a junction with the Cambrian line from Dolgellau to Pwllheli. Here, Ivatt Class 2 2-6-0 No. 46428 takes on water at the station on 1 April 1954 before departing with its train of blood-and-custard coaches. The station closed on 7 December 1964 along with the rest of the line northwards to Caernarfon. Trains on the Cambrian line still pass the site of the station today.

the Ffestiniog Railway but it had closed completely by the Second World War.

Other closures along the line had happened even earlier with the Llanberis branch losing its passenger service in 1930 and the Nantlle branch two years later. Despite this, excursion traffic still penetrated the Llanberis branch until the early 1960s. After the war, the opening of Butlins Holiday Camp at Penychain brought a surge of summer traffic to the line with through trains operating from as far afield as Euston.

Following the Beeching Report in early 1963, the Caernarfon to Afon Wen line and its remaining freight-only branches were doomed. First to go were the freight-only branches to Nantlle and Llanberis, which closed completely in December 1963 and September 1964 respectively. The Caernarfon to Afon Wen line saw complete closure in December 1964 although the northerly branch from Caernarfon to Menai Bridge clung on until January 1970, its life extended by the investiture of the Prince of Wales at Caernarfon Castle in 1969.

◄ Although possessing only one platform, Chwilog station, the penultimate stop before Afon Wen, boasted a substantial station building. Seen here in August 1956, the platform and stationmaster's house still survive today.

▲ Some of the early Derby lightweight diesel multiple units saw service between Caernarfon and Afon Wen. Here a northbound service waits at Llangybi while the southbound steam-hauled train clears the passing loop in August 1956.

◄ The southern terminus of the Lon Eifion cycleway is at the site of Bryncir station. Here there is a small car park alongside the old platforms and restored water tower. The nearby station house is now a holiday cottage.

WALKING AND CYCLING THE LINE

THE LINE TODAY

After lying dormant for many years, 12 miles of the Caernarfon to Afon Wen railway now has a new lease of life. First to arrive on the scene was the traffic-free Lôn Eifion footpath and cycleway, which runs along the trackbed of the line from Caernarfon to Bryncir. Today it forms part of National Cycle Network Route 8.

A railway also returned to part of the route in 2000 when the first stage of the ambitious narrow gauge Welsh Highland Railway project was opened from Caernarfon to Waunfawr. The railway, now open throughout to Porthmadog via Beddgelert, follows the trackbed of the standard gauge Caernarfon to Afon Wen line as far as Dinas, where it strikes off in an easterly direction into the Snowdonia National Park. North of Dinas a request halt is provided at Bontnewydd. Most WHR trains include cycle wagons for cyclists using the Lon Eifion cycleway, which parallels the line as far as Dinas. Car parking is available at Caernarfon and Dinas. The steam locomotives hauling the trains are massive (by narrow gauge standards) Beyer-Garratt articulated locos rehabilitated from South Africa.

Lôn Eifion and the Welsh Highland Railway part company at Dinas, the former continuing its southerly route to Groeslon, where the Welsh Rock Café and the Inigo Jones Slate Works are located alongside the cycleway. Continuing south past Penygroes, where the platforms still survive, there are fine views of Snowdonia to the east and Bwlch Mawr to the west before the cycleway terminates at the site of Bryncir station. Here there is a small car park adjacent to the old platforms and restored water tower.

PLACES TO VISIT

HERITAGE RAILWAYS
Welsh Highland Railway
Harbour Station, Porthmadog, Gwynedd, LL49 9NF
Tel 01766 516000
Website www.welshhighlandrailway.net
Route Caernarfon to Porthmadog
Length 19½ miles

OTHER ATTRACTIONS
Caernarfon Castle World Heritage Site
Castle Ditch, Caernarfon, Gwynedd LL55 2AY
Tel 01286 677617
Website www.caernarfon-castle.co.uk

Caernarfon Airworld Museum
Dinas Dinlle, Caernarfon, Gwynedd LL54 5TP
Tel 01286 830800
Website www.air-world.co.uk

Glynllifon Gardens and Country Park
Clynnog Road, Caernarfon, Gwynedd LL54 5DY
Tel 01286 830222
Website www.gwynedd.gov.uk

Criccieth Castle
Castle Street, Criccieth LL55 0DP
Tel 01766 522227
Website www.cadw.wales.gov.uk

PRACTICAL INFORMATION

NEAREST RAILWAY STATIONS
Bangor, Caernarfon (Welsh Highland Railway), Dinas (Welsh Highland Railway),

TOURIST INFORMATION
Caernarfon Tourist Information Centre
Oriel Pendeitsh, Stryd y Castell, Caernarfon, LL55 1SE
Tel 01286 672232
Website www.gwynedd.gov.uk

OS MAPS
Landranger Nos 115, 123

CYCLE HIRE
Menai Cycles
1 Slate Quay, Caernarfon, Gwynedd LL55 2PB
Tel 01286 676804
Website www.beicsmenai.co.uk

THE MAWDDACH TRAIL

Barmouth to Dolgellau

*Once an important through route to West Wales, the Ruabon to Barmouth railway closed early in 1965.
An 8-mile western section is now a traffic-free multi-use path along the Mawddach Estuary.*

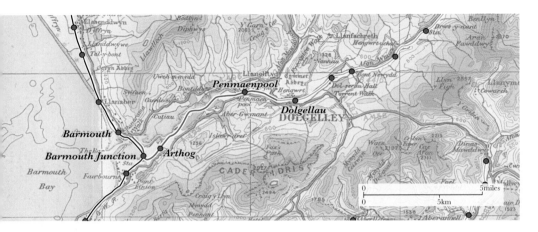

▼ Formerly known as Barmouth Junction, Morfa Mawddach station was the junction between the Cambrian Coast line, seen curving away to the right, with the line to Dolgellau and Ruabon. BR Standard Class 4 4-6-0 No. 75006 is seen approaching the station with the 10.20am train from Barmouth to Chester with through coaches for Birkenhead on 7 June 1963. Three old camping coaches can be seen parked in the station bay.

Although the railway line from Ruabon to Barmouth was built in fits and starts by several independent companies, it was the mighty Great Western Railway that had the foresight to see it as a through route to West Wales. First to open was the Vale of Llangollen Railway, which first ran between Ruabon and Llangollen in 1862, followed by the Llangollen & Corwen Railway along the scenic Dee Valley in 1865. Next was the Corwen & Bala Railway, which reached Bala in 1868. All three railways were operated from the start by the GWR before being absorbed in 1896. The next link in the chain was the Bala & Dolgelly Railway, which also opened in 1868 and was again worked from the start by the GWR, being absorbed by them in 1877.

Meanwhile, a branch line had already been opened from Barmouth Junction alongside the Mawddach Estuary to Penmaenpool by the Cambrian Railways in 1865. Financial difficulties had prevented them from continuing the line to Dolgellau. The 1-mile missing link in this through route of 54½ miles, the Penmaenpool to Dolgellau section, was finally completed by the Bala & Dolgelly Railway with GWR backing in 1870.

▶ Opened in 1867, the 900-yd single-track Barmouth Bridge carries the Cambrian Coast line across the Mawddach Estuary. A steel swing bridge to allow shipping to pass replaced a wooden drawbridge in 1901. The bridge was closed for repairs in the mid-1980s after it was found to be infested by marine worms. Walkers and cyclists pay a small toll to use the attached footbridge.

Two other railways formed junctions with the Ruabon to Barmouth Junction line. The first to open was the Denbigh, Ruthin & Corwen Railway, which started running throughout in 1865 and was absorbed by the London & North Western railway in 1879. The last line to open was the GWR-backed Bala & Festiniog Railway, which opened throughout in 1883.

Despite being mainly single-track throughout, the Ruabon to Barmouth line was an important through route for GWR trains to West Wales. Until the Second World War holiday traffic on summer Saturdays was particularly heavy with through carriages to Barmouth or Pwllheli from Paddington, Birkenhead, Birmingham and Manchester.

Closures along the line started in 1953 when passenger trains from Corwen to Denbigh ceased to run. However, the route was still used for a few more years by Land Cruise trains that ran in the summer on the circular Rhyl – Corwen – Barmouth – Afon Wen – Caernarfon – Rhyl route. Goods trains ceased in 1962.

▼ The old GWR signalbox at Penmaenpool has been restored as a birdwatching hide.

▲ Nestling alongside the Mawddach Estuary, Penmaenpool was, and still is, a delightful spot. Although the railway line, timber platform and assorted sheds have disappeared since this 1963 photograph, the scene remains much the same today. The wooden toll bridge is still open for light vehicles and pedestrians while the signalbox is now an RSPB observation post.

Next to go was the Bala to Ffestiniog line, which closed to passengers in 1960 and completely in 1961. The main line struggled on for a few more years but its lifeblood was draining away with freight diverted via the more southerly Cambrian main line from Shrewsbury to Barmouth via Machynlleth. Another victim of the 'Beeching Axe', closure of the whole line was scheduled for 18 January 1965 but flooding during the previous December cut the line at several places, leaving just the eastern section from Ruabon to Llangollen and the isolated Dolgellau to Bala section to soldier on to the end.

Since closure, several long sections of the Ruabon to Barmouth line have come back to life – the Llangollen Railway operates a 7½-mile heritage line from Llangollen to Carrog with an extension to Corwen currently under construction. Farther west the 2ft-gauge Bala Lake Railway operates along 4½ miles of trackbed from Llanuwchllyn to the outskirts of Bala.

▼ A GWR '2301' Class 0-6-0, otherwise known as a 'Dean Goods', and a later Collett '2251' Class 0-6-0 simmer outside the little two-road engine shed at Penmaenpool in pre-BR days. The shed was originally opened in 1869 but closed on 18 January 1965. It has since been demolished.

▼ An ex-GWR Mogul heads a train for Dolgellau alongside the Mawddach Estuary near Arthog Halt on 17 September 1959. Fortunately, users of the Mawddach Trail can now enjoy the same view after the Snowdonia National Park authorities purchased the trackbed following closure.

▲ Close to the eastern outskirts of Dolgellau, the Mawddach Trail crosses the Afon Wnion, a tributary of the Afon Mawddach, on this rusting railway girder bridge. The river banks here are a popular spot for fishermen.

WALKING AND CYCLING THE LINE

THE LINE TODAY

One of the most scenic closed railway routes in Britain, the 8-mile section of line from Morffa Mawddach station to Dolgellau is now a multi-use traffic-free path along the southern shore of the Mawddach Estuary. Known as the Mawddach Trail it starts in Barmouth by crossing the Afon Mawddach on a footbridge attached to the 900yd-long Barmouth Bridge. Pedestrians and cyclists are required to pay a toll to cross the bridge. At the south end of the bridge, Morfa Mawddach station (once named Barmouth Junction) is still served by trains on the Cambrian Coast line from Machynlleth to Pwllheli. From the car park here, where the old curving platform still survives, the route of the Trail swings eastwards to follow closely the south shore of the Mawddach Estuary to Penmaenpool. With dramatic views across to Snowdonia, the estuary, much loved by William Wordsworth, is an important breeding site for wetland birds such as redshank and merganser and is recommended for birdwatchers.

Six miles along the trail from Morfa Mawddach station is Penmaenpool, once the short-lived terminus of the Cambrian branch line, which opened in 1865. Although the wooden station platforms have long gone, a GWR lower quadrant signal and the restored signalbox still lend a railway atmosphere to this delightful spot. Here the George III Hotel is a perfect place to stop for refreshments and to relax and enjoy the view across the estuary. Nearby is the 1879-built wooden toll bridge across the river and the Penmaenpool Wildlife Centre, which uses the signalbox as an observation point. From the car park here the Mawddach Trail continues eastwards along the railway trackbed to the western outskirts of Dolgellau where there is a small car park at the junction with the A493. From here the A470 follows the route of the railway into the town.

PLACES TO VISIT

HERITAGE RAILWAYS
Talyllyn Railway
Wharf Station, Tywyn, Gwynedd LL36 9EY
Tel 01654 710472
Website www.talyllynrailway.co.uk
Route Tywyn Wharf to Nant Gwernol
Length 7¼ miles

OTHER ATTRACTIONS
RNLI Museum
Pen-y-Cei, Barmouth LL42 1HB
Tel 01341 280737

Cymer Abbey
Llanelltyd, Nr Dolgellau
Website www.cadw.wales.gov.uk

Fairbourne Railway
Beach Road, Fairbourne, Gwynedd LL38 2EX
Tel 01341 250362
Website www.fairbournerailway.com

Corris Railway and Museum
Station Yard, Corris, Machynlleth,
Powys SY20 9SH
Tel 01654 761303
Website www.corris.co.uk

Bala Lake Railway
The Station, Llanuwchllyn,
Gwynedd LL23 7DD
Tel 01678 540666
Website www.bala-lake-railway.co.uk

PRACTICAL INFORMATION

NEAREST RAILWAY STATIONS
Barmouth, Morfa Mawddach

TOURIST INFORMATION
Barmouth Tourist Information Centre
The Old Library, Station Road, Barmouth,
Gwynedd LL42 1LU
Tel 01341 280787
Website www.visitmidwales.co.uk

Dolgellau Tourist Information Centre
Ty Meirion, Eldon Square, Dolgellau,
Gwynedd LL40 1PU
Tel 01341 422888
Website www.visitmidwales.co.uk

OS MAP
Landranger No. 124

CYCLE HIRE
Birmingham Garage
Dolgellau Road, Barmouth,
Gwynedd LL42 1EL
Tel 01341 280644

SWANSEA & MUMBLES RAILWAY

First conceived as a horsedrawn tramway to carry minerals and limestone along the shore of Swansea Bay from Oystermouth to the Swansea Canal, the 4ft-gauge Oystermouth Railway, as it was then called, became the first fare-paying passenger-carrying railway in the world in 1807. Passengers were initially carried along the track in a horsedrawn railway stagecoach but the service ceased in around 1826 following competition from a new turnpike road.

The railway lay dormant until 1855 when it was relaid with conventional standard gauge rails and the horsedrawn passenger service was reintroduced. Steam haulage was instituted in 1877 and the line, now known as the Swansea & Mumbles Railway,

▲ Until the line was extended to a new pier at Mumbles Head in 1898, the western terminus of the railway was at Oystermouth. Here, passengers board tramcar No. 10 on the 3.18pm from Southend to Rutland Street on 12 December 1959.

▶ With only three weeks to go before closure, business is brisk for the Swansea & Mumbles Railway at the Rutland Street Terminus in Swansea. Seen here on 12 December 1959 are tramcars Nos 6 and 1, between them capable of seating 212 passengers.

was extended to a new pier at Mumbles Head in 1898. The next major development in the history of the railway came in 1929 when it was electrified using overhead transmission operating at 640V DC. A fleet of large double-deck tramcars, seating over 100 passengers each, was delivered by Brush Electrical and these remained in service until the line closed.

The end came for the Swansea & Mumbles Railway in 1958 when the local bus operator, wishing to rid itself of any competition, purchased the line. Permission to close it came a year later and, despite strong local protests, the last tram returned to the Rutland Street terminus on 5 January 1960. Sadly, the railway and tramcars were rapidly dismantled, thus ending an important piece of railway history.

▼ From 1898, the western terminus of the railway was at Mumbles Head Pier, where tramcar No. 12 is seen in May 1959. The section of line from the preceding station, Southend, to the Pier was closed in October of that year, three months before closure of the rest of the railway.

SOUTH WALES MINERAL RAILWAY

Briton Ferry to Glyncorrwg

Originally built to Brunel's broad gauge, the unique South Wales Mineral Railway was closed in three stages between 1910 and 1970. Today, mountain bikers enjoy the scenery of the Afan and Corrwg valleys.

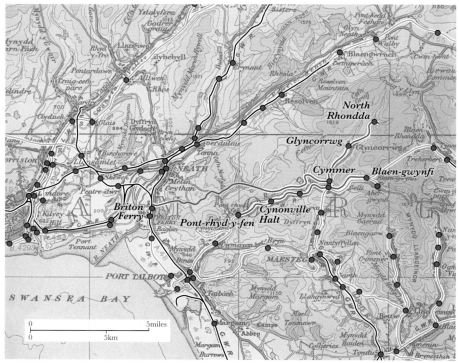

▲ Opened in 1863, the 1,109-yd Gyfylchi Tunnel on the South Wales Mineral Railway was built to Brunel's broad gauge. It was closed in 1947 after a landslip, when the line between Cymmer and Tonmawr was also closed. The single-track tunnel was the scene of a serious head-on collision between two trains in 1902. The tunnel, seen here at the eastern portal, is now partially flooded and home to colonies of bats. A track to the tunnel leads through woods from the Afan Forest Visitor Centre in the valley below at Cynonville.

The South Wales Mineral Railway was built solely to convey coal from mines at the top end of the narrow Corrwg Valley the 12 miles or so down to new docks at Briton Ferry. Leased from the outset by the Glyncorrwg Coal Company and engineered by Isambard Kingdom Brunel, the railway was built to broad gauge standards (7ft 0½in) with the last 1½ miles down to Briton Ferry being operated by a 1 in 10 cable-worked incline. The line between Briton Ferry and collieries at Tonmawr was opened in 1861, followed by the mountainous section through Gyfylchi Tunnel and up the Afan Valley to Glyncorrwg, which opened in 1863.

In 1872 the SWMR was converted to standard gauge but it was never a financial success and the opening of the Port Talbot Railway's branch to Tonmawr in 1898 soon brought about the railway's downfall. The SWMR was taken over by the Port Talbot Railway in 1908 (by then part of the GWR) which then closed the Briton Ferry Incline. Traffic from the SWMR was then diverted via a connection with the PTR's branch at Tonmawr.

Despite being built as a mineral railway, a short-lived passenger service was introduced on the SWMR in 1918 between Cymmer (already served by trains on the GWR's line from Tondu and the ex-Rhondda & Swansea Bay's line from Aberavon) and the village of Glyncorrwg. The regular passenger service ceased in 1930 but workmen's trains continued to operate from Cymmer to Glyncorrwg and along an extension to the North Rhondda Colliery until the late 1950s.

▶ Henry Casserley's delightful photo of Glyncorrwg level crossing was taken during his visit on 11 July 1958. Full of period detail with children playing in the street it also features a 1934 Hillman Minx.

▼ Ex-GWR 0-6-0 pannier tank No. 9617 departs from Glyncorrwg propelling three workmen's coaches up the valley to North Rhondda Colliery on 11 July 1958. On the left, railway photographer Henry Casserley clicks away, watched by a BR employee.

▼ The old SWMR station at Cymmer is now a café and bar. Regular passenger services from here to Glyncorrwg (1918–1930) were short-lived but workmen's trains continued to run until the 1950s.

▲ This bridge over the Afon Afan at Cymmer was built in 1878 to link the Glyncorrwg branch of the South Wales Mineral Railway with the GWR's line down to Tondu and Bridgend. Unusually for the period, it was built of iron resting on stone piers.

The old SWMR route was further shortened in 1947 when the section between Cymmer and Tonmawr via the Gyfylchi Tunnel was closed due to a landslip. Coal traffic from North Rhondda was then diverted onto the GWR line to Tondu via a bridge over the valley at Cymmer. This remaining section of the SWMR closed in 1970 when the last of the pits shut down.

WALKING AND CYCLING THE LINE

THE LINE TODAY

Much of the route of the old South Wales Mineral Railway can still be explored today. Although a fairly steep climb, much of the incline from the cemetery at Briton Ferry is now a footpath that passes over several of Brunel's original bridges on its 1½-mile course. The trackbed of several mineral railways can still be visited around Tonmawr but the SWMR route comes to a dead end near here at the western end of the now bricked-up Gyfylchi Tunnel.

To continue our exploration of the SWMR it is now necessary to visit the Afan Forest Country Park visitor centre at Cynonville in the neighbouring Afan Valley. Here there is a car park, café, campsite, cycle-hire facilities and the South Wales Miners' Museum. From the visitor centre, there are a network of cycle trails – some of them serious mountain bike rides – and scenic walks, some of which not only follow the SWMR trackbed but also that of the Rhondda & Swansea Bay Railway's line up from Aberavon. The eastern portal of Gyfylchi Tunnel can be reached on foot from the visitor centre via a footbridge over the fast-flowing Afon Afan, followed by a 20-minute scenic climb through woodlands. There are many picnic sites in the valley, including one on the platform of Cynonville station.

From the eastern portal of Gyfylchi Tunnel the SWMR trackbed is now a well-surfaced forest trail as far as Cymmer. Here the physical link between the SWMR and the GWR, the girder bridge across the Afan, still stands. Nearby is the old station building (now a café and bar) and platform from where miners once started their journey up the Corrwg Valley to North Rhondda Colliery. From Cymmer to Glyncorrwg and up the narrowing valley to North Rhondda the trackbed is now a footpath and cycleway. Half a mile south of Glyncorrwg is the newly opened Glyncorrwg Mountain Bike Centre, which houses a café and biking facilities at the start of two world-class mountain bike trails.

PLACES TO VISIT

HERITAGE RAILWAYS

Swansea Vale Railway
Upper Bank Works, Pentrechwyth,
Swansea SA1 7DB
Tel 01792 461000
Website http://homepage.ntlworld.com/michael.
meyrick/
Route Six Pit Junction to Upper Bank Station
Length 2 miles

OTHER ATTRACTIONS

South Wales Miners Museum
Afan Forest Park, Cynonville,
Port Talbot SA13 3HG
Tel 01639 850564
Website www.southwalesminersmuseum.co.uk

Neath Museum and Art Gallery
Gwyn Hall, Orchard Street,
Neath SA11 1DU
Tel 01639 645726
Website www.npt.gov.uk

Margam Country Park
Margam, Port Talbot SA13 2TJ
Tel 01639 881635
Website www.npt.gov.uk

National Waterfront Museum
Oystermouth Road, Maritime Quarter,
Swansea SA1 3RD
Tel 01792 638950
Website www.museumwales.ac.uk

PRACTICAL INFORMATION

NEAREST RAILWAY STATION

Briton Ferry (Llansawel)

TOURIST INFORMATION

Swansea Tourist Information Centre
Plymouth Street,
Swansea SA1 3QG
Tel 01792 468321
Website www.visitswanseabay.com

OS MAP

Landranger No. 170

CYCLE HIRE

Afan Forest Visitor Centre
Cynonville, Port Talbot
SA13 3HG
Tel 01639 851100
Website www.skylinecycles.co.uk

◀ Workmen's trains continued to operate from Glyncorrwg to North Rhondda until the late 1950s. Here 0-6-0 pannier tank No. 9617 has just arrived at North Rhondda Halt after propelling its set of 1921 Swindon-built workmen's coaches up the valley on 11 July 1958.

GLYN VALLEY TRAMWAY
Chirk to Glyn Ceiriog

During a relatively short working life of 62 years, the little Glyn Valley Tramway was an important link with the outside world for the granite quarries and local residents of the beautiful Ceiriog Valley.

▲ To deal with increased granite traffic, a fourth steam loco was purchased by the Glyn Valley Tramway in 1921. Built by the Baldwin Locomotive Works in the USA for use on military light railways in France during the First World War, this 4-6-0 tank locomotive was converted to the GVT's unusual gauge of 2ft 4¼ in by Beyer Peacock and began working on the line in 1921.

Although slate had been quarried in the remote Ceiriog Valley since the 16th century, the industry was a very local affair. The opening of the Ellesmere Canal to nearby Chirk in 1799 changed all this and much larger markets suddenly became tantalisingly closer. However, there remained one problem – how to transport the slate over the 6 miles between the quarries at Glyn Ceiriog and the canal at Chirk.

Although various schemes were put forward to build a horsedrawn tramway along the valley to Chirk, it was a turnpike road that was built first. Partly funded by the Cambrian Slate Company, it opened in 1863 with a verge that was wide enough to accommodate a tramway in the future. Finally, in 1870, the Glyn Valley Tramway was formed and the gauge selected was a curious 2ft 4¼in – exactly half that of the standard gauge. The horsedrawn line opened in 1873 alongside the road from Glyn Ceiriog to Pontfaen and thence across private land up an 800-yd 1 in 25 incline to railway

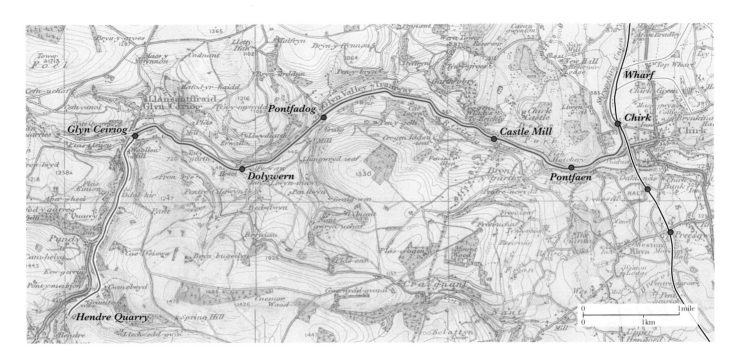

interchange sidings and a canal wharf south of Chirk. This arrangement worked fairly well until a granite quarry was opened at Hendre, 3 miles to the southwest of Glyn Ceiriog. Initially carried by packhorse to the tramway's railhead, the increased heavy traffic of granite setts put enormous pressure on the line.

The year 1888 was a turning point for the line – steam haulage, in the shape of two steam tram locomotives, was introduced and a new route into Chirk was opened along with a 3-mile extension from Glyn Ceiriog to quarries at Hendre and Pandy. Passenger services recommenced in 1891 with new stations provided at Chirk, adjacent to the GWR station, and Glyn Ceiriog and roadside waiting rooms at Pontfadog and

▼ The Glyn Valley Tramway ordered two steam tram engines from Beyer, Peacock of Manchester for the opening of the new route into Chirk in 1888; a third was added to the line in 1892. Here, 'Dennis' (named after the railway's chief engineer) stands at Chirk station with a mixed train for Glyn Ceiriog in the late 19th century.

▼ Beyer Peacock steam tram engine 'Glyn' and its driver pose for an Edwardian photographer on the Glyn Valley Tramway. The open four-wheeled carriages were particularly popular in the summer when, on Bank Holidays, trains were packed to capacity.

▲ Built in 1888, a 3-mile extension from Glyn Ceiriog to Hendre Quarry crossed the Afon Ceiriog on this girder bridge near Upper Pandy. Now owned by the National Trust, the trackbed is a well-surfaced footpath leading up the valley.

Dolywern. The line prospered into the 20th century, being especially popular on Bank Holidays, when long trains of carriages were often packed full of day trippers. Sadly, the end came quickly for the tramway in the early 1930s when a combination of reduced demand for granite and a competing bus service soon led to its demise. Passenger services ceased in 1933 and the line closed completely in 1935. Apart from a couple of coaches, which have since been preserved on the Talyllyn Railway, all locomotives and rolling stock were scrapped and the rails lifted.

▲ A mixed train from Chirk has just arrived at Glyn Ceiriog station on 7 October 1931. The track in the foreground leads to the granite quarry at Hendre. Passenger services on the Glyn Valley Tramway ceased on 6 April 1933.

WALKING AND CYCLING THE LINE

THE LINE TODAY

Despite closure over 75 years ago there is still much to be discovered along the route of the tramway today. From the site of the Blackpark Canal basin on the Shropshire Union Canal, the course of the line can be followed through woodland adjoining the present main line where the only overbridge on the tramway still stands. From Pont-Faen to Glyn Ceiriog along what is now the B4500 the Glyn Valley Tramway was a true roadside tramway and today, when travelling up the valley, the wide roadside verge on the left of the road clearly marks the line's route. At Pontfadog the old GVT roadside waiting room, complete with sparse period furniture, has been restored by the Glyn Valley Tramway Group and is open to the public. At Dolywern an 1888 diversion of the line cuts

through the grounds of a Leonard Cheshire Home – with the appropriate permission it is possible to see the old girder bridge over the Afon Ceiriog and the GVT waiting room. At Glyn Ceiriog, where the former engine shed awaits restoration and the station building is a private residence, there is a small photographic display of the tramway in the Glyn Valley Hotel.

South of Glyn Ceiriog the route of the 1888 extension can be followed between the Coed-y-Glyn granite quarry and Hendre Quarry. This section of the GVT was given to the National Trust in 1948 and is now a well-maintained footpath and cycleway. Highlights of the path are the girder bridge over the Afon Ceiriog at Upper Pandy and the remains of old quarry buildings hidden away in the undergrowth near Hendre Quarry.

PLACES TO VISIT

HERITAGE RAILWAYS
Llangollen Railway
Llangollen Railway Station, Llangollen LL20 8SN
Tel 01978 860979
Website www.llangollen-railway.co.uk
Route Llangollen to Carrog
Length 7½ miles

OTHER ATTRACTIONS
Chirk Castle (NT)
Chirk LL14 5AF
Tel 01691 777701
Website www.nationaltrust.org.uk

The Glyn Valley Hotel
Llanarmon Road, Glyn Ceiriog,
Llangollen LL20 7EU
(Contains a small 'Museum' dedicated to the Glynn Valley Tramway)
Tel 01691 718896
Website www.glynvalleyhotel.co.uk

Plas Newydd Museum
Hill Street, Llangollen,
Denbighshire LL20 8AW
Tel 01978 862834
Website www.denbighshire.gov.uk

PRACTICAL INFORMATION

NEAREST RAILWAY STATION
Chirk

TOURIST INFORMATION
Wrexham Tourist Information Centre
Lambpit Street, Wrexham LL11 1AR
Tel 01978 292015
Website www.wrexham.gov.uk

Llangollen Tourist Information Centre
Y Capel, Castle Street,
Llangollen LL20 8NU
Tel 01978 860828
Website www.llangollen.org.uk

OS MAPS
Landranger Nos 125/126

◀ Beyond Upper Pandy, the National Trust-owned trackbed of the Glyn Valley Tramway continues as a narrow footpath to the site of Hendre Quarry. Here, old quarry buildings still lurk in the undergrowth and even a short length of rail can be discovered in the grass by inquisitive lovers of old railways.

NORTHERN ENGLAND

◀ BR Standard Class 4 2-6-4 tank No. 80117 drifts into Ravenscar with a train for Scarborough in July 1957. Originally called Peak, the station at Ravenscar was in an exposed position at the summit of the line and was constantly buffeted by North Sea gales during the winter months. Today only the original up platform survives.

KESWICK RAILWAY FOOTPATH
Cockermouth to Penrith

Originally conceived as part of a mineral-carrying coast-to-coast through route, the Cockermouth to Penrith railway survived mainly on seasonal tourist traffic. Its closure in 1972 was extremely short-sighted.

Railways first reached the ancient Cumbrian market town of Cockermouth in 1847 with the opening of the Cockermouth & Workington Railway. Built to carry coal to the docks at Workington, it was absorbed into the London & North Western Railway in 1866. At the eastern edge of the Cumbrian Fells, the Lancaster & Carlisle Railway (later also part of the LNWR) had opened through the market town of Penrith in 1846. Several schemes were soon put forward to build railways across the Lake District, one of which was an extension of the South Durham & Lancashire Union Railway (soon to become part of the North Eastern Railway) that had opened across the Pennines via Stainmore in 1861.

▲ Passenger services west of Keswick ceased on 18 April 1966 and from that date the town was served by an 18¼-mile branch line from Penrith. Before closure the railway closely followed the shore of Bassenthwaite Lake to the station of that name, and on to Cockermouth. It is seen here two years after closure in 1968. The trackbed of the railway beside the lake has since disappeared under road improvements to the A66.

Authorised in 1861, the nominally independent Cockermouth, Keswick & Penrith Railway was not only designed to take advantage of tourist traffic – it was the only railway built across the Lake District – but also to carry mineral traffic to and from the northeast of England via the Stainmore line. The heavily graded 31¼-mile single-track line opened to goods in 1864 and to passengers the following year and, apart from mineral traffic, was worked from the outset by the LNWR.

Mineral traffic was transported by the North Eastern Railway via a new connecting spur at Red Hills Junction near Penrith.

Passing through some of the most beautiful scenery anywhere in Britain, it is not surprising that tourist traffic was particularly heavy on this line. Trainloads of Victorian tourists were soon flocking to the town of Keswick where a large railway hotel was also built. Founded in 1875, the Keswick Convention – a large annual gathering of Evangelical Christians – also brought increased passenger traffic to the line. Seasonal traffic became so

▼ The station building, awning and down platform at Keswick station are now incorporated into the former railway hotel, which originally opened in 1869. The western end of the Keswick Railway Path to Threlkeld starts here.

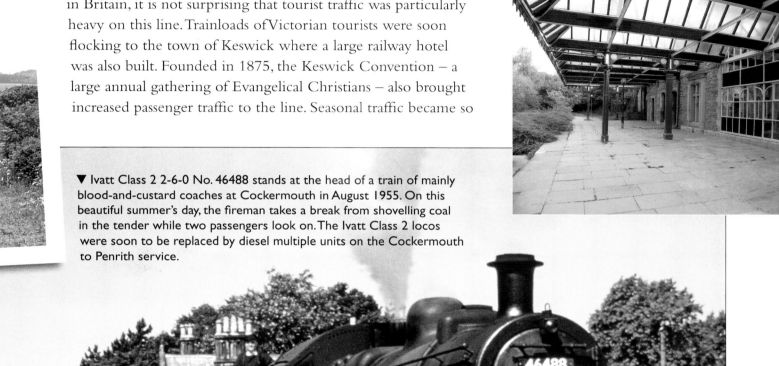

▼ Ivatt Class 2 2-6-0 No. 46488 stands at the head of a train of mainly blood-and-custard coaches at Cockermouth in August 1955. On this beautiful summer's day, the fireman takes a break from shovelling coal in the tender while two passengers look on. The Ivatt Class 2 locos were soon to be replaced by diesel multiple units on the Cockermouth to Penrith service.

heavy that by the beginning of the 20th century 13½ miles of track had been doubled. Despite this improvement, passenger trains, usually hauled by underpowered veteran steam locos, were still painfully slow.

Mineral traffic, mainly pig-iron going east and coke going west, was also heavy in the early years but despite a boom that was caused by, and lasted until after, the First World War, this traffic dramatically decreased, never to be revived. Despite this loss, other goods traffic, including livestock, forest products and stone from the many quarries in the area, kept the line busy until after the Second World War.

By the 1950s competition from road transport and the changing habits of holidaymakers had led to a serious drop in both passenger and freight traffic on the line. Although Keswick was still served by through carriages in the summer from Euston, Manchester and Newcastle until the early 1960s, the introduction of new diesel multiple units in 1955 failed to stem the flow and it was hardly surprising, given the huge losses incurred, that the line was listed for closure in the Beeching Report of 1963. First to go were freight through trains, which ceased in 1964, followed by complete closure of the line west of Keswick in 1966. Strong local protests halted closure of the Penrith to Keswick section, which was subsequently singled with remaining stations becoming unstaffed halts. This sad state of affairs finally came to an end on 6 March 1972 when the remaining diesel service was withdrawn. In more recent years proposals to reopen the railway have come to nothing.

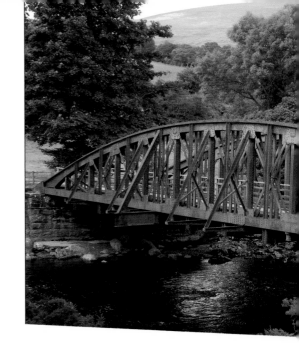

▲ When it opened in 1864, the 18¼-mile section of the CK&PR between Keswick and Penrith included 78 bridges, of which eight cross and recross the River Greta on the 4-mile Keswick Railway Path to Threlkeld.

◀ Prior to the introduction of newly built Ivatt Class 2 2-6-0s in the late 1940s, motive power on the Penrith to Cockermouth line was usually in the hands of ancient ex-LNWR locos. Here a 'Cauliflower' 0-6-0 of 1887 vintage waits to depart from Keswick with a train for Penrith on 13 June 1947. The platform and awning on the left still exist as part of the Keswick Hotel.

◀ A Derby-built two-car diesel multiple unit pulls out of Threlkeld station with a train for Penrith and Carlisle in 1968. By this date the line between Penrith and Keswick had been singled and all stations reduced to unstaffed halts. A sign of the times is the isolated passing loop and lack of signal arms. Threlkeld station is now the eastern end of the Keswick Railway Path.

WALKING AND CYCLING THE LINE

THE LINE TODAY
Sadly much of the route of the line from Cockermouth and along the west shore of Bassenthwaite Lake to Braithwaite, 2 miles west of Keswick, has been swallowed up during major improvements to the A66 trunk road. With views over the lake to Skiddaw this must have been one of the most scenic railway lines in the UK and its loss is still greatly mourned.

Fortunately a 4-mile stretch of the CK&PR trackbed between Keswick and Threlkeld was purchased by the Lake District National Park Authority and is now a popular traffic-free footpath and cycleway known as the Keswick Railway Footpath. Car parking is available at either end of the path, which threads its way up the wooded Greta Valley, crossing and recrossing the river on bridges no fewer than eight times. Wheelchair access is also available from Keswick.

Keswick railway station is of particular interest to lovers of old railways. Here, the platform and awning has been incorporated into the adjoining Keswick Hotel, and there are numerous bowstring bridges and a short tunnel along the route.

East of Threlkeld the trackbed of the line follows a route south of the river across private land to Troutbeck. Here the summit of the line reached 889ft above sea level, although part of the route has disappeared beneath the A66. East of Penruddock, deep cuttings still scar the landscape where the line once made an enormous loop around limestone quarries at Flusco and Blencow. On the southwestern outskirts at Penrith the CK&PR railway embankment runs north of the A66 near to its junction with the M6, but nothing now remains of the Red Hills curve, which was last used in 1926.

PLACES TO VISIT

HERITAGE RAILWAYS
Ravenglass & Eskdale Railway
Ravenglass, Cumbria CA18 1SW
Tel 01229 717171
Website www.ravenglass-railway.co.uk
Route Ravenglass to Dalegarth
Length 7 miles

OTHER ATTRACTIONS
Wordsworth House (NT)
Main Street, Cockermouth
Cumbria CA13 9RX
Tel 01900 820884
Website www.wordsworthhouse.org.uk

Keswick Museum and Art Gallery
Fitz Park, Station Road, Keswick,
Cumbria CA12 4NF
Tel 017687 73263
Website www.allerdale.gov.uk

Cars of the Stars
Standish Street, Keswick,
Cumbria CA12 5LS
Tel 017687 73757
Website www.carsofthestars.com

Mirehouse, Keswick
Cumbria CA12 4QE
Tel 017687 72287
Website www.mirehouse.com

Newlands Adventure Centre
Stair, Keswick,
Cumbria CA12 5UF
Tel 017687 78463
Website www.activity-centre.com

Keswick Launch Company
29 Manor Park, Keswick,
Cumbria CA12 4AB
Tel 017687 72263
Website www.keswick-launch.co.uk

PRACTICAL INFORMATION

NEAREST RAILWAY STATIONS
Maryport, Workington

TOURIST INFORMATION
Keswick Tourist Information Centre
Moot Hall, Market Square, Keswick CA12 5JR
Tel 017687 72645
Websites www.lakedistrict.gov.uk
and www.visitcumbria.com

OS MAPS
Landranger Nos 89, 90

CYCLE HIRE
Keswick Bikes
The Workshop, Southey Hill,
Keswick CA12 5ND
Tel 017687 75202
Website www.keswickbikes.co.uk

Keswick Motor Company
Lake Road, Keswick,
Cumbria CA12 5BX
Tel 017687 72064
Website www.keswickmotorcompany.co.uk

THE LONGDENDALE TRAIL
Manchester to Hadfield and Penistone via Woodhead Tunnel

Closure of the electrified trans-Pennine freight route between Manchester and Sheffield in 1981 must rate as yet another short-sighted decision. Hopes for its early reopening are probably still a pipe dream.

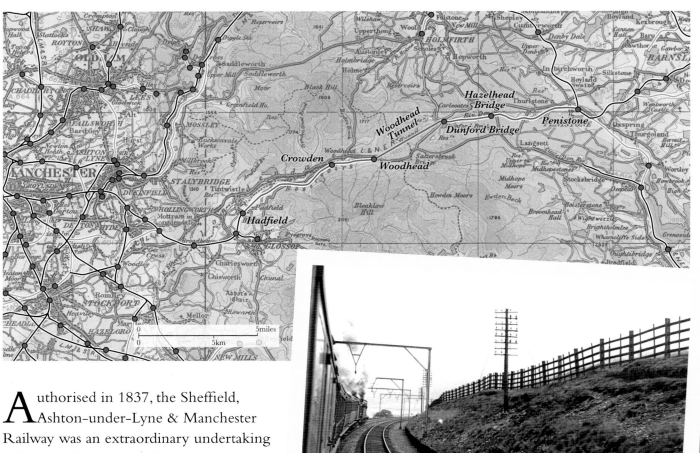

▲ Electrification of the Woodhead line was started by the LNER in 1936 but the outbreak of war brought this to a temporary halt. Here LNER Class 'J11' 0-6-0 No. 5286 pilots Class 'K3' 2-6-0 No. 202 under the unfinished 1.5kV DC catenary masts near Dinting with the 12.30pm Manchester to Sheffield train on 15 September 1945.

Authorised in 1837, the Sheffield, Ashton-under-Lyne & Manchester Railway was an extraordinary undertaking of its time. Designed to link two major centres of population across the Pennines, it tested the skills of its Victorian engineers to the limit and included the construction of the 3-mile Woodhead Tunnel – at that time the longest in Britain.

Initially consisting of a single bore, the tunnel was excavated by hundreds of navvies, billeted in temporary camps on the bleak Pennine fells – drunken behaviour was rife and 26 of them lost their lives in accidents. The railway, also featuring graceful viaducts at Etherow and Dinting, opened through the tunnel from Manchester London Road to Sheffield in 1845. It soon became apparent that the single-bore Woodhead Tunnel could not cope with the amount of traffic, so a second bore, parallel to the first, was opened in 1852. During its construction a further 28 navvies died in an outbreak of cholera.

► Once an important trans-Pennine railway route, the trackbed of the Woodhead line has now been reduced to a footpath and cycleway between Hadfield and Woodhead. Seen here alongside Woodhead Reservoir, the Longdendale Trail is a popular recreational route with local people but it would be better utilised as a freight-carrying railway once again.

Although the second tunnel helped to speed up the flow of traffic, the 3-mile-long single-bore tunnels became 'hell holes' for the drivers and firemen of steam locomotives.

Meanwhile the Sheffield, Ashton-under-Lyne & Manchester Railway had merged with two other railway companies and had become the Manchester, Sheffield & Lincolnshire Railway (MS&LR) in 1847. The railway had already transformed the Longdendale Valley

▲ Coal was the lifeblood of the Woodhead line until the decline of Britain's coal industry. Here Class 76 (formerly EM1) Bo-Bo electric locomotives Nos 76010 and 76012 head a westbound merry-go-round coal train through Hadfield on 22 July 1976. Hadfield is now the eastern terminus of the line from Manchester.

▶ Sporting the BR Inter-City logo, Class 76 Bo-Bo No. 76040 heads a mixed freight alongside Woodhead Reservoir, about ¾ mile west of Woodhead Tunnel on 9 June 1977. Passenger services between Manchester and Sheffield via Woodhead and Penistone had ceased in 1970 and rerouted via the more southerly Hope Valley route.

▼ Operating on a pre-war 1.5kV DC system, the electrified Woodhead line was obsolete the day it opened. Looking magnificent in its early BR black livery with lion rampant, Class EM1 No. 26023 heads past Torside with a westbound express of blood-and-custard coaches in 1954.

between Dinting and Woodhead but in 1848 Manchester Corporation started the building of six enormous reservoirs along the valley from Arnfield to Woodhead. Completed in 1884, the reservoirs still supply the residents of Manchester and Salford with fresh drinking water.

Alongside the reservoirs, the Woodhead line was doing brisk business for the fast-expanding MS&LR – in 1897 the company changed its name to the Great Central Railway ahead of the opening of its extension to London Marylebone. The movement of coal from the South Yorkshire coalfields was of prime importance to the

▼ With only three years to go before closure, two Class 76 Bo-Bo electric locos approach Woodhead Tunnel with an eastbound empty merry-go-round coal train on 9 June 1977. The ugly pylons carrying the National Grid end here as the electricity cables go underground via the old northbound single-bore railway tunnel to Dunford Bridge. Today Woodhead is the end of the Longdendale Trail from Hadfield – the 1950s station buildings have gone but the platforms still remain.

▶ The western portal of Woodhead Tunnel marks the end of the Longdendale Trail from Hadfield. Closed in 1981, the tunnel portal still proudly proclaims its opening date by British Railways in 1954.

WALKING AND CYCLING THE LINE

THE LINE TODAY

Now forming part of the Trans Pennine Trail (National Cycle Network Route 62), 6½ miles of trackbed of the Woodhead line from Hadfield to the western portals of the Woodhead Tunnels is now a traffic-free cycleway and footpath known as the Longdendale Trail. The route closely follows the south shores of Valehouse, Torside and Woodhead reservoirs and is paralleled by giant electricity pylons marching up the valley. When completed in the 19th century the reservoirs were the largest artificial expanse of water in the world.

Car parking for the trail is at Crowden (on the A628) and Torside (on the B6105) – at the former there is also a campsite and at the latter a picnic area and information point. The trail is also suitable for people with disabilities and for horse riders. Circular walks or rides are also possible following paths around the nearby reservoirs.

The trail ends at the western portals of the three Woodhead Tunnels, where the old north bore carries the trans-Pennine National Grid beneath the Peak District National Park. While the old south bore is flooded and in a dangerous state, the newer double-track tunnel opened to traffic in 1955 is currently the subject of great debate – plans to reroute the National Grid through this tunnel have met with strong opposition from campaigners who want to see it reopened as a railway. Visitors to the tunnel mouth can still see the stone plaque set above the entrance that proudly proclaims, 'B.R. 1954'.

PLACES TO VISIT

HERITAGE RAILWAYS
Kirklees Light Railway
Park Mill Way, Clayton West, Nr Huddersfield,
West Yorkshire HD8 9XJ
Tel 01484 865727
Website www.kirkleeslightrailway.com
Route Clayton West to Shelley
Length 2 miles

OTHER ATTRACTIONS
Holmfirth Postcard Museum
47 Huddersfield Road,
Holmfirth HD7 1JH
Tel 01484 682231

The Picturedrome
Market Walk, Holmfirth,
West Yorkshire HD9 7DA
Tel 01484 689759
Website www.picturedrome.net

PRACTICAL INFORMATION

NEAREST RAILWAY STATION
Hadfield

TOURIST INFORMATION
Holmfirth Tourist Information Centre
49–51 Huddersfield Road, Holmfirth,
West Yorkshire HD9 3JP
Tel 01484 222444
Website www.kirklees.gov.uk/visitors

Manchester Tourist Information Centre
Carver's Warehouse, 77 Dale Street,
Manchester M1 2HG
Tel 0871 222 8223
Website www.visitmanchester.com

OS MAP
Landranger No. 110

CYCLE HIRE
Longdendale Valley Cycles
105 Station Road, Hadfield
Derbyshire SK13 1AA
Tel 01457 854672
Website www.hikers-and-bikers.co.uk/
longdendale-valley-cycles/

▼ The final stretch of the 6½-mile Longdendale Trail heading east towards Woodhead. The sound of double-headed LNER freight locomotives struggling up the grade to the tunnel with their heavy freight trains is now little more than a fading memory to a few railway enthusiasts.

company and, under its general manager, Sir Sam Fay, the GCR opened the Wath Marshalling Yard in 1907 and vast coal-handling export facilities at Immingham in 1912. Coal trains were also the lifeblood of the Woodhead line – coal from South Yorkshire was carried to a depot at Mottram for distributon throughout the northwest of England.

The difficulties of operating heavy coal trains over the steeply graded Woodhead line had already become apparent to the Great Central before the First World War. Double-heading of steam locomotives was a necessity and the asphyxiating journey for train crews through the smoky single-bore Woodhead tunnels can only be imagined. Plans to electrify the line had been around for years but in 1936 the LNER (successor to the GCR) made a start on converting the line to take current from overhead catenaries at 1.5kV DC. Work stopped during the Second World War but recommenced in 1945. A new double-track Woodhead tunnel was constructed and new EM1 and EM2 electric locomotives were built at Gorton Works in Manchester. The electrified line was opened in 1954 but by that time major developments in railway electrification had already made the line's technology obsolete. This factor, together with the run-down of the South Yorkshire coalfields in the 1970s, soon put the Woodhead line's future in doubt. Passenger services between Manchester and Sheffield ceased in 1970 and the last freight train ran on 17 July 1981. Today, all that is left of this once-important trans-Pennine route is a suburban passenger service between Manchester and Hadfield.

TEES VALLEY RAILWAY PATH

Middleton-in-Teesdale to Barnard Castle

Built primarily to convey stone from quarries in the upper Tees Valley, the picturesque branch line to Middleton-in-Teesdale became yet another victim of the Beeching Report when it closed in 1964.

▲ A busy scene at Middleton-in-Teesdale station c.1930 with goods wagons from all of the Big Four railway companies in the sidings. On the left an ancient lorry tips a load of stone into a railway wagon while on the right is the narrow gauge tramway from the Middleton Quarry.

Once an important railway junction, the historic town of Barnard Castle is now 15 miles from the nearest railway station at Bishop Auckland. Railways first came to the town in 1856 when the Stockton & Darlington Railway opened a line from Darlington. Next on the scene was the South Durham & Lancashire Railway, which opened a single-track line from Bishop Auckland to Tebay via Barnard Castle and Kirkby Stephen in 1861. A year later the Eden Valley Railway had opened from Kirkby Stephen to Penrith, thus completing an important trans-Pennine route that linked the northeast with the northwest. Both railways were taken over by the S&DR in 1862, which itself was absorbed by the North Eastern Railway a year later.

The final link in the railway network around Barnard Castle came in 1868 when the Tees Valley Railway opened its branch line from the town up the scenic Tees Valley to Middleton-in-Teesdale. Along with three intermediate stations on the 8¾-mile line, at Cotherstone, Romaldkirk and Mickleton, the outstanding engineering features were the Lunedale and Baldersdale viaducts. The lifeblood of the railway was stone, and several short branches were built to link the quarries at Middleton, Park End, Crossthwaite and Greengates with the branch line. Narrow gauge feeder tramways were also built to Lunedale

▼ Ex-Great Northern Railway Class 'D3' 4-4-0 No. 4347 waits to depart from Middleton-in-Teesdale with the 2.10pm train to Barnard Castle and Durham on 4 June 1935. The turntable, water tower and small engine shed can be seen on the left. Passenger traffic on the branch line was never heavy, with steam-hauled trains being replaced by diesel multiple units in 1957.

▼ Heading a joint Railway Correspondence & Travels Society/ Stephenson Locomotive Society Enthusiasts' special, ex-LMS Fowler Class 4 2-6-4 tank No. 42405 gets ready to run round its train at Middleton-in-Teesdale on 30 September 1963. Passenger services on the branch to Barnard Castle and Darlington ceased just over a year later.

◄ The North Eastern Railway staff at little Romaldkirk station pose for their photograph in the early 20th century. Despite covering only a small village, the station was still served by six diesel multiple unit trains each weekday in the early 1960s.

▼ The verges of the Tees Valley Railway Path, seen here north of Romaldkirk, are a profusion of wild flowers in the summer, while ponds containing toads and frogs can be seen in the ditches alongside the track.

Quarry and to the Grassholme and Selset reservoirs during their construction at the beginning of the First World War.

Passenger traffic on the line was never heavy, although it did attract Victorian and Edwardian tourists wishing to visit the famous High Force waterfall farther up the valley. By the 1950s increasing amounts of stone were being transported by road and, to reduce ever-increasing losses, steam haulage of passenger trains was phased out in 1957 in favour of new diesel multiple units – but even these failed to halt the downward spiral. Closure of the railways through Barnard Castle started even before the publication of Beeching's report – the trans-Pennine route from Bishop Auckland to Penrith via Barnard Castle was the first to go when it closed in January 1962 (the branch from Kirkby Stephen to Tebay had already

▼ Completed in 1868, this five-arched railway viaduct near Mickleton now carries the Tees Valley Railway Path over the River Lune.

▼ The Tees Valley Railway Path from Middleton-in-Teesdale ends in the village of Cotherstone. The station building and platform, seen here in 1969 after the track was lifted, still survive as a private residence.

closed in 1952). British Railways were so keen to rid themselves of this route that within a very short time track had been lifted and most of the viaducts, including the famous Belah Viaduct, had been demolished. From that date trains for Barnard Castle and Middleton-in-Teesdale started and ended their journeys at Darlington but by 1963 this line had also been listed for closure by Dr Beeching. The end finally came on 30 November 1964, when all passenger services ceased, although goods traffic continued until April the following year.

▼ The site of the level crossing at Romaldkirk is still guarded by an old North Eastern Railway signal, while the station building on the right is now a private residence.

◀ With its train of two clerestory coaches, ex-North Eastern Railway Class 'J21' No. 899 stands at Barnard Castle station with the 1.03pm Penrith to Darlington on 4 June 1935. First introduced in 1886, the last members of this once-numerous class survived until 1962. Closed in 1964, the busy junction station at Barnard Castle with its attractive overall roof is now just a fading memory for local inhabitants.

WALKING AND CYCLING THE LINE

THE LINE TODAY

The track of the Middleton-in-Teesdale branch was lifted in 1967 and since then 6 miles of the trackbed has been converted into a traffic-free footpath and cycleway known as the Tees Valley Railway Path. The station building at Middleton survives but there is now a mobile home park on the site. The Railway Path, a profusion of wild flowers in the summer, starts a short distance to the east of here and within ½ mile it crosses the River Lune on a five-arch viaduct that was built in 1868. Mickleton station, a ½ mile farther to the east, has long ago disappeared but there is now a car park and picnic site here. A farther 2 miles along the Railway Path is Romaldkirk, where the old station building is now a private residence complete with its own railway signal. Bearing south from here the Railway Path soon crosses the River Balder on a nine-arched viaduct before ending at the village of Cotherstone where the station building, now a private residence, and platform still survive. Walkers can join the Teesdale Way LDP at Cotherstone to complete their journey to Barnard Castle. Sadly, all traces of the once-busy junction station here have long disappeared beneath a car park and factory.

Parking for users of the Tees Valley Railway Path is located at Middleton-in-Teesdale, Mickleton, Romaldkirk and Cotherstone. There are also public houses serving refreshments at all of these locations.

PLACES TO VISIT

HERITAGE RAILWAYS
Weardale Railway
Stanhope Station, Stanhope, Bishop Auckland,
Co. Durham DL13 2YS
Tel 01388 526203
Website www.weardale-railway.org.uk
Route Stanhope to Wolsingham
Length 5¼ miles

OTHER ATTRACTIONS
Rokeby Park
Tel 01609 748612
Website www.rokebypark.com

The Bowes Museum
Barnard Castle,
Co. Durham DL12 8NP
Tel 01833 690606
Website www.thebowesmuseum.org.uk

Egglestone Abbey (English Heritage)
nr Barnard Castle
Website www.english-heritage.org.uk

PRACTICAL INFORMATION

NEAREST RAILWAY STATION
Bishop Auckland

TOURIST INFORMATION
Barnard Castle Tourist Information Centre
Woodleigh, Flatts Road, Barnard Castle,
Co. Durham DL12 8AA
Tel 01833 690909
Website www.visitnortheastengland.com

Middleton-in-Teesdale Tourist Information Centre
10 Market Place, Middleton-in-Teesdale,
Co. Durham DL12 0QG
Tel 01833 641001
Website www.visitnortheastengland.com

OS MAP
Landranger No. 92

CYCLE HIRE
Dale Bike Hire
(mobile bike hire in Teesdale),
Wolsingham, Durham DL13 3AH
Tel 01388 527737
Website www.dalebikehire.co.uk

YORK TO SELBY RAILWAY PATH
York to Selby

Opened in 1871 to shorten the railway journey between King's Cross and York, the York to Selby line was itself closed in 1983 with the opening of a new high-speed route to the west.

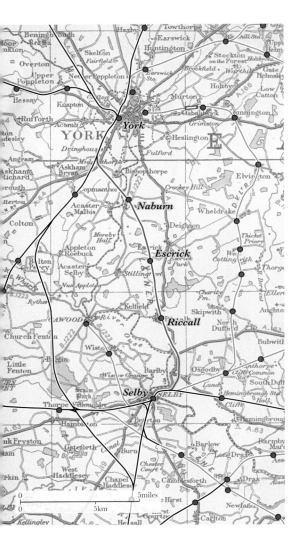

Cocooned in their air-conditioned trains, most travellers along the East Coast Main Line between Doncaster and York today are totally unaware of the complicated history of this route. Railways first reached York in 1839 when George Hudson's York & North Midland Railway, engineered by Robert Stephenson, opened its line from Leeds to a temporary terminus outside the city walls. A new station opened in 1841 inside York's city walls, by then the terminus of a through route from London to York via Rugby and Derby. From the south the Great Northern Railway had reached Doncaster (initially via Lincoln)

► Opened in 1871, the railway swing bridge at Naburn allowed ships to pass through on their way up the River Ouse to York. The control cabin on top of the bridge has been removed since closure of the line in 1983.

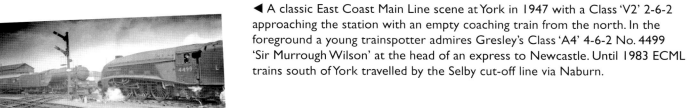

◄ A classic East Coast Main Line scene at York in 1947 with a Class 'V2' 2-6-2 approaching the station with an empty coaching train from the north. In the foreground a young trainspotter admires Gresley's Class 'A4' 4-6-2 No. 4499 'Sir Murrough Wilson' at the head of an express to Newcastle. Until 1983 ECML trains south of York travelled by the Selby cut-off line via Naburn.

▲ Just south of Bishopthorpe, the old swing bridge at Naburn is now adorned by a large wire sculpture, *Fisher of Dreams*, designed by local artist Peter Rogers.

from London in 1849 – a year later it was running through trains from London to York via Doncaster and over a new route through Knottingly and Burton Salmon.

From the north, York was served by the North Eastern Railway, a company formed by various mergers including the York, Newcastle & Berwick Railway and George Hudson's York & North Midland Railway. The most northerly link in the East Coast Main Line chain was the North British Railway, which had opened its first line from Edinburgh to Berwick in 1846.

▶ South of Naburn, the station at Escrick, seen here in the early 20th century, also closed to passengers in 1953 and to goods in 1961. The station site today features a grass maze, while a scale model of the planet Neptune – part of the scale model of the solar system found along the railway path – is located south of the station.

▼ A short distance south of the swing bridge was Naburn station, seen here in the early 20th century. It closed to passengers on 8 June 1953 but the building has survived and is now a café and hostel alongside the York to Selby Railway Path. An eye-catching part of the scale model of the solar system found along the railway path is the planet Saturn, located north of the station.

THE.STATION. ESCRICK

NEILS · SERIES · No 1484

Despite there now being a through route – albeit operated by three railway companies – between London King's Cross and Edinburgh, journey times were painfully slow. However, it took until 1871 before matters improved significantly. In that year the North Eastern Railway opened a new cut-off from Shaftholme Junction, north of Doncaster, to Chaloner's Whin Junction, on the Leeds line south of York. The new line via Selby was more direct than the previous route via Knottingly but was hampered by speed restrictions over the swing bridges across the River Ouse at Selby and Naburn. Intermediate stations between York and Selby were also opened at Naburn, Escrick and Riccall. A new station, then the largest in the world, was opened by the NER at York in 1877 with ECML trains being hauled south of here to King's Cross via the Selby cut-off by Great Northern Railway locomotives.

The route of the East Coast Main line south of York remained virtually unchanged for more than 100 years, although the intermediate stations at Naburn and Escrick had closed on 8 June 1953 and that at Riccall on 15 September 1958. The next major development came

▼ Near Riccall, north of Selby, walkers and cyclists now follow the route once taken by the 'Flying Scotsman' as it streaked through behind a Gresley 'A4' Pacific on its journey between Edinburgh and King's Cross.

in September 1983 when a completely new high-speed cut-off was opened between Temple Hirst Junction, south of Selby, to Colton Junction on the Leeds to York line. Designed to avoid the new Selby coalfield and the severe speed restriction at Selby, the cut-off slashed journey times on the ECML. The 1871 cut-off via Naburn was then closed completely, although Selby is still served by trains between York and Hull via the new cut-off and West Hambleton Junction.

▼ Between Riccall and Selby the trackbed of the old ECML has disappeared beneath improvements to the A19 trunk road. Between these points the York to Selby Railway Path parallels the road on a separate track.

◄ A scale model of the solar system is spread out along 6.4 miles of the York to Selby Railway Path. The model of Saturn, left, can be found south of Naburn swing bridge.

WALKING AND CYCLING THE LINE

THE LINE TODAY

Soon after closure in 1983, the York to Selby railway line became one of the first railway routes to be opened as a cycleway by the charity Sustrans. Bought for the princely sum of £1, the trackbed was only the second such venture for the newly formed organisation, which has created the National Cycle Network.

Forming part of National Cycle Network Route 65, the 15-mile York to Selby Railway Path initially runs from York railway station along the River Ouse and past the Millennium Bridge before turning away past York Racecourse to join the old trackbed near Bishopthorpe. Of particular interest to both walkers and cyclists young and old is the scale model of the solar system, which is spread out along 6.4 miles of the path. The scale of the model is 575,872,239:1, so every 100 metres along the track corresponds to more than 57 million kilometres in space. At this scale the speed of light corresponds to 1.16mph so it's possible to complete a cycle ride down the path before even starting it and getting younger in the process!

Other highlights along the path are an organic nursery and café at Naburn station and the turf maze at Escrick station, where there is also a car park. Just south of Bishopthorpe the old swing bridge at Naburn is now adorned by a large wire sculpture. The path can be included as part of a circular walking or cycling tour using the railway service between York and Selby for one half of the journey. Note that the railway path stops at the village of Riccall where there is a car park. From here to Selby the cycleway runs parallel with the A19 via Barlby.

PLACES TO VISIT

HERITAGE RAILWAYS
Derwent Valley Light Railway
c/o Yorkshire Museum of Farming,
Murton Lane, Murton, York YO19 5UF
Tel 01904 489966
Website www.dvlr.org.uk
Route Within Murton Park
Length ½ mile

OTHER ATTRACTIONS
National Railway Museum
Leeman Road,
York YO26 4XJ
Tel 08448 153139
Website www.nrm.org.uk

York Minster
Church House, Ogleforth, York YO1 7JN
Tel 0844 9390011
Website www.yorkminster.org

Jorvik Viking Centre
Coppergate,
York YO1 9WT
Tel 01904 543400
Website www.jorvik-viking-centre.co.uk

Yorkshire Farming Museum
Murton Park, Murton Lane,
York YO19 5UF
Tel 01904 489966
Website www.murtonpark.co.uk

Selby Abbey
The Crescent, Selby,
Yorkshire YO8 4PU
Tel 01757 703123
Website www.selbyabbey.org.uk

PRACTICAL INFORMATION

NEAREST RAILWAY STATIONS
York, Selby

TOURIST INFORMATION
York Tourist Information Centre
York Railway Station, Outer Concourse,
York YO24 1AY
Tel 01904 550 095
Website www.visityork.org

Selby Visitor Information Centre
52 Micklegate, Selby,
Yorkshire YO8 4EQ
Tel 01757 212181
Website www.selbytourism.co.uk

OS MAP
Landranger No. 105

CYCLE HIRE
Europcar
Platform 1, York Railway Station,
York YO24 1AY
Tel 01904 656181
Website www.autohorn.co.uk

Bob Trotter Cycles
13–15 Lord Mayor's Walk,
York YO31 7HB
Tel 01904 622868
Website www.bobtrottercycles.com

PENNINE VIADUCTS

The scenic trans-Pennine route from Darlington and Barnard Castle to Penrith via Stainmore Summit closed on 22 January 1962. In its haste to rid itself of the loss-making line, British Railways had lifted the track and demolished most of the viaducts in a very short time. Included in this orgy of destruction was the iconic Belah Viaduct west of Barras, which is seen here from the driving compartment of a Penrith-bound diesel multiple unit on 14 October 1961. Although double-track, only one train at a time was allowed to cross the graceful 16-span iron structure. Today only the stone buttresses remain on either side of the valley.

The spine of northern England, the north–south range of the Pennines, was by far the biggest natural obstacle to be overcome by England's 19th-century railway engineers. With a combination of tunnels and viaducts, six major railway routes had tamed the mighty Pennines by 1876. Many of the viaducts (and tunnels) are still in use and their survival today is a fitting testimony not only to the optimistic Victorian railway promoters but also to the thousands of navvies who toiled over their construction.

The building of the Settle & Carlisle railway by the Midland Railway was a wonder of the Victorian Age. Opened in 1876, this heavily graded mainline had a workforce of around 6,000 navvies who built 23 viaducts – including the famous 24-arch Ribblehead Viaduct – and constructed 13 tunnels along the 72-mile route. The line was saved from closure in 1984 and the viaducts restored to their former glory.

Sadly, the same cannot be said for the once-important trans-Pennine line from Darlington to Penrith, which closed in 1962. In a desperate bid to rid itself of the loss-making line once and for all, British Railways embarked on an orgy of destruction and within 18 months of closure the track had been lifted and many viaducts demolished – of these the greatest tragedy was the hurried demolition of the graceful iron Belah Viaduct west of Barras.

Fortunately we now live in a more enlightened society and a few fine viaducts on long-closed Pennine railway lines have since been saved for posterity. The Northern Viaduct Trust has saved three viaducts on the Kirkby Stephen to Tebay line and incorporated them in a new footpath and cycleway.

◀ The South Durham & East Lancashire Railway opened its line from Kirkby Stephen to Tebay in 1861. Built originally as a part of a trans-Pennine mineral-carrying line, it closed to passengers in 1952 and to freight in 1962. Not to be confused with the nearby viaduct on the Settle to Carlisle line, the 14-arch Smardale Viaduct, seen here, has recently been restored by the Northern Viaduct Trust. A footpath across the viaduct leads to a wildlife reserve managed by the Cumbria Wildlife Trust.

▲ Designed by Sir Thomas Bouch and completed in 1858, Hownes Gill Viaduct replaced earlier inclined planes on the Stanhope & Tyne Railway southwest of Consett in County Durham. The graceful 750-ft viaduct crosses the valley on 12 arches with a maximum height of 150ft. It is now a public footpath.

SCARBOROUGH & WHITBY RAILWAY PATH

Scarborough to Whitby

Nearly abandoned before completion and with a working life of only 80 years, the Scarborough to Whitby railway now has a new lease of life as a footpath and cycleway along the rugged Yorkshire coastline.

▼ Between 1900 and 1910, the North Eastern Railway erected large tile maps of their system at various stations throughout the northeast and at King's Cross, London. Made by Craven Dunnill of Jackfield in Shropshire, each map consisted of 64 8in-square tiles and, needless to say, contained a few errors including a line that was never built! Twelve of these beautiful maps still exist, nine of which are still at their original stations including Scarborough (seen here) and Whitby.

A railway first reached the fishing port of Whitby as early as 1836 when the horsedrawn Whitby & Pickering Railway, engineered by Robert Stephenson, opened for business. Steam haulage was introduced when the railway was taken over by the York & North Midland Railway in 1845. The York & North Midland then became part of the North Eastern Railway that opened the Esk Valley line to Grosmont, where it connected with the Whitby & Pickering line, in 1863. The Esk Valley line from Middlesbrough is still open for passenger services while the Whitby & Pickering line from Grosmont to Pickering is now the North Yorkshire Moors Railway heritage line.

Farther south along the coast, the York & North Midland had opened its railway from York to Scarborough in 1845. A year later the

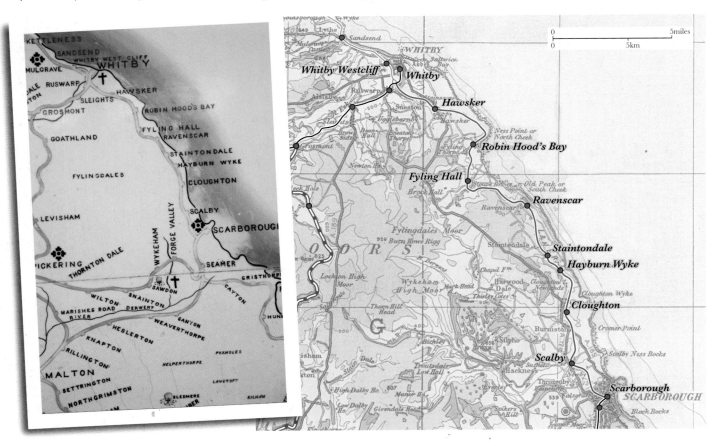

company opened the line from Seamer Junction, west of Scarborough, to Filey, Bridlington and Hull. Both of these lines are still open.

The third railway to reach Scarborough was the Forge Valley line to Pickering, which was opened by the North Eastern Railway (NER), in 1882. The railway had a short working life and closed on 3 June 1950.

Last, but not least, was the Scarborough & Whitby Railway that almost failed to be completed. Work started on this scenic coastal line in 1872 but progress was slow and six years later it was nearly abandoned when the company ran into financial difficulties. At the last minute the owner of Raven Hall, an 18th-century mansion overlooking Robin Hood's Bay, stepped in and rescued the company. Construction work recommenced and the line was open for business in 1885. Worked from the outset by the North Eastern Railway, the steeply graded line was linked at its southern end to the grand Scarborough station via a tunnel. Arrangements at Whitby, where the

▼ Ivatt Class 4 2-6-0 No. 43073 has just emerged from Ravenscar Tunnel at the start of the descent to Robin Hood's Bay with the 2.57pm Scarborough to Middlesbrough train on 13 July 1957. Diesel multiple units were soon to replace steam-hauled services on the line. On the far left is the 18th-century Raven Hall Hotel with its magnificent sea views across to Robin Hood's Bay.

120ft-high Larpool Viaduct – built with more than five million bricks – carried the line over the River Esk to Whitby West Cliff station, were much more complicated. From here a steeply graded reverse spur linked the line under the viaduct to the Whitby & Pickering station.

Whitby West Cliff was also served by trains from the north by the Whitby, Redcar & Middlesbrough Railway, a coast-hugging railway, also worked by the NER from the outset. With its numerous viaducts and tunnels it was costly to maintain and it closed on 5 May 1958.

In the meantime, the Scarborough & Whitby Railway had been taken over by the NER in 1898, which heavily promoted the line for its coastal scenery. During the 1920s and 1930s LNER Sentinel steam railcars were a common sight on the line, taking tourists on circular tours from Scarborough via Pickering, Grosmont and Whitby. Excursions from farther afield also took the circular route and, of

▼ As early as the 1930s, the steeply graded line from Scarborough to Whitby was used by the LNER as a testing ground for a pioneering diesel-electric railcar. Steam power was replaced by new diesel multiple units in 1958 with the service operating from Middlesbrough along the Esk Valley Line to Whitby, thence reversing up to West Cliff and again reversing there to continue the journey down to Scarborough. Seen here at Hayburn Wyke station in 1958, the DMU service took around 2½ hours to complete the 58½-mile journey.

◄ The beautifully restored station at Cloughton is now a tea room and also offers B&B accommodation. This BR Mk 1 coach also provides self-catering accommodation at the station, which is located alongside the Scarborough to Whitby Railway Path.

▼ The Stephenson Locomotive Society's Whitby Moors Railtour halts at Robin Hood's Bay station on 6 March 1965 behind restored Class 'K4' 2-6-0 No. 3442 'The Great Marquess' and Class 'K1' 2-6-0 No. 62005. This was the last day of services on the line. The station buildings here are now a holiday let.

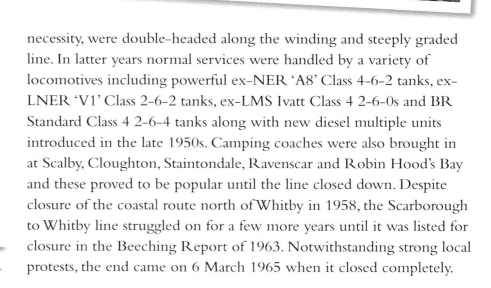

necessity, were double-headed along the winding and steeply graded line. In latter years normal services were handled by a variety of locomotives including powerful ex-NER 'A8' Class 4-6-2 tanks, ex-LNER 'V1' Class 2-6-2 tanks, ex-LMS Ivatt Class 4 2-6-0s and BR Standard Class 4 2-6-4 tanks along with new diesel multiple units introduced in the late 1950s. Camping coaches were also brought in at Scalby, Cloughton, Staintondale, Ravenscar and Robin Hood's Bay and these proved to be popular until the line closed down. Despite closure of the coastal route north of Whitby in 1958, the Scarborough to Whitby line struggled on for a few more years until it was listed for closure in the Beeching Report of 1963. Notwithstanding strong local protests, the end came on 6 March 1965 when it closed completely.

▼ Preserved Class 'K1' 2-6-0 No. 62005 heads a train destined for the North Yorkshire Moors Railway under the magnificent Larpool Viaduct near Whitby in 2007. Built from over five million bricks, the viaduct now carries Route 1 of the National Cycle Network over the River Esk.

WALKING AND CYCLING THE LINE

THE LINE TODAY

Fortunately, most of the trackbed of the Scarborough to Whitby line is now a footpath and cycleway, 23 miles in length, known as the Scarborough to Whitby Railway Path. With superb scenery, especially on the coastal section between Ravenscar and Robin Hood's Bay, the path is a popular destination during summer months and is now part of National Cycle Network Route 1 and the Moor to Sea Cycle Route. However, with its long gradients and, in places, uneven surface it is not recommended for the complete novice.

The path starts at a supermarket car park on Falsgrave Road in Scarborough and reaches open country at Scalby before twisting and turning up through Cloughton (where there is a pub), Hayburn Wyke and Staintondale to the cliffs at Ravenscar. Here there are two car parks and refreshments can be taken at Raven Hall Hotel overlooking the North Sea. The path then takes a loop inland before reaching Robin Hood's Bay where there are spectacular sea views. From the Bay the path takes an inland route to the village of Hawsker, where there is a cycle-hire centre, before ending on the famous Larpool Viaduct at Whitby.

Of particular interest to lovers of old railways is the beautifully restored station at Cloughton, which is now a tea room. A BR Mk 1 coach also provides self-catering accommodation here. The platform and stationmaster's house still survive at Hayburn Wyke as does the station building at Staintondale, which is now a private residence. One platform still survives at Ravenscar while the extensive station buildings at Robin Hood's Bay are now a holiday let. At Hawsker, the last station on the line before Whitby, the station buildings and platform still survive. Here, Trailways run a cycle-hire centre and offer luxury self-catering accommodation in a converted InterCity 125 dining car. The railway path ends at Whitby by crossing the magnificent 13-arch Larpool Viaduct, now owned by Sustrans.

PLACES TO VISIT

HERITAGE RAILWAYS

North Yorkshire Moors Railway
2 Park Street, Pickering YO18 7AJ
Tel 01751 472508
Website www.nymr.co.uk
Route Pickering to Grosmont
Length 18 miles

OTHER ATTRACTIONS

Scarborough Maritime Heritage Centre
36 Eastborough, Scarborough, YO11 1NJ
Tel 07790979067
Website www.scarboroughsmaritimeheritage.
org.uk

Rotunda Museum
Vernon Road, Scarborough YO11 2NH
Tel 01723 384503
Website www.scarboroughmuseumstrust.org.uk

North Bay Miniature Railway
Burniston Road, Scarborough, YO12 6PF
Tel 01723 368791
Website www.nbr.org.uk

Ravenscar Coastal Centre (NT)
Peakside, Ravenscar, YO13 0NE
Tel 01723 870423
Website www.nationaltrust.org.uk

Whitby Abbey
Abbey Lane, Whitby YO22 4JT
Tel 01947 603568
Website www.english-heritage.org.uk

Whitby Museum
Pannett Park, Whitby, YO21 1RE
Tel 01947 602908
Website www.whitbymuseum.org.uk

PRACTICAL INFORMATION

NEAREST RAILWAY STATIONS
Scarborough, Whitby

TOURIST INFORMATION

Scarborough Tourist Information Centre
Brunswick Shopping Centre, Westborough,
Scarborough, North Yorkshire YO11 1UE
(also at Sandside, Scarborough, North Yorkshire
YO11 1PP)
Tel 01723 383636

Whitby Tourist Information Centre
Langborne Road, Whitby,
North Yorkshire YO21 1YN
Tel 01723 383636
Website www.discoveryorkshirecoast.com

OS MAPS
Landranger Nos 94, 101

CYCLE HIRE

Trailways
The Old Railway Station, Hawsker, Whitby
North Yorkshire YO22 4LB
Tel 01947 820207
Website www.trailways.info

CONSETT & SUNDERLAND RAILWAY PATH

Consett to Sunderland

The Stanhope & Tyne mineral railway was bedevilled by inclined planes along its route. In the mid-20th century it acquired cult status with enthusiasts keen to witness the power of Consett iron-ore steam trains.

▼ Ex-North Eastern Railway Class 'Q7' 0-8-0 No. 63460 powers up the gradient towards Consett with an enthusiasts' special on 28 September 1963. By then preserved, No. 63460 was the last survivor of this powerful class of 15 locos that did such sterling work on the Tyne Dock to Consett iron-ore trains for nearly 40 years.

Primitive railways in the form of horsedrawn tramways running on wooden rails had been used in northeast England since the 17th century. Their primary task was to carry coal from local pits down to wharves on the River Tyne, where it was transferred onto coastal sailing ships for onward distribution. A breakthrough came at the end of the 18th century when iron rails were first used on a colliery tramway. Albeit a freight-carrying concern, the first public railway was the Stanhope & Tyne Railway, which opened for business between South Shields and Upper Weardale via Consett, in 1834. Built primarily to transport lime from kilns at Stanhope and coal from the numerous collieries along its route to the docks at South Shields, the 34-mile railway included numerous inclined planes and a vertical wagon lift at Hownes Gill with the stretches in between being worked by horses. Only the last 9 miles to South Shields were hauled by a locomotive, and journey times over the whole line were wretchedly slow. The Stanhope & Tyne soon fell on hard times because it had to pay landowners a toll for crossing their land; it went bankrupt in 1840 and was dissolved the following year.

In 1841. the newly formed Pontop & South Shields Railway took over 24½ miles of the S&T between Leadgate, east of Consett, and South Shields, while the western end from Stanhope to their ironworks at Consett was sold to the Derwent Iron Company. The P&SSR was itself taken over by the Newcastle & Darlington Junction Railway (soon to become the York & Newcastle Railway) in 1847. Despite the building of a viaduct across Hownes Gill in 1858, the numerous inclined planes on the line continued to hold up progress until 1893 when the North Eastern Railway (formed by various regional amalgamations in 1854) opened a new deviation line via Beamish and a connection with the East Coast Main Line at South Pelaw Junction near Chester-le-Street. Primarily a freight-carrying line, passenger services were withdrawn on 23 May 1955.

▼ Consett station was closed to passengers on 23 May 1955 but iron-ore and coal trains continued to run over the heavily graded line from Tyne Dock until 1976. Here, an enthusiasts' special, having just arrived from South Pelaw Junction behind a Class 'Q7' 0-8-0, is set to head off from Consett on the rest of its journey behind Class 'K1' 2-6-0 No. 62027 on 28 September 1963.

▼ Westinghouse air-pump-fitted BR Standard Class '9F' 2-10-0 No. 92097 passes through Washington with a train of iron-ore bogie wagons in 1962. Sister engine No. 92063 worked the last steam-hauled Tyne Dock to Consett iron-ore train on 19 November 1966. Probably the most successful steam locomotive class built in Britain, many of the 9Fs were no more than 10 years old when scrapped.

▼ Heavy coal and iron-ore trains from Tyne Dock halted at South Pelaw Junction, where they were divided before the 1 in 36 climb up to Annfield and Consett. Here, BR Standard Class '9F' 2-10-0 No. 92062 is seen at South Pelaw with a coal train for Consett on 21 September 1965.

From the 1920s until the 1960s, the line became famous for the heavily laden iron-ore or coal trains that operated 24 hours every day to feed the giant steelworks at Consett. These massive trains were hauled initially by Class 'Q7' 0-8-0s or 'O1' 2-8-0s fitted with Westinghouse air-pumps – these operated the doors of bogie iron-ore hoppers, each with a capacity of 56 tons. Loaded trains from Tyne Dock would halt at South Pelaw Junction where they were split in two for the arduous 1 in 36 climb to Annfield Plain and Consett. Banking assistance was also provided by another Class 'O1', 'Q6' or 'Q7'. In the early 1960s, the 'O1s' and 'Q7s' were replaced by more powerful BR Standard Class '9F' 2-10-0s, also fitted with air pumps and banked in the rear by English Electric Type 4 diesels. Steam haulage ended on 19 November 1966 and the iron-ore trains, diverted via Gateshead to South Pelaw Junction, were then double-headed by new specially fitted BR Sulzer Type 2 diesels until 26 March 1976, when the line from South Pelaw to Consett was closed. From that date, new trains, hauled by a pair of Class 37s, operated from Redcar until the closure of Consett steelworks in 1980.

▶ Completed in 1992, *King Coal* is a striking sculpture found beside the path at Pelton Fell. Designed by artist David Kemp, the material for it came from dismantled local industries, including stone from the bridge at Consett station.

▶ A view from the footplate of BR Standard Class '9F' 2-10-0 No. 92062 as it powers up the 1 in 36 gradient towards Annfield with a heavy load of coal wagons from Tyne Dock to Consett on 21 September 1965. A total of 10 locos of this class were fitted with Westinghouse air-compressors for working iron-ore trains from Tyne Dock to Consett.

WALKING AND CYCLING THE LINE

THE LINE TODAY

Since closure, much of the route of the Stanhope & Tyne Railway between Consett and the southern outskirts of Washington has been converted into a footpath and cycleway known as the Consett & Sunderland Railway Path. Downhill nearly all the way from Consett, its 22-mile route now forms part of National Cycle Network Route 7 and the 'C2C' challenge route. Highlights along the path include the Beamish Open Air Museum and specially commissioned pieces of sculpture. Some of the most ambitious pieces of artwork commissioned by Sustrans, they include the famous *Terris Novalis* by Tony

Cragg – a theodolite and engineer's level reproduced at 20 times life size – the giant *Lambton Worm* and *The Jolly Drovers Maze* by Andy Goldsworthy and *The Old Transformers* and *King Coal* by David Kemp.

Beamish Open Air Museum includes the 1867-built railway station from Rowley, near Consett, which was dismantled after closure and rebuilt on the new site.

The final section of the path from Washington to Sunderland closely follows the north bank of the River Wear, where it finally passes the Stadium of Light and an impressive artwork trail.

PLACES TO VISIT

HERITAGE RAILWAYS
Tanfield Railway
Sunniside, Gateshead,
Tyne & Wear NE16 5ET
Tel 0845 463 4938
Website www.tanfield-railway.co.uk
Route Sunniside to East Tanfield
Length 3 miles

OTHER ATTRACTIONS
Bowes Railway Centre
Springwell Village, Gateshead,
Tyne & Wear NE9 7QJ
Tel 0191 4161847
Website www.bowesrailway.co.uk

Derwentcote Steel Furnace
Rowlands Gill, Co. Durham NE39 1BA
Tel 0191 2691200
Website www.english-heritage.org.uk

Vindomora Roman Fort
Ebchester, Co. Durham

Beamish Open Air Museum
Beamish, Co. Durham DH9 0RG
Tel 0191 3704000
Website www.beamish.org.uk

Monkwearmouth Station Museum
North Bridge Street, Sunderland SR5 1AP
Tel 01801 0191 567 7075
Website www.twmuseums.org.uk

PRACTICAL INFORMATION

NEAREST RAILWAY STATIONS
Chester-le-Street, Sunderland

TOURIST INFORMATION
Sunderland Tourist Information Centre
50 Fawcett Street,
Sunderland SR1 1RF
Tel 0191 5532000
Website www.visitsunderland.com

OS MAP
Landranger No. 88

CYCLE HIRE
Darke Cycles
113 High Street West,
Sunderland SR1 1TR
Tel 01919 5108155
Website www.peterdarkecycles.com

RAILS TO ROSEDALE
Battersby Junction to Rosedale

*Built to transport ironstone from quarries around Rosedale to the ironworks of Teeside,
the Rosedale mineral railway was one of the highest and most remote lines in Britain.*

▲ The loaded wagons from Rosedale
were lowered down Ingleby Incline on
a rope, starting their descent from the
centre road that lies between the more
steeply inclined 'kips' for the ascending
wagons. The speed of ascent and
descent was controlled by a brakeman
in the drum house.

▲ Formerly named Ingleby Junction,
Battersby Junction was once an
important marshalling point for
ironstone trains from Rosedale. Here,
a Class 37 diesel is seen at the head
of an engineers' train for the Esk Valley
line on 5 July 1965. By some amazing
act of providence the scenic line from
Middlesbrough to Whitby via Battersby
is still open. The large engine shed on
the left has since been demolished
but several rows of railway workers,
cottages have survived. A mile south of
the station, the trackbed of the mineral
railway to Ingleby Incline and Rosedale
is easily followed on foot or bike.

The presence of large quantities of high-grade ironstone in the
North Yorkshire Moors around Rosedale had been known for
centuries, but it was only in the mid-19th century that the means of
transporting it to the ironworks of County Durham became possible.

By 1858 the North Yorkshire & Cleveland Railway (NY&CR)
had reached the foot of the Cleveland Hills at Ingleby Junction (later
renamed Battersby Junction). From here a line owned by the Ingleby
Mining Company ran southwards for 3 miles to a tippler at the foot
of an incline from its ironstone mines high on the hillside. In the same
year, the NY&CR, itself taken over by the North Eastern Railway in
1859, bought the mining company's line and received authorisation to
extend it via an incline to large ironstone deposits around Rosedale.
Opened in 1861, the main engineering work on the 14-mile line

was the self-acting Ingleby Incline, which had a gradient at the top of 1 in 5 and a length of nearly 1 mile. From the mines at Rosedale West, loaded wagons of ironstone were hauled over the 11-mile stretch of moorland line by former Stockton & Darlington Railway 0-6-0 locomotives based at Rosedale engine shed. The loaded wagons were then lowered down the self-acting incline with their weight counterbalanced by empty wagons making the return journey – around 200 wagonloads a day could be processed in this way. At the foot of the incline, assembled trains of ironstone were then conveyed via Battersby Junction to ironworks around County Durham.

Vast quantities of ironstone were soon being carried over the railway, now owned by the North Eastern Railway, and in 1865 a 4½-mile branch was opened from Blakey Junction to new workings at East Rosedale. Enormous profits were also being made by the

▼ Opened in 1861, Ingleby Incline had a gradient at the top of 1 in 5 and a length of nearly 1 mile. Loaded wagons from Rosedale were lowered down the self-acting incline with their weight counterbalanced by empty wagons making the return journey. The line and the incline closed in 1928, only a year after this photograph was taken.

WALKING AND CYCLING THE LINE

THE LINE TODAY

Despite closure more than 80 years ago, it is remarkable that nearly all of the route of this mineral railway can still be walked or cycled. The 2-mile straight and level section of the line from Bank Foot, a mile south of Battersby station, to the foot of the Ingleby Incline is now a Forestry Commission track. Walking up the 1,400-yd incline is hard work and cyclists will have to dismount towards the top where the gradient rises to 1 in 5. The drum house and railway cottages at the top have long since disappeared but visitors to the summit are rewarded with far-reaching views across to the Tees Valley from a height of 1,375ft.

For the next 7 miles the trackbed of the railway meanders through cuttings and across embankments over Blakey Moor, more than 1,000ft above sea level, to the site of Blakey Junction. The views from here across Farndale to Rudland Ridge are simply stunning. What must have been the most remote railway junction in the British Isles, Blakey Junction lies only half a mile south of the famous Lion Inn, today a popular watering hole for walkers and cyclists.

From Blakey Junction the trackbed of the line can be followed in a southeasterly direction along the side of Blakey Ridge and past the site of Sheriff's Pit Ironstone Mine to Bank Top, high above the village of Rosedale Abbey. Above the railway here are the remains of large calcine kilns where the mined ironstone was once roasted to reduce its weight. The former engine shed at Bank Top was dismantled in 1939 and the stone was used to build the village hall in Hutton-le-Hole in neighbouring Ryedale.

Back at Blakey Junction, the branch line to Rosedale East loops high around the head of Rosedale to the site of the High Baring East Mines. Ruins of railway workers' cottages, workshops and kilns seen en route are a stark reminder of this once-important mining industry.

PLACES TO VISIT

HERITAGE RAILWAYS
North Yorkshire Moors Railway
2 Park Street, Pickering YO18 7AJ
Tel 01751 472508
Website www.nymr.co.uk
Route Pickering to Grosmont
Length 18 miles

OTHER ATTRACTIONS
Ryedale Folk Museum
Hutton-le-Hole, York YO62 6UA
Tel 01751 417367
Website www.ryedalefolkmuseum.co.uk

Lion Inn
High Blakey Ridge, Kirkbymoorside,
North Yorkshire YO62 7LQ
Tel 01751 417320
Website www.lionblakey.co.uk

The Moors National Park Centre
Lodge Lane, Danby, North Yorkshire YO21 2NB
Tel 01439 772737
Website www.visitthemoors.co.uk

Captain Cook's Monument
Easby Moor, Great Ayton
Website www.great-ayton.org.uk

PRACTICAL INFORMATION

NEAREST RAILWAY STATION
Battersby

TOURIST INFORMATION
The Moors National Park Centre
Lodge Lane, Danby, North Yorkshire YO21 2NB
Tel 01439 772737
Website www.visitthemoors.co.uk

OS Maps
Landranger Nos 93, 94

◀ In winter the high-altitude and exposed Rosedale branch was often blocked by heavy snow, and two four-wheel snow ploughs were built in 1888 specially for the line. Up to three engines, sandwiched between the two ploughs, were often required to clear the line.

▶ Compared to today's tranquil scene, the mining operations at East Rosedale were a hive of industrial activity. Seen here about 1920 are the drift workings at East Rosedale, where the calcine dust, produced during the roasting process in the kilns, is being reclaimed and loaded into wagons for transport to Teeside. By 1927 nearly ¼ million tons of this dust had been reclaimed.

▼ A 4½-mile branch from Blakey Junction to ironstone mines at Rosedale East opened in 1865. Although it closed over 80 years ago, there is still much of interest to be seen by visitors today, including derelict workers' cottages, workshops, calcine kilns, goods sheds and railway cottages.

mines' investors and these continued, albeit in an erratic fashion due to the fluctuations in demand, until the 1920s. By then falling demand for the ironstone, worked-out mines and industrial unrest all contributed to the railway's demise. The line finally closed in 1928 and by the following year it was completely abandoned. However, despite the passage of time, much of the route of the mineral railway from Battersby to Rosedale can still be traced easily today.

▲ At more than 1,000ft above sea level, remote Blakey Junction must have been an inhospitable place in winter. Walkers and cyclists along the line today have but a short detour from here to the famous Lion Inn.

The Works. Rosedale.

THE KIELDER FOREST BORDER RAILWAY TRAIL

Riccarton Junction to Reedsmouth Junction

Serving only scattered and sparsely-populated rural communities, the Border Counties Railway never lived up to its promoter's expectations. Fortunately much of the line's infrastructure has survived since closure.

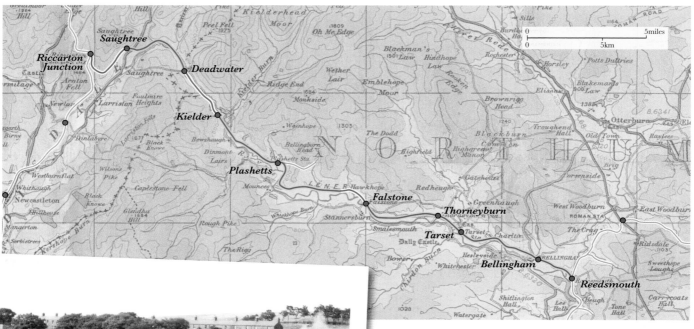

▲ The lonely railway outpost of Riccarton Junction, seen here in 1956. With no road access it was once a self-contained railway community with its own school, post office and co-op general stores. Even doctors had to travel by train from Newcastleton or Hawick to visit patients. The station closed on 5 January 1969, along with the rest of the Waverley Route.

The brainchild of a local landowner, W. H. Charlton Esq. of Hesleyside Hall, the 42-mile single-track Border Counties Railway opened throughout between Hexham, on the Newcastle & Carlisle Railway, to Riccarton Junction, on the newly opened Border Union Railway, on 1 July 1862. The discovery of coal deposits at Plashetts, just inside the English side of the Border, had been the original *raison d'être* for building the line, but these soon proved to be of poor quality and the hoped–for traffic never lived up to expectations. The railway, which had been absorbed by the North British Railway prior to opening, did however offer an alternative, albeit longer and slower, route between Edinburgh and Newcastle. By using running powers over the North Eastern Railway's line from Newcastle to Hexham, the North British offered a through service to Edinburgh via Riccarton Junction and its Waverley Route.

It was never a great success and even the fastest train took just under five hours to complete the circuitous journey.

The only other railway to penetrate the North Tyne Valley was the Wansbeck Railway, which opened throughout between Morpeth and Reedsmouth via Scotsgap in 1865. By that date the railway had also been absorbed by the North British, who saw it as another way of penetrating North Eastern Railway territory to Newcastle via the Blyth & North Tyne Railway. Serving only isolated farming communities, the meandering line was never a success and passenger services ceased in 1952.

Apart from the towns of Bellingham and Hexham, the Border Counties line served a sparsely populated region with stations often sited some distance from the villages they served. Passenger traffic between Bellingham and the remote Riccarton Junction was negligible,

▼ In later years, diesel multiple units occasionally visited the line with enthusiasts' and ramblers' specials. The arrival of one of these specials at Falstone just before closure has certainly brought out the crowds. Falstone station, platform and signalbox have all survived intact.

▼ Two stops on from Riccarton Junction is Deadwater station, which is now a private residence. The trackbed south of here forms the 3-mile Kielder Forest Border Railway Trail to Kielder.

although ramblers' specials or troop trains for nearby training grounds occasionally brought the line to life. By the early 1950s there were only three return journeys each way on a weekday, all originating in Newcastle, with one terminating at Riccarton and the other two at Hawick. Goods traffic included the conveyance of sheep to markets at Bellingham and Hexham, coal from mines north of Hexham and stone and limestone from several rail-linked quarries. Perhaps the most unusual traffic was that of large artillery pieces from the Armstrong Whitworth factory in Newcastle to firing ranges in the nearby hills.

After the Second World War, the future for this loss-making line looked bleak and its fate was sealed by flood damage to the Border Counties Bridge over the River Tyne at Hexham in 1948. Although the bridge was temporarily repaired, its poor condition and the prohibitive cost of proper repairs was the final nail in the coffin and the line closed to passengers on 15 October 1956. A weekly goods service from Hexham to Riccarton continued until September 1958, when the line south of Reedsmouth and west of Bellingham was completely closed. However, one passenger train still visited Bellingham each September when a diesel multiple unit excursion ran from Newbiggin-by-the-Sea for the annual Redesdale Show. Reedsmouth and Bellingham also continued to be served by a weekly goods train via the Wansbeck line from Morpeth until November 1963, when that line closed west of Woodburn. At the northern end of the Border Counties line, Riccarton Junction on the Waverley Route from Edinburgh to Carlisle closed on 5 January 1969.

◀ Following withdrawal of freight services, the line between Bellingham and Riccarton Junction closed in September 1958. From then until closure in November 1963, Bellingham was served by a weekly goods train via the Wansbeck line and Redesmouth Junction. On the final day before closure, 9 November 1963, Ivatt Class 4 2-6-0 No. 43129 is seen at Bellingham with the RCTS/SLS 'Wansbeck Wanderer' enthusiasts' special.

▼ Seen here midway between Deadwater and Kielder, the traffic-free Kielder Forest Border Railway Trail is popular with walkers and cyclists. Car parking and cycle hire are available in the village of Kielder.

WALKING AND CYCLING THE LINE

THE LINE TODAY

Despite closure more than 50 years ago, much of the route and infrastructure of the Border Counties Railway can still be traced today. From the car park of the Waverley Route Heritage Association at Whitrope (north of the Border) it is possible to walk south along the trackbed of the Waverley Route for 2 miles through forestry plantations to the eerily silent Riccarton Junction. Inaccessible by road, Riccarton Junction is one railway pilgrimage worth making. Here the island platform has been partially restored with a short length of track, station nameboard and a (disconnected) red telephone box. Apart from this and the ruins of the stationmaster's house, nothing now remains of this lonely railway outpost that was once inhabited by more than 100 people.

From Riccarton Junction the trackbed of the Border Counties line, now a forestry track, swings eastward to Saughtree where the remote station and platform have been restored along with a short length of track. At Deadwater the station building is now a private residence and

from here to Kielder the trackbed is a 3-mile traffic-free footpath and cycleway known as the Kielder Forest Border Railway Trail. At Kielder, where the seven-arch skew viaduct has been preserved, there are car parking, cycle-hire and refreshment facilities. Between Kielder and Falstone much of the railway, including the site of Plashetts station, was submerged beneath the Kielder Water Reservoir during its construction in the late 1970s. Falstone station site, where the station building, platform and signalbox still survive, is now owned by the Forestry Commission. Farther east, Thorneyburn and Tarset station buildings are now private residences. At Bellingham, the most important station on the line, the station buildings (now council offices), goods shed and platform survive intact. The former station yard is now a car park and also houses the Bellingham Heritage Centre, which has a permanent exhibition on the Border Counties Railway. At Reedsmouth, former junction with the Wansbeck line, the large signalbox and base of the water tower have been converted into private residences.

PLACES TO VISIT

HERITAGE RAILWAYS
South Tynedale Railway
Alston Railway Station,
Alston CA9 3JB
Tel 01434 381 696
Website www.strps.org.uk
Route Alston to Kirkhaugh
Length 2¼ miles

OTHER ATTRACTIONS
Waverley Route Heritage Association
Signal Box Cottage,
Whitrope, Hawick,
Roxburghshire TD9 9TY
Website www.wrha.org.uk

Kielder Castle
Kielder, Northumberland NE48 1ER
Tel 01434 250209
Website www.visitkielder.com

Tower Knowe
Falstone, Northumberland NE48 1BX
Tel 0845 155 0236
Website www.visitkielder.com

Bellingham Heritage Centre
Station Yard, Woodburn Road, Bellingham,
Northumberland NE48 2DF
Tel 01434 220050
Website www.bellingham-heritage.org.uk

PRACTICAL INFORMATION

NEAREST RAILWAY STATION
Hexham

TOURIST INFORMATION
Bellingham Tourist information Centre
The Heritage Centre, Hillside, Bellingham,
Northumberland NE48 2GR
Tel 01434 220616
Website www.visitnorthumberland.com

OS MAPS
Landranger Nos 79, 80

CYCLE HIRE
The Bike Place
Station Road, Kielder
Northumberland NE48 1EG
Tel 01434 250457
Website www.thebikeplace.co.uk

SCOTLAND

◄ In latter steam years, the St Combs branch was operated by Ivatt Class 2 2-6-0 locomotives. Here, fitted with statutory cowcatcher, No. 46460 makes a spirited departure from Fraserburgh in 1958. The heavy amount of railborne freight traffic once originating from the fishing port of Fraserburgh is clearly demonstrated by the busy goods yard.

LONGNIDDRY TO HADDINGTON RAILWAY PATH

Longniddry to Haddington

Originally built as a double track line to appease the wealthy townsfolk of Haddington, the short branch line from Longniddry never lived up to expectations and became an early casualty of post-war closures.

▼ Although it was closed to passengers in 1949, the Haddington branch was often visited by enthusiasts specials until its complete closure in 1968. Here, ex-NBR Class 'J35' 0-6-0 No. 64489 is seen in the Haddington bay at Longniddry with a special train on 11 June 1960.

When planning the route of its new railway from Edinburgh to Berwick, the North British Railway directors considered two options – either build along the coast or via the wealthy county town of Haddington. The latter option was eventually rejected due to higher construction and operating costs and on 4 July 1844, the North British Railway was authorised to build a main line from Edinburgh to Berwick via Drem with a 4-mile branch line from Longniddry to Haddington. Both lines opened to the public on 22 June 1846.

Unusually for a short branch line, the Longniddry to Haddington line was built with double tracks. This extra expense was incurred not only to appease the townsfolk of Haddington for losing their main line status, but also to convey large amounts of agricultural traffic. Sadly, the latter never materialised and the line was singled in 1856. The Haddington branch soon became a sleepy backwater with around 10 return trains each weekday making

◄ Despite being only a short branch line, the Haddington branch was originally built with double tracks. This road overbridge near Merryhatton clearly demonstrates the original width of the line, which was singled in 1856.

▼ Another enthusiasts' special visited Haddington on 29 August 1964. It is seen here waiting to depart from the station behind veteran ex-NBR Class 'J36' 0-6-0 No. 65234. The platform and station building still survive.

the short 10-minute trip to Longniddry, where passengers changed trains for Edinburgh or Berwick. This pattern continued until after the Second World War, but by then increasing competition from road transport had seen passenger numbers on the branch drop dramatically.

The end came in 1949 when the Haddington branch became one of the earliest casualties of branch-line closures under British Railways' new management. Passenger services were withdrawn on 5 December that year but freight continued for nearly 20 years more, until the line was closed completely on 30 March 1968.

▼ The woodland and hedgerows alongside the Longniddry to Haddington railway path offer shelter to a wide diversity of wildlife. The path can also be accessed at Cottyburn, about 1½ miles southeast of Longniddry, where there is a small car park and picnic site.

WALKING AND CYCLING THE LINE

THE LINE TODAY

The trackbed of the Haddington branch was purchased by East Lothian Council in 1978 and is now a traffic-free footpath, cycleway and bridle path. The railway path starts at Longniddry station where there is a car park, which is still open for passengers on the Edinburgh to Berwick main line, and ends near Haddington Hospital. There are several stone bridges along the route that clearly demonstrate the branch line's original double-track construction. There is a diversion at the western outskirts of the town where the new A1 dual carriageway crosses over the trackbed. Although the station site at Haddington is now an industrial estate, the platform and station building have somehow miraculously survived alongside new industrial units. Plans to reopen the line for commuter traffic to Edinburgh have so far come to nothing.

PLACES TO VISIT

Museum of Flight
East Fortune Airfield,
East Lothian EH39 5LF
Tel 0131 247 4238
Website www.nms.ac.uk

Lennoxlove House
Haddington, EH41 4NZ
Tel 01620 823 720
Website www.lennoxlove.com

Glenkinchie Distillery
Pencaitland, Tranent,
East Lothian EH34 5ET
Tel 01875 342004
Website www.discovering-distilleries.com

Myreton Motor Museum
Aberlady, East Lothian EH32 0PZ
Tel 01875 870288
Website www.myretonmotormuseum.co.uk

PRACTICAL INFORMATION

NEAREST RAILWAY STATION
Longniddry

TOURIST INFORMATION
North Berwick Tourist Information Centre
Quality Street, North Berwick,
East Lothian EH39 4HJ
Tel 01620 892197
Website www.visitscotland.com

OS MAP
Landranger No. 66

CYCLE HIRE
Law Cycles
2 Law Road, North Berwick,
East Lothian EH39 4PL
Tel 01620 890643
Website www.lawcycles.co.uk

Leith Cycle Company
276 Leith Walk, Edinburgh EH6 5BX
Tel 0131 202 8261
Website www.leithcycleco.com

◄ The railway path from Longniddry ends near Haddington Hospital because the remaining section of the line has now been built over. The station site is now an industrial estate, but the platform and station building, seen here, still survive among industrial units.

WEST FIFE CYCLE WAY
Dunfermline to Alloa

The Stirling & Dunfermline Railway served the West Fife coalfields and provided a through route between Edinburgh and Stirling until 1968. The western section, from Stirling to Alloa, reopened in 2008.

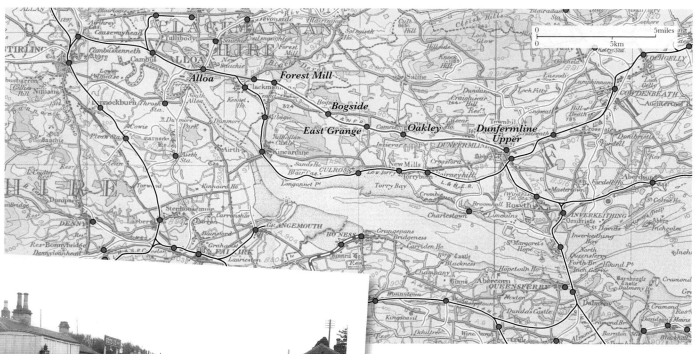

▲ The small station at Bogside closed on 15 September 1958. The North British Railway added 'Fife' to the nameboard to avoid confusion with the other Bogside in Renfrewshire.

Authorised in 1846, the Stirling & Dunfermline Railway (S&DR) opened in three stages: Dunfermline Upper to Alloa on 28 August 1850; branches to Alloa Harbour and Tillicoultry on 3 June 1851; Alloa to Stirling on 1 July 1852. Built to tap into the coalfields of West Fife, the 20½-mile line was double track throughout, with intermediate stations at Oakley, East Grange, Bogside, Forest Mill, Alloa, Cambus and Causewayhead. The S&DR was taken over by the Edinburgh & Glasgow Railway in 1858, which was itself absorbed by the North British Railway in 1865.

A short branch line was also later opened from Oakley to the Comrie Colliery and Roxio Coking Plant. By the early 20th century, there were 8 or 9 return services each weekday between Dunfermline and Stirling, the majority being through trains to and from Edinburgh, including one that conveyed a through carriage to and from Aberfoyle for day trippers to the Trossachs.

▲ The Stirling & Dunfermline Railway reached Alloa in 1850. The once-busy station, seen here at the east end on 20 June 1937, serving trains to Stirling, Dunfermline Upper and Dunfermline Lower via Kincardine, closed on 7 October 1968. In 2008, a new station was built at Alloa for the reopening of the line to Stirling.

▶ The West Fife Cycle Way, or Alloa to Dunfermline Link, is part of a network of cycle paths in Clackmannanshire.

▼ Alloa engine shed, located east of Alloa station, was once a sub-shed of Dunfermline. It was built in 1885 and closed at the end of 1966, the end of steam in Scotland. Here, ex-NBR Class 'J36' 0-6-0 No. 9670 was spotted on shed during a visit by Henry Casserley on 20 June 1937.

▼ Most passenger trains between Dunfermline Upper and Stirling originated or ended in Edinburgh via the Forth Bridge and Dunfermline Lower. Although geographically only a short distance apart, the circuitous 2½-mile rail journey between Dunfermline's two stations took six minutes. Here, LNER Class 'V3' 2-6-2 tank No. 7618 enters Upper station with a train for Stirling on 2 October 1946.

▶ Despite closure only just over 40 years ago, very little now remains of the railway's infrastructure. However, keen-eyed enthusiasts of lost railways will usually find a few traces from the past – here, hidden in the undergrowth at the site of East Grange station, is a British Railways' electrical junction box.

By the 1960s, steam had been replaced by DMUs but the frequency of trains remained roughly the same as 50 years before, with most trains running through from or to Edinburgh. Station closures started as early as 1930 when Forest Mill was closed; Causewayhead shut in 1955 and Bogside and East Grange on 15 September 1958. Passenger services were completely withdrawn between Dunfermline Upper and Stirling on 7 October 1968, but parts of the line remained open for freight well into the 1980s. At the eastern end, the section from Dunfermline Upper to Comrie Colliery remained open until 1986.

However, that is not the end of the story as the Stirling to Alloa section was reopened to both freight and passengers in May 2008. Merry-go-round coal trains also travel via Alloa to Longannet power station on the north shore of the Firth of Forth.

WALKING AND CYCLING THE LINE

THE LINE TODAY

The county of Fife now has around 300 miles of cycle routes, some of them along disused railways, including the 8-mile traffic-free West Fife Cycle Way between Dunfermline and Clackmannan. Sadly, the station site at Dunfermline Upper was cleared after the closure of the line to Comrie Colliery in 1986. In Dunfermline, the West Fife Cycle Way starts at a car park close to the site of Upper station and proceeds in a westerly direction to Oakley, where the Comrie Colliery branch once veered off in a northerly direction. Although nothing remains of the station here, the abutments of the branch-line bridge can still be seen. Continuing westwards, the cycleway follows a fairly straight and level course to the outskirts of Clackmannan, passing under or over a fair number of road bridges en route. Apart from these bridges and the spectacular viaduct over Comrie Burn, nearly all of the railway's lineside infrastructure has long since gone, with the exception of the signalbox at the site of Bogside station. The cycleway, prone to flooding in winter, ends at the B910 on the outskirts of Clackmannan.

PLACES TO VISIT

HERITAGE RAILWAYS
Bo'ness & Kinneil Railway
Bo'ness Station, Union Street, Bo'ness,
West Lothian EH51 9AQ
Tel 01506 822298
Website www.srps.org.uk
Route Borrowstounness (Bo'ness) to Manuel
Length 5 miles

OTHER ATTRACTIONS
Culross Palace (NTS)
Culross, Fife KY12 8JH
Tel 0844 493 2189
Website www.nts.org.uk

Dunfermline Abbey
Dunfermline KY12 7PE
Tel 01383 724586
Website www.dunfermlineabbey.co.uk

Dunfermline Museum
Viewfield Terrace, Dunfermline,
Fife KY12 7HY
Tel 01383 721814
Website www.culture24.org.uk

PRACTICAL INFORMATION

NEAREST RAILWAY STATIONS
Alloa, Dunfermline

TOURIST INFORMATION
Dunfermline Tourist Information Centre
1 High Street,
Dunfermline KY12 7DL
Tel 01383 720999
Website www.visitscotland.com

OS MAPS
Landranger Nos 58, 65

CYCLE HIRE
Flying Fox Bikes & Outdoors
103 Stirling Street, Alva,
Clackmannanshire FK12 5EF
Tel 01259 763109
Website www.flyingfoxbikes.com

▼ West of Bogside, the West Fife Cycle Way dives under this double-track road bridge at Slack where there is an access point and small car park.

◄ Despite closure to passengers in 1968, Dunfermline Upper station, seen here in the 1930s, remained fairly intact until the early 1990s. Demolition followed the closure of the line to Comrie Colliery via Oakley in 1986.

▼ The signal box at Bogside still stands guard over the West Fife Cycle Way today. The windows and frames have a nice touch of *trompe-l'oeil*. In the distance, the bridge that once carried a forestry track over the line has been filled in.

LOCHABER NARROW GAUGE RAILWAY

Fort William to Loch Treig

The remote and inaccessible Lochaber Narrow Gauge Railway lasted just over 50 years.
Today, intrepid walkers of the line are rewarded with stunning views and fascinating railway relics.

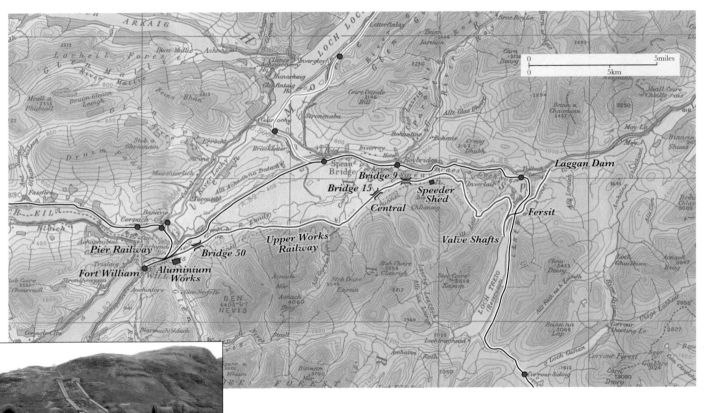

▲ The Upper Works Railway closed in 1976 but a few tangible remains can still be found near the site of 'Possil Park' close to the main power house at the aluminium works in Fort William. Overlooked by the pipes carrying millions of gallons of water from distant Loch Treig, this 3ft-gauge wagon chassis and pile of track await their future.

By 1921, demand for aluminium in Britain had far outstretched supply from existing factories at Foyers, on Loch Ness, and at Kinlochleven, at the head of Loch Leven. Requiring vast amounts of electricity to produce each ingot of the material, the British Aluminium Company finally decided on a new factory that was to be built at Fort William. Electricity would come from hydro-electric power generated at the plant from 860 million gallons of water each day flowing along a 15-mile tunnel, bored through solid rock, from Loch Treig. A dam was to be built across Loch Treig to raise the water height from 784ft to 814ft. The loch was also to be fed by water through a 6-mile tunnel from a new dam at Loch Laggan and from mountain streams diverted into the main tunnel at 12 intakes between Loch Treig and the plant.

◀ Just to the east of 'Central', the truncated remains of curving Bridge 15 once carried the Upper Works Railway high over Allt Leachdach. Today, this dangerous structure is definitely out of bounds to walkers.

▼ Hunslet 0-4-2 saddle tank No. 2 'Lady Morrison' of the Pier Railway propels a load of cryolite from the pier on Loch Linnhe to the British Aluminium Company's works at Fort William on 25 May 1961. The brakeman standing on the first wagon appears to be in charge. The Pier Railway was soon to fall into disuse, with raw materials and aluminium ingots being carried to and from Fort William on the West Highland Line.

▶ Accessible on foot, the trackbed of the railway from the Laggan Dam is now a private road between the car park at Fersit, Treig Dam and the valve intakes at the head of Loch Treig. Remnants of a loading platform sit left and the main line of the UWR to Fort William runs on the hillside behind.

▼ Bridge 9 is is one of the best preserved on the line – this American-style curving steel trestle bridge with 3ft-gauge track still in situ straddles a deep gulley that carries the foaming torrents of Allt Beinn Chlianaig. Walkers are advised not to attempt to cross this structure.

◀ A speeder or locomotive shed was located near Adit 3 high above Monessie Gorge. Seen here on 24 May 1961, the shed was reached by a track from Roy Bridge. The wagon in the siding would carry a hut to provide shelter for men and materials.

This massive undertaking was not helped by the total lack of access roads along the route of the pipeline on the lower slopes of the Nevis range of mountains. To overcome this, a 21-mile 3ft-gauge Light Railway was built by the contractors Balfour Beatty to carry men and materials to various construction sites and adits along the route of the proposed tunnel and to the dams. Construction of the Upper Works Railway (UWR), as it was known, from Base Camp in Fort William to Fersit at the head of Loch Treig, commenced in 1925 and continued as work progressed on the hydro-electric scheme until its completion during the Second World War. A total of 53 bridges, mainly American-style trestle types, were built to carry the little railway across roaring mountain streams as it hugged the contours at around 650ft above sea level. It was later extended to Loch Laggan, where another dam was being built.

A 2-mile 3ft-gauge line, known as the Pier Railway, was also built from the aluminium smelter at Fort William down to a new concrete pier located at the head of Loch Linnhe. Here raw materials were shipped in and the finished product shipped out. Fort William was also connected with the outside world by the West Highland Railway, which had opened from Glasgow in 1894. The building of the dam at the head of Loch Treig involved diverting the West Highland Line along the top of an enormous stone embankment at this point.

During construction, Balfour Beatty used its own fleet of narrow gauge steam locomotives to haul materials to the various sites along the line, with workers being conveyed in converted motor cars known as speeders. Battery-powered locomotives were also used on the various 2ft-gauge lines in and around the tunnel adits.

Aluminium production started at Fort William in 1929 and the British Aluminium Company was soon employing its own fleet of locomotives – two 0-4-2 saddle tanks were employed on the Pier Railway while the Upper Works Railway used small diesel-mechanical locos to haul materials and Wickham speeders to convey men. After the Second World War, the Pier Railway remained in use, carrying alumina and cryolite to the aluminium plant until the early 1960s, when the line fell out of use. By that date all raw materials and the finished

WALKING AND CYCLING THE LINE

THE LINE TODAY

Exploring the Upper Works Railway today is not a task for the faint-hearted. Only the western section is suitable for experienced mountain bikers, while walkers attempting to explore the whole route should wear suitable clothing and footwear as much of the ground is very boggy. Many of the trestle bridges across the mountain streams still survive – some even complete with track still in situ – but they are much too dangerous to cross and many have been fenced off. Fortunately, the entire route of the railway is marked as 'dismantled tramway' on OS Landranger Map No. 41.

At the western end, the route of the railway can be accessed from a track that runs around the perimeter of the aluminium works at Fort William. Here, just beyond the power house, lies the site of 'Possil Park', where the shed that housed the speeders still survives complete with 3ft-gauge track embedded in the concrete floor. From here the route of the railway can be followed on mountain bike or on foot across rebuilt Bridges 50 and 51 to Torlundy, where there is a car park for mountain bike trails in Leanachan Forest. The trackbed of the railway can also be accessed on foot or mountain bike from the Nevis Range Ski and Gondola Centre 2 miles east of Torlundy. In parts a forest track, the route of the UWR traverses the upper slopes of Leanachan Forest for 6 miles before emerging at Bridge 15 (see page 223).

The remote Upper Works Railway can also be accessed from several other points. Bridge 15 can be reached by mountain bike or on foot from Spean Bridge via the lane to Corriechoille and thence up a steep Forestry Commission track. Close to the fenced-off Bridge 15, inquisitive lovers of old railways will find remains of the railway track still embedded in the boggy ground. It was here that a speeder reversing triangle known as 'Central' was once located. Farther east, Bridges 9 (page 224) and 10 can also be reached on foot or mountain bike via a steep forestry track from Insh, 1 mile east of Corriechoille. On a sharp bend in the track, the boggy route of the UWR can be followed eastwards on foot to the bridges, both of which are unsafe to cross. The UWR can also be accessed from a car park at Fersit, reached along a lane from the A86 not far from Tulloch station. From the car park the trackbed of the railway is now a private road, which can be followed on foot down to the Treig Dam and beyond to the valve shafts at the head of Loch Treig. In the hills above, the boggy trackbed of the railway can be explored on foot as it winds its way westwards around the contours of Beinn Chlianaig.

PLACES TO VISIT

HERITAGE RAILWAYS

The Jacobite
c/o West Coast Railways, Jesson Way,
Crag Bank, Carnforth, Lancashire LA5 9UR
Tel 0845 128 4681
Website www.westcoastrailways.co.uk
Route Fort William to Mallaig
Length 42 miles

OTHER ATTRACTIONS

Ben Nevis Distillery
Lochy Bridge, Fort William PH33 6TJ
Tel 01397 700 200
Website www.bennevisdistillery.com

Old Inverlochy Castle
Inverlochy, Fort William
Website www.inverlochycastle.co.uk

Nevis Range Gondola and Ski Centre
Torlundy, Fort William PH33 6SQ
Tel 01397 705 825
Website www.nevisrange.co.uk

West Highland Museum
Cameron Square, Fort William PH33 6AJ
Tel 01397 702 169
Website www.westhighlandmuseum.org.uk

Glenfinnan Station Museum
Station Cottage, Glenfinnan PH37 4LT
Tel 01397 722295
Website www.glenfinnanstationmuseum.co.uk

PRACTICAL INFORMATION

NEAREST RAILWAY STATIONS

Fort William, Tulloch

TOURIST INFORMATION

Fort William Tourist Information Centre
15 High Street, Fort William PH33 6DH
Tel 0845 2255 121
Website www.visitscotland.com

OS MAP

Landranger No. 41

CYCLE HIRE

Off Beat Bikes
High Street, Fort William
Tel 01397 704 008
Website www.offbeatbikes.co.uk

Nevis Cycles
4 Lochy Crescent, Inverlochy, Fort William
PH33 6NG
Tel 01397 705555
Website www.neviscycles.co.uk

▲ The valve intakes at Loch Treig can be reached on foot along the trackbed of the Upper Works Railway from a car park at Fersit, a distance of 1½ miles to the north. The West Highland Line between Tulloch and Corrour runs along the opposite shore of the loch. Each day, 860 million gallons of water flow from here down the 15-mile tunnel to the aluminium works at Fort William.

product were being carried on the West Highland Line – a practice that still continues today. The Upper Works Railway, by now used for maintenance of the hydro–electric scheme, was not in a good state of repair but it struggled on until 1971, when a landslip caused by heavy rain swept away Bridge 43 east of Fort William. With new access roads to the area already being built by the Forestry Commission, the end was in sight for the Upper Works Railway – the bridge was never repaired but several locomotives and speeders, stranded on the wrong side, continued to operate along the line for several more years until 1976, when the last section of track was finally lifted. In recent years a proposal to open a miniature railway along a section of the UWR has failed to materialise.

▲ The eastern terminus of the Upper Works Railway was at the valve intakes at the head of Loch Treig. On the left is a railway-linked slipway operated by a winch. Apart from the disappearance of the railway track and the speeder hut on the right, the scene today (see view above) is exactly the same.

FORMARTINE & BUCHAN WAY

Dyce to Fraserburgh and Peterhead

In hindsight, the closure of the railways to Fraserburgh and Peterhead was a mistake. Although the lines are now enjoyed by walkers and cyclists, their reopening for their true purpose is seriously overdue.

▼ BR Standard Class 4 2-6-4 tank No. 80112 arrives at Dyce with a train from Peterhead/Fraserburgh on 12 June 1955. Dyce station on the Aberdeen to Inverness main line has been reopened and serves nearby Aberdeen Airport. The station buildings on the right have since been demolished to make way for a car park.

The first railway to be built north of Aberdeen was the Great North of Scotland Railway's (GNoSR) main line to Huntly, which opened in 1854. Previous to this the Great North of Scotland (Eastern Extension) Company had already received authorisation to build a line from Dyce to Peterhead and Fraserburgh, but the company went bankrupt before construction work had started. Other schemes were put forward but it was not until 1858 that the Formartine & Buchan Railway was finally authorised to build its line from Dyce, on the GNoS mainline, to Peterhead. Progress in building the line was slow due mainly to bad weather in the winter of 1860/61, which

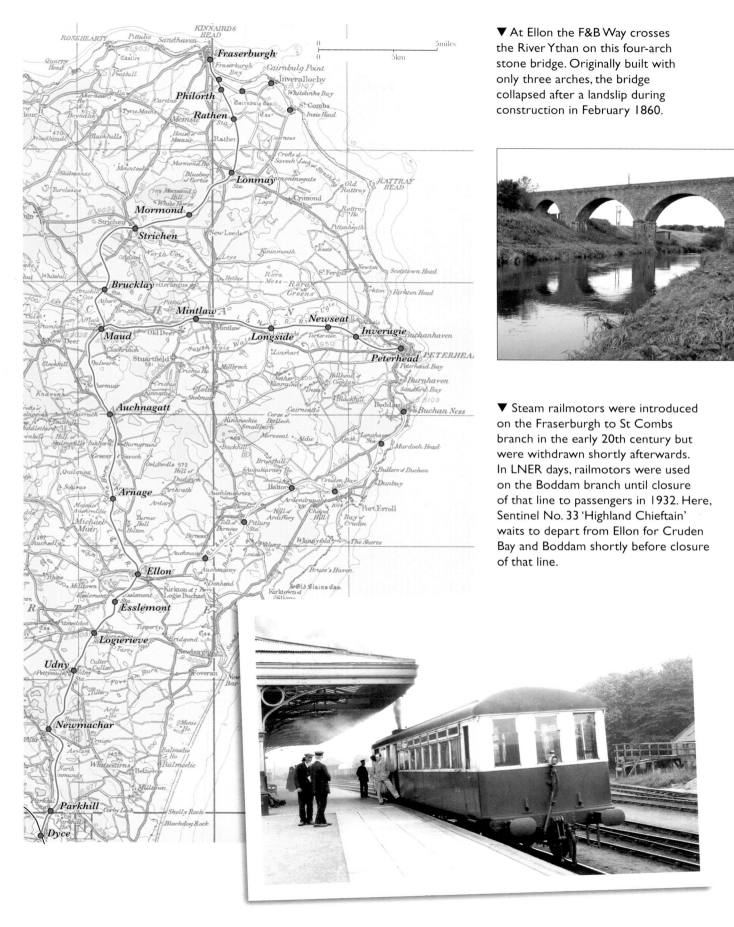

▼ At Ellon the F&B Way crosses the River Ythan on this four-arch stone bridge. Originally built with only three arches, the bridge collapsed after a landslip during construction in February 1860.

▼ Steam railmotors were introduced on the Fraserburgh to St Combs branch in the early 20th century but were withdrawn shortly afterwards. In LNER days, railmotors were used on the Boddam branch until closure of that line to passengers in 1932. Here, Sentinel No. 33 'Highland Chieftain' waits to depart from Ellon for Cruden Bay and Boddam shortly before closure of that line.

brought about the collapse of the new viaduct at Ellon. Operated from the outset by the GNoSR, the 44¼-mile line was opened throughout to Peterhead on 3 July 1862, with a short branch to the harbour opening three years later.

The 16-mile branch line to Fraserburgh was opened from Brucklay (renamed Maud Junction) on 24 April 1865 and a year later the Formartine & Buchan (F&B) was absorbed by the Great North of Scotland. A second branch line was opened in 1897 from Ellon to Boddam, on the coast only 3 miles south of Peterhead. At Cruden Bay, the GNoSR also built a large hotel and golf course, which was connected with Cruden station by a narrow gauge electric tramway. The third branch line to be built was the 5-mile Fraserburgh to St Combs light railway, which opened in 1903. The railway network north of Aberdeen was now complete.

For the next 100 years, passenger services on the Peterhead and Fraserburgh lines remained

▶ Until the introduction of DMUs in 1959, trains for Peterhead and Fraserburgh were divided at Maud Junction, seen here during LNER days in 1937. The goods yard, on the left, is now a car park, but the turntable pit, just out of the image, still survives. The Peterhead platforms are on the right; those for Fraserburgh are on the left.

▼ Apart from the growth of vegetation and the removal of track, the scene is much the same today. Seen here in May 1998, the four platforms and station buildings at Maud Junction remain beautifully preserved. A railway museum, once located on the island platform, is now closed.

fairly constant, with 4 or 5 return trains to and from Aberdeen each weekday; trains were normally divided at Maud Junction. Goods traffic in the form of agricultural produce, coal and fish was an important source of revenue – refrigerated fish trains originating at the ports of Peterhead and Fraserburgh travelled overnight to fish markets in London. The Cruden Bay experiment was never a success and the line from Errol closed to passengers on 31 October 1932 and to goods on 7 November 1945. Steam haulage ended in June 1959 when diesel multiple units were introduced between Aberdeen and Fraserburgh/ Peterhead and on the St Combs branch. Goods trains were also being handled by the North British Type 2 diesels that were based at Kittybrewster shed in Aberdeen. One of the most unsuccessful diesel classes ever introduced by British Railways, they were also pressed into service to replace failed DMUs.

Listed for closure in the Beeching Report of 1963, both the Maud Junction to Peterhead line and the St Combs branch closed to passengers on 3 May 1965. Despite strong local protests, the Aberdeen to Fraserburgh service clung on to life for only another five months, until that was also closed to passengers on 4 October. Although by now suffering from increased road competition, freight trains continued to operate from Peterhead until 7 September 1970. Fraserburgh continued

▶ North British Type 2 diesel D6141 has just arrived under the overall roof at Peterhead station on 6 June 1963. This scene, full of period detail including weighing machine, posters, bicycle and gas lamps was finally swept away following closure when the station site was redeveloped. Probably the most unsuccessful of BR diesel classes, the NB Type 2s had a very short working life.

▼ Here, BR Standard Class 4 2-6-4 tank No. 80029 leaves Peterhead with the 12.38pm train for Aberdeen on 12 June 1959. The short train would have joined the Fraserburgh portion at Maud Junction. Peterhead once had a busy freight yard as witnessed here by the long lines of vans awaiting collection of the day's fish.

▶ Following total closure in 1979, the 54 miles of trackbed of the Fraserburgh and Peterhead lines was bought by Grampian Regional Council. It was reopened as a footpath and cycleway in 1987 as the Formartine & Buchan Way. Now managed by Aberdeenshire Council, most sections are also available for horse riding but permits are necessary for this activity.

WALKING AND CYCLING THE LINE

THE LINE TODAY

With amazing foresight, Grampian Regional Council bought the trackbed of the Dyce to Peterhead/Fraserburgh lines following closure in 1979. The purchase was initially seen as a way of safeguarding the route for possible reopening. In the meantime, it has become a 54-mile footpath, known as the Formartine & Buchan Way, popular with local walkers, cyclists and commuters and part of National Cycle Network Route 1.

Much of the infrastructure of the line, including bridges, station buildings (now converted as private residences) and platforms, has survived. With investment, it could be reopened and provide the inhabitants of Fraserburgh, Peterhead and expanding Ellon with an alternative to the A90.

At its southern end, Dyce station, on the Aberdeen to Inverness line, has been reopened to serve nearby Aberdeen Airport. Here the platforms that once served the F&B line have been covered over by a car park from where the Way starts. The first station on the line was at Parkhill, which closed on 3 April 1950, although remains of the platforms can still be seen today. New Machar station building is now a private residence, while north of here is the summit of the line where the F&B Way passes through a deep and long cutting. From here the line drops on a gradient of 1 in 80 through Udny, Logierieve and Esslemont, where the station buildings and platforms all still survive, to Ellon en route passing over the River Ythan on a stone viaduct (this collapsed before the line opened and had to be rebuilt). At Ellon, former junction for the Boddam branch, part of the platform still survives. Continuing northwards, the platforms and station buildings at Arnage and Auchnagatt also still remain.

Maud Junction, junction for the Peterhead and Fraserburgh lines, is still worthy of a railway pilgrimage – here the four platforms, station buildings and even the turntable pit are patiently waiting for the line's reopening. Sadly, the railway museum on the island platform has now closed but there is a large car park adjoining the site.

On the Peterhead branch the station buildings and platforms at Mintlaw, Longside and Newseat still survive, unlike the large station site at Peterhead, which has completely disappeared following redevelopment.

Back at Maud Junction, the line to Fraserburgh continues in a northerly direction before swinging eastwards around Mormond Hill near Strichen. En route, Brucklay station and platform are passed before the line crosses the North Ugie Water on a tall rusting girder bridge at Strichen. From Strichen station, now a private residence, the F&B Way continues on its way past the stations and platforms at Mormond, Lonmay, Rathen and Philorth before arriving at its destination in Fraserburgh. Sadly the once vast station site has now disappeared beneath roads and industrial buildings, although the two-road GNoSR engine shed still survives in a different guise.

PLACES TO VISIT

HERITAGE RAILWAYS
Alford Valley Railway
Alford, Aberdeenshire AB33 8TN
Tel 07879 293934
Website www.alfordvalleyrailway.org.uk
Route Alford to Haughton Park
Length 1½ miles

Keith & Dufftown Railway
Dufftown Station, Dufftown, Banffshire AB55 4BA
Tel 01340 821181
Website www.keith-dufftown-railway.co.uk
Route Keith Town to Dufftown
Length 11 miles

OTHER ATTRACTIONS
Grampian Transport Museum
Alford, Aberdeenshire AB33 8AE
Tel 019755 62292
Website www.gtm.org.uk

Peterhead Maritime Heritage Centre
Tel 01779 473000
Website www.zincweb.co.uk/pmh

Fraserburgh Heritage Centre
Quarry Road, Fraserburgh, Aberdeenshire AB43 9DT
Tel 01346 513802
Website www.fraserburghheritage.com

PRACTICAL INFORMATION

NEAREST RAILWAY STATION
Dyce

TOURIST INFORMATION
Fraserburgh Tourist Information Centre
Saltoun Square, Fraserburgh AB43 9DA
Tel 01346 518315
Website www.visitscotland.com

OS MAPS
Landranger Nos 30, 38

▲ (Top of page) Closed to passengers on 4 October 1965, Auchnagatt station platform still survives today alongside the Formartine & Buchan Way between Maud and Fraserburgh. Despite the passage of time, the station nameboard posts and lamp brackets are still standing as memorials to a railway line that should never have been closed.

to be served by freight trains for another seven years until complete closure on 8 October 1979. By that date any remaining fish railway traffic had been lost to road transport. A hoped-for reopening of the lines to Peterhead and Fraserburgh in anticipation of the North Sea oil boom never materialised, even though the trackbed had been purchased by Grampian Regional Council (later superseded by Aberdeenshire Council).

◀ Until complete closure of the line, the rusting girders of the skew bridge across the North Ugie Water near Strichen still saw the passage of freight trains from Fraserburgh. Now only walkers and cyclists can enjoy the view from the top.

◀ A two-car diesel multiple unit from the St Combs branch spills out its passengers at Fraserburgh station at 2pm on the last day of service, Saturday 1 May 1965. Opened as a light railway in 1903, the official closing date for the St Combs branch was Monday 3 May 1965, as there were no Sunday services. The overall-roof station at Fraserburgh has sadly since been demolished to make way for roads and industrial units.

ALONG THE LOCHWINNOCH LOOP

Johnstone to Dalry via Lochwinnoch

Opened in 1905 as a relief line for the congested Glasgow to Ayr main line, the Lochwinnoch Loop had a short working life of just over 60 years. The trackbed now forms part of National Cycle Network Route 7.

Linking Scotland's biggest city, Glasgow, with the Firth of Clyde coast at Ayr, the Glasgow, Paisley, Kilmarnock & Ayr Railway was authorised in 1837 with shares being offered at £12 10s. Opened in stages between 1839 and 1840, the 33-mile route of the railway between Paisley and Ayr took it in a southwesterly direction from Glasgow to Johnstone and then along the eastern side of a valley

▶ A mixed freight headed by G&SWR 4-4-0 No. 84 rumbles into Kilbarchan station in the early 20th century. Under LMS management, nearly all former G&SWR locomotives had been withdrawn by 1933. Only one survives today – 0-6-0 tank No. 9 has been preserved and can be seen at the new Riverside Museum in Glasgow, which opens in 2011.

formed by three small lochs and the River Garnock. The section between Paisley and Glasgow (Bridge Street) was a joint line known as the Glasgow & Paisley Railway. The GPK&AR expanded in 1846 when it took over the Kilmarnock & Troon Railway; it was granted the authority to purchase the Paisley & Renfrew a year later, before merging with the Glasgow, Dumfries & Carlisle Railway in 1850 to form the Glasgow & South Western Railway.

By the end of the 19th century, the line's capacity between Glasgow and Ayr had become stretched to the limit and quadrupling it was out of the question due to the confined geography of the valley and lochs. To overcome this, a 13-mile loop line was opened on 1 June 1905 along the western shores of the lochs from Elderslie Junction to Brownhill Junction via stations at Johnstone North, Kilbarchan, Lochwinnoch and Kilbirnie. The latter town was already served by the Caledonian Railway's short branch line from Giffen, which had already opened in 1889. Complete closure of this branch came in 1930.

Passenger services on the loop line remained fairly constant for the next 60 years, with around 10-12 return trains each day running between Glasgow St Enoch, Ayr and Largs or Kilmarnock.

▼ Opened in 1905, the four stations along the new Glasgow & South Western Railway's loop line each had a wide island platform reached via a subway from the road below. Here, two youngsters proudly pose at their new station at Kilbarchan soon after opening. The overgrown platform and subway entrance in the road below still survive today.

Lochwinnoch station was also popular with Glaswegian day trippers visiting Castle Semple Loch on summer weekends. Although cost-cutting diesel multiple units were introduced in the early 1960s, the line was listed for closure in the 1963 Beeching Report. The end came on 27 June 1966 when passenger trains were withdrawn. Freight services remained until 1971, when the line north of Kilbirnie was completely closed. The short section from Brownhill Junction to Kilbirnie remained open to serve Glengarnock steelworks until 1977.

◀ ▼ Between Kilbarchan and Lochwinnoch, this road overbridge has recently been strengthened by a short tunnel to allow walkers and cyclists unimpeded progress along the railway path. The path forms part of National Cycle Network Route 7.

▲ Lochwinnoch station, seen here from a Glasgow-bound train on a sunny 5 July 1957, was located in a delightful spot on the west shore of Castle Semple Loch. Today the whole site has disappeared beneath modern housing although the loch is still a popular destination for Glaswegians at weekends.

▼ Built as a double-track line to relieve the overcrowded Glasgow to Ayr railway across the valley, the Glasgow & South Western loop had a short working life of around 60 years. Just west of Lochwinnoch the railway path along the route of the loop crosses the River Calder on this fine stone bridge.

WALKING AND CYCLING THE LINE

THE LINE TODAY

Since closure, the trackbed of the former loop line between Johnstone and Kilbirnie has been resurfaced as a traffic-free cycleway and footpath that now forms part of National Cycle Network Route 7. This level multi-use path also forms part of the Lochs & Glens Cycle Route that passes Castle Semple Loch, Barr Loch and Kilbirnie Loch. At Castle Semple Loch is a visitor centre with a car park, picnic site, watersports centre and boat and cycle-hire facilities. The route is easily accessed by rail from stations at Johnstone, Lochwinnoch and Glengarnock on the Glasgow to Ayr main line.

Despite having opened only just over 100 years ago, little now remains of the four stations along the line. The railway bridge and part of the island platform survive at Kilbarchan, as does the street entrance below. A station was never opened at Castle Semple but a private platform once existed for the use of the nearby estate. At Lochwinnoch the station site has disappeared beneath modern housing but the bricked-up entrance to the old island platform can still be seen in the bridge below. At Kilbirnie, at the southern end of the line, the island platform still survives alongside National Cycle Network Route 7.

PLACES TO VISIT

HERITAGE RAILWAYS
Scottish Industrial Railway Centre
Dunaskin Heritage Centre,
Dalmellington, Ayrshire
Tel 01292 269260 or 01292 313579 (evenings)
Website www.arpg.org.uk
Route Within site at Dunaskin

OTHER ATTRACTIONS
Castle Semple Country Park and Visitor Centre
Lochlip Road, Lochwinnoch,
Renfrewshire PA12 4EA
Tel 01505 842 882
Website www.clydemuirshiel.co.uk

Weaver's Cottage (NTS)
The Cross, Kilbarchan PA10 2JG
Tel 0844 493 2205
Website www.nts.org

Kelburn Country Centre
Kelburn Castle, Fairlie,
Ayrshire KA29 0BE
Tel 01475 568 685
Website www.kelburnestate.com

Blackshaw Farm Park
West Kilbride,
Ayrshire KA23 9PG
Tel 01294 823014

PRACTICAL INFORMATION

NEAREST RAILWAY STATIONS
Johnstone, Glengarnock

TOURIST INFORMATION
Paisley Tourist Information Centre
9A Gilmour Street,
Paisley PA1 1DD
Tel 0141 889 0711
Website www.visitscotland.com

OS MAPS
Landranger Nos 63, 64

CYCLE HIRE
RT Cycles and Fishing
73 Main Road, Glengarnock,
Ayrshire KA14 3AA
Tel 01505 682191
Website www.cyclerepairman.co.uk

▶ Between Lochwinnoch and Kilbirnie, the loop line passed through a 2-mile cutting obscuring views of Kilbirnie Loch. Today, cyclists and walkers can enjoy the same journey through the cutting on a well-asphalted surface.

▲ Seen from a Glasgow-bound train in July 1957, the station building at Kilbirnie has just received a new lick of paint. The line's station buildings and subway shelters were built of timber, which explains their total lack of survival today.

▶ The layout of stations along the loop, such as at Kilbirnie, was of a common design with wide island platforms accessed by stairs and a subway from the road below. Sadly the elegant timber subway shelters and station buildings with their wide awnings have long since rotted away.

PAISLEY & CLYDE RAILWAY PATH

Johnstone to Princes Pier

A direct competitor with the Caledonian Railway, the Glasgow & South Western Railway's circuitous route to Princes Pier ended its days carrying trans-Atlantic ocean-liner passengers to and from Glasgow.

▶ The Paisley & Clyde Railway Path passes under the A761 near the site of Bridge of Weir station. The Bridge of Weir Railway made an end-on junction with the new Greenock & Ayrshire Railway when the latter opened from Princes Pier in 1869. The station building did not survive its closure.

▲ Bridge of Weir station seen from a Glasgow-bound train on 5 July 1957. Despite closure of the line beyond Kilmacolm in 1965, Bridge of Weir remained open for passengers until 10 January 1983.

The circuitous route from Glasgow St Enoch to Princes Pier at Greenock had its beginnings in the 3½-mile Bridge of Weir Railway, which opened from Johnstone on the Glasgow & South Western Railway's main line to Ayr and to Bridge of Weir in 1864. A year later the Bridge of Weir Railway was vested in the G&SWR.

In the meantime, the G&SWR had its eye on reaching the growing seaport of Greenock on the south shore of the Clyde, although the

◄ Seen here before the line was singled, Kilmacolm station became the terminus of regular passenger services from St Enoch from February 1959 until January 1983. The road bridge and station building still survive – the latter is now a public house. (see below).

Caledonian Railway was already working the nominally independent Greenock & Wemyss Bay line, which had opened in 1865. Despite strong opposition from the Caledonian Railway, the G&SWR-backed Greenock & Ayrshire railway was authorised in 1865 to build a line from Princes Pier in Greenock to Bridge of Weir, where it would make an end-on connection with the branch from Johnstone.

The line opened completely on 23 December 1869 and before long a no-holds-barred price war had broken out between the CR and the G&SWR for the lucrative passenger traffic from Glasgow to

▲ The former station building at Kilmacolm is now a welcome sight for thirsty travellers along the Paisley & Clyde Railway Path.

▼ Ex-LMS Class 5 4-6-0 No. 45158 'Glasgow Yeomanry' and BR Standard Class 5 4-6-0 No. 73123 double-head a boat train for Princes Pier near Kilmacolm in May 1964. Locomotives were forced to travel tender first on the line following closure of the engine shed and turntable at Princes Pier in May 1959.

▼ Greenock Lynedoch, seen here in July 1957, was the penultimate station on the line. Located adjacent to a Tate & Lyle sugar refinery, the station closed on 2 February 1959. The platforms survive intact today. From Lynedoch the line descended steeply through a tunnel to the terminus at Princes Pier.

▲ The road bridge at Kilmacolm is now the gateway to the Paisley & Clyde Railway Path towards Bridge of Weir. It's hard to imagine that less than 50 years ago heavily laden double-headed boat trains stormed through here en route to the Ocean-Liner Terminal at Princes Pier.

the Clyde steamboat piers at Greenock. Fares became so low that the only winners eventually were the passengers. In the end the G&SWR held the trump card despite their longer route – at Princes Pier their passengers could embark directly onto the steamboats while CR passengers had to walk from Greenock station to Custom House Quay. Despite the high numbers of passengers being carried on the Greenock & Ayrshire line, receipts were disappointing due to the heavy discounting of ticket prices; freight also did not fair well despite optimistic forecasts by the railway's promoters. In the end the CR and G&SWR agreed to fix their fares and share their revenue on the two competing routes. The Greenock & Ayrshire eventually became part of the G&SWR in 1872.

To compete with the excellent facilities at Princes Pier, the Caledonian Railway opened an extension to a new pier at Gourock in 1889. Faced with this renewed competition, the G&SWR built a new grand terminal at Princes Pier in 1894 – both companies also ran their own fleet of Clyde paddle steamers, and competition between the two rivals continued into London Midland & Scottish and London & North Eastern Railway days up to the outbreak of the Second World War. Nationalisation of the railways in 1948 saw Clyde steamer traffic withdrawn from Princes Pier, although the route from St Enoch was still used for boat trains to connect with trans-Atlantic liners that called there.

Closure of the line from Johnstone to Princes Pier came in stages: local passenger services between Kilmacolm and Princes Pier ended on 2 February 1959; the last boat train from St Enoch to Princes

▶ An empty boat train returns to Glasgow St Enoch high above Port Glasgow in May 1964. The lead engine in this back-to-back duo of Stanier Class 5 4-6-0s is No. 45476. By that date the line had been singled and had only 18 months to go before complete closure. Sadly, the nine-arch viaduct has since been demolished.

▶ Routes on the National Cycle Network are marked at regular intervals by attractive mileposts such as this one on the Paisley & Clyde Railway Path (Route 75) at Bridge of Weir. Nearby the path crosses the River Gryfe on a substantial stone viaduct.

WALKING AND CYCLING THE LINE

THE LINE TODAY

Known as the Paisley & Clyde Railway Path, the trackbed of the former Glasgow & South Western Railway from Johnstone to Greenock forms part of a mainly traffic-free 21-mile footpath and cycleway on National Cycle Network Route 75. At Johnstone the junction with NCN Route 7 (see page 240) is marked by a large multi-coloured sculpture. At Bridge of Weir the railway path dives under a steel bridge carrying the A761 before crossing the River Gryfe on a fine stone viaduct. From here the

railway path traverses pleasant countryside on embankments along the river valley to Kilmacolm, where the former station building is now the Pullman Tavern public house. Beyond Kilmacolm the path continues in a northwesterly direction alternating through cuttings and along embankments to the built-up suburbs of Port Glasgow and Greenock. Here, alongside the Clyde, NCN Route 75 continues on its non-railway route to Gourock, from where there are ferries across the Firth to Dunoon.

PLACES TO VISIT

RIVERSIDE MUSEUM
(Opening 2011)
Tel 0141 287 2720
Website www.glasgowmuseums.com

OTHER ATTRACTIONS
Paisley Museum & Art Gallery
High Street, Paisley PA1 2BA
Tel 0141 887 1010
Website www.renfrewshire.gov.uk

Finlaystone Country Estate
Langbank, Renfrewshire PA14 6TJ
Tel 01475 540505
Website www.finlaystone.co.uk

Newark Castle
Port Glasgow PA14 5NH
Tel 01475 741858
Website www.historic-scotland.gov.uk

McLean Museum & Art Gallery
15 Kelly Street, Greenock,
Inverclyde PA16 8JX
Tel 01475 715624
Website www.museumsgalleriesscotland.org.uk

PRACTICAL INFORMATION

NEAREST RAILWAY STATIONS
Johnstone, Port Glasgow, Greenock

TOURIST INFORMATION
Paisley Tourist Information Centre
9A Gilmour Street, Paisley PA1 1DD
Tel 0141 889 0711
Website www.visitscotland.com

Helensburgh Visitor Information Centre
The Clock Tower, Helensburgh,
Dunbartonshire, G84 7PA, Scotland
Tel 08452 255121
Website www.visitscotland.com

OS MAPS
Landranger Nos 63, 64

▲ With only two months to go before complete closure of the line, BR Standard Class 5 4-6-0 No. 73121 rests under the overall roof at Princes Pier station with a boat train from St Enoch. Designed by Scottish architect James Miller, the Italianate station was demolished to make way for a container terminal following closure of the line in 1965.

Princes Pier Greenock,
with G. & S. W. Ry. Co's. Steamer "Neptune"

◀ Faced with renewed competition from the Caledonian Railway's new steamboat pier at Gourock, the G&SWR opened their new Princes Pier terminal in 1894. The railway company and its successor, the LMS, continued to operate a Clyde steamboat service from here until the Second World War. After the war it was used until the 1960s as an ocean-liner terminal for trans-Atlantic liners.

Pier ran in November 1965; the line beyond Kilmacolm was closed completely in September 1966; passenger services on the truncated branch to Kilmacolm were withdrawn on 3 January 1983. Princes Pier was also demolished to make way for a container terminal, which was linked by rail to the former Caledonian Railway's line to Wemyss Bay at Cartsburn Junction. Even this rail link has now gone.

THE END OF THE LINE

Despite dieselisation of many railway routes in Scotland in the early 1960s, steam still clung to life in central and southern Scotland until the early summer of 1967. With the Beeching Axe threatening many rural and cross-country lines, these final years were to witness a terrible rundown of many of Scotland's railways – railway photographers from all over the UK descended on these final bastions of steam to record the dying moments of this once mighty national treasure that had by then been reduced to sheer decrepitude. R.I.P.

▼ After years of sterling service, veteran Caledonian Railway locomotives seen at the Carnbroe dump on 1 September 1962. The line-up consists of (from front to rear): Drummond 0-6-0 No. 57369; McIntosh 0-4-4T No. 55267; Drummond 0-6-0s Nos 57389 and 57417; McIntosh 0-6-0Ts Nos 56313, 56298 and 56356; Drummond 0-6-0s Nos 57418, 57288 and 57271; McIntosh 0-6-0 No. 57564.

▲ BR Standard Class 4 2-6-4 tank No. 80093 simmers among the weeds near tiny Loch Tay shed on 4 August 1965 while her crew stock up with coal from the adjacent wagon. The Loch Tay branch from Killin closed prematurely on 27 September of that year following a landslip on the Callander & Oban line in Glen Ogle.

▲ Not many weeds here at Rankinston in Ayrshire, but definitely an end-of-the-line feel about the place. The line beyond the bridge to Holehouse Junction had been ripped up in 1950 or thereabouts, but this stub-end of the branch from Belston Junction served Littlemill Colliery. Trains had to come as far as Rankinston and reverse to get into any of the collieries. Here ex-LMS 'Crab' 2-6-0 No. 42908 waits with its loaded coal wagons at the site of Rankinston station on 3 August 1965 before propelling them all the way back to Belston Junction. No one has quite worked out why a permanent way gang is working on the line at this point as the buffer stop was only a few yards farther on.

INDEX

ACKNOWLEDGEMENTS

The author and AA Publishing would like to thank the following photographers and organisations for their assistance in the preparation of this book.

r= right; l = left; t = top; b = bottom; m = middle

Ben Ashworth: 37b; 38tl; 102/103b; 114mr; 129t; 150/151b

Hugh Ballantyne: 24/25b; 26tl; 30mr; 33tl; 61mr; 61bl; 74; 100/101b; 107tr; 106/107b; 112/113b; 115mr; 120/121t; 123t; 130mr; 131bl; 136tl; 154tl; 154m; 188ml; 198/199; 201tr

Henry Casserley: 12mr; 18/19b; 22t; 23bl; 24ml; 53t; 55b; 60tl; 71tr; 72mr; 77br; 100b; 104b; 118ml; 124t; 125mr; 127tl; 129br; 132mr; 140ml; 141tl; 148/149t; 149ml; 157mr; 168mr; 170mr; 177mr; 181tl; 196ml; 197mr; 212ml; 217t; 218; 219t; 239tr; 240l; 241t; 242bl; 244tl

Richard Casserley: 31tr; 44/45b; 58m; 58b; 60b; 65b; 76bl; 78m; 92/93t; 96/97t; 96b; 142bl; 151mr; 157tr; 159bl

Colour-Rail: 29tl; 29mr; 32b; 46; 50/51b; 57br; 64b; 76/77m; 92b; 95t; 98; 117mr; 119b; 120b; 130b; 134/135b; 138; 143b; 146/147; 167b; 172b; 177b; 197b; 208tl; 210; 233t; 243b; 245br; 246/247t

Mike Esau: 17t; 28b; 41b; 43t; 50mr; 63b

Kenneth Field: 182/183b

John Goss: 32tl; 36ml; 39tl; 56bl; 57t; 57mr; 58tr; 62tl; 63tr; 64tr; 108/109m; 126ml; 248b; 249t; 249br

Tony Harden: 66b; 67tl; 69b; 83t; 82/83b; 84ml; 84b; 86/87b; 87t; 141m; 144/145m; 161b; 162/163m; 176ml; 178t; 179mr; 184mr; 184b; 203b; 206ml; 207mr; 216ml; 220/221t; 229br; 231tl; 236m; 237b; 241br; 243tl; 247bl

Tom Heavyside: 171m; 172tr; 173

Colin Hogg: 6b, 13b

Julian Holland: 7b; 12bl; 13 tr; 15br; 16mr; 19br; 20b; 20mr; 21tl; 22bl; 25tr; 26tr; 26/27b; 30bl; 31br; 35br; 36bl; 37mr; 41tl; 41tr; 42tr; 42b; 49tr; 49ml; 50/51t; 53bl; 54bl; 67tr; 68bl; 68/69t; 72/73; 73br; 83br; 85tl; 85b; 101bl; 103tr; 104tr; 104/105m; 106b; 108tl; 108/109b; 111tl; 113tr; 113br; 141bl; 142/143t; 142mr; 145tr; 144/145b; 146tl; 148b; 150br; 151tr; 153tl; 156ml; 157b; 158/159t; 162t; 163bl; 213tl; 214/215b; 215b; 217br; 219mr; 220bl; 220/221b; 222bl; 223tl; 224t; 224/225b; 226/227t; 229tr; 233br; 234/235t; 234/235m; 238tl; 238b; 238br; 240r; 242tr; 243tr; 244/245t; 246t

Roger Holmes: 45t

Ken Hoole Collection: 202tr; 204tl; 205ml

Alan Jarvis: 35t; 49b; 116b; 117t; 152/153b; 154/155b

Michael Mensing: 10; 14/15b; 15mr; 110ml; 111b; 115b; 124b; 137br; 164; 166tr; 168b; 191b; 192/193b; 223b; 224/225t; 227br

Milepost 92½: 9; 34b; 38b; 90bl; 130/131t; 167mr; 168/169t; 171tr; 174t; 174/175; 178; 179b; 180/181b; 183tl; 183m; 185b; 186/187b; 187tl; 190bl; 193tl; 200/201; 202ml; 207b; 208/209b

Brian Morrison: 71b

Gavin Morrison: 1, 2/3; 193mr; 228b; 230/231; 232/233b

W. Redshaw Collection/Oakwood Press: 89tr; 89b

Brian Sharpe: 77tl; 78tl; 79; 80tr; 80b; 91t; 91b; 93bl; 94ml; 97ml; 97br; 122bl; 123b; 125t; 126b; 127ml; 128/129b; 131t; 133; 135tr; 136/137b; 188bl; 189; 194; 205tr; 205b

Frank Spaven: 235bl

Stewart E. Squires/Oakwood Press: 88t

Andrew Swift: 19tl; 19mr; 21mr; 40br; 52b; 54tr; 95bl; 119mr; 152mr; 160tl; 161mr

Every effort has been made to trace copyright holders, and we apologise in advance for any unintentional omissions or errors.
We would be pleased to apply any corrections in a following edition of this publication.